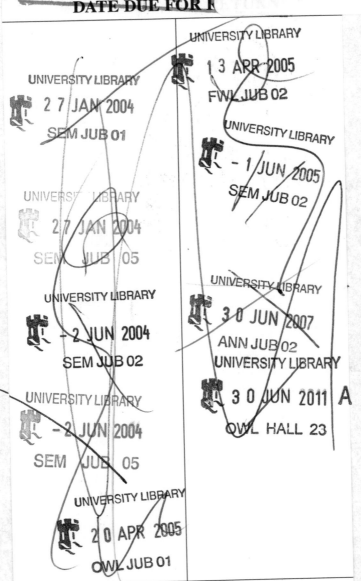

Studies in language and linguistics

General editors: GEOFFREY LEECH *Lancaster University*
and JENNY THOMAS *Bangor University*

Already published:

A Dictionary of Stylistics
KATIE WALES

The Communicative Competence of Young Children
SUSAN H. FOSTER

Linguistic Purism
GEORGE THOMAS

Women, Men and Language
Second edition
JENNIFER COATES

Lexical Ambiguity in Poetry
SOON PENG SU

Understanding Metaphor in Literature
GERARD STEEN

English Spelling and the Computer
ROGER MITTON

Conversational Routines in English: Convention and Creativity
KARIN AIJMER

Learner English on Computer
Edited by SYLVIANE GRANGER

Learner English on Computer

Edited by SYLVIANE GRANGER

Longman
London and New York

Addison Wesley Longman Limited
Edinburgh Gate
Harlow, Essex CM20 2JE
England

and Associated Companies throughout the world

Published in the United States of America
by Addison Wesley Longman Inc., New York

First published 1998

ISBN 0 582 29883–0 Paper

British Library Cataloguing-in-Publication Data

A catalogue record for this book is
available from the British Library

Library of Congress Cataloging-in-Publication Data

Learner English on computer / edited by Sylviane Granger.
p. cm. — (Studies in language and linguistics)
Includes bibliographical references and index.
ISBN 0–582–29883–0 (pbk.)
1. English language—Study and teaching—Foreign speakers—Data processing. 2. English language—Errors of usage—Data processing. 3. English language—Computer-assisted instruction. 4. Computational linguistics. I. Granger, Sylviane, 1951– . II. Series: Studies in language and linguistics (London, England)
PE1128.A2L364 1998
428′.00285—dc21 97–36716
CIP

Set by 35 in 9/11pt Palatino
Produced through Longman Malaysia, TCP

In the final analysis if linguistics
is not about language as it is
actually spoken and written by
human beings, then it is about
nothing at all.

Michael Stubbs

Contents

Contributors

Jan Aarts, Department of Language and Speech, University of Nijmegen, Netherlands

Bengt Altenberg, Department of English, Lund University, Sweden

Doug Biber, Department of English, Northern Arizona University, USA

Sylvie De Cock, Centre for English Corpus Linguistics, Université Catholique de Louvain, Belgium

Adam Gadsby, ELT Division, Addison Wesley Longman, England

Patrick Gillard, ELT Division, Addison Wesley Longman, England

Przemysław Kaszubski, School of English, Adam Mickiewicz University, Poland

Geoffrey Leech, Department of Linguistics and Modern English Language, Lancaster University, England

Gunter Lorenz, Didaktik des Englischen, University of Augsburg, Germany

Tony McEnery, Department of Linguistics and Modern English Language, Lancaster University, England

Fanny Meunier, Centre for English Corpus Linguistics, Université Catholique de Louvain, Belgium

John Milton, Language Centre, Hong Kong University of Science and Technology, Hong Kong

Stephanie Petch-Tyson, Centre for English Corpus Linguistics, Université Catholique de Louvain, Belgium

Paul Rayson, Department of Computing, Lancaster University, England

Randi Reppen, Department of English, Northern Arizona University, USA

Håkan Ringbom, Department of English, Åbo Akademi University, Finland

Marie Tapper, Department of English, Lund University, Sweden

Christopher Tribble, Institute of English Language Education, Lancaster University/Centre for Applied Language Studies, University of Reading, England

Tuija Virtanen, Department of English, Åbo Akademi University, Finland

Editor's acknowledgements

I am indebted to the Université Catholique de Louvain for granting me a year's sabbatical in 1995–96, a year which was crucial for the development of my views on computer learner corpus research. I have particularly good memories of the time I spent carrying out research at the Universities of Lancaster and Nijmegen and would like to thank G. Leech and J. Aarts for the warm welcome I received in both places. I am especially grateful to the Fonds National de la Recherche Scientifique, the Commissariat Général aux Relations Internationales and the British Council for their financial support during this time. I would also like to thank the contributors to this volume for their diligence in keeping to deadlines and their patience in complying with my editorial demands. Special thanks go to Sylvie De Cock and Estelle Dagneaux for their meticulous examination of the typescript, and to Stephanie Petch-Tyson, who provided numerous suggestions for improvement. Finally, I would like to thank my family – my husband Guy and my two sons, David and Tony, for putting up with my year-long exile with only a minimum of bad grace!

Publisher's acknowledgements

We are indebted to Cambridge University Press for permission to use our Table 13.1 'A typical example of vocabulary tabulation' from *Study Writing* by L. Hamp-Lyons and B. Heasley (1987: 71); and Addison Wesley Longman for our Table 13.2 'A vocabulary table with graded stylistic information' from J. Arnold and J. Harmer *Advanced Writing Skills* (1978: 57).

List of abbreviations

BNC	British National Corpus
CA	Contrastive Analysis
CALL	Computer-Assisted Language Learning
CIA	Contrastive Interlanguage Analysis
CLC	Computer Learner Corpus
DDL	Data-Driven Learning
EA	Error Analysis
EFL	English as a Foreign Language
ELT	English Language Teaching
ESL	English as a Second Language
HKUST	Honk Kong University of Science and Technology
ICE	International Corpus of English
ICLE	International Corpus of Learner English
IL	Interlanguage
KIIC	Key Item In Context
KWIC	Key Word In Context
LD	Lexical Density
LLC	Longman Learners' Corpus
LOB Corpus	Lancaster-Oslo/Bergen Corpus
LOCNESS	Louvain Corpus of Native English Essays
MIQ	Multiple-Items Queries
MSL	Mean Sentence Length
MTTR	Mean Type/Token Ratio
MTUL	Mean T-Unit Length
NL	Native Language
NS	Native Speaker
NNS	Non-Native Speaker
POS	Part Of Speech
SGML	Standard Generalized Markup Language
SLA	Second Language Acquisition
UG	Universal Grammar

Preface

Geoffrey Leech

Learner corpora: what they are and what can be done with them

This is the first book devoted to the idea of collecting a corpus, or computer textual database, of the language produced by foreign language learners: a collection known as a learner corpus. To begin with a hypothetical but realistic example, let us suppose that higher education teacher X, in a non-English speaking country, teaches English to her students every week, and every so often sets them essays to write, or other written tasks in English. Now, instead of returning those essays to students with comments and a sigh of relief, she stores the essays (of course with the students' permission) in her computer, and is gradually building up, week by week, a larger and more representative collection of her students' work. Helped by computer tools such as a concordance package, she can extract data and frequency information from this 'corpus', and can analyse her students' progress as a group in some depth. More significant (since teacher X is also interested in building up a research profile) are the research questions which open up once the corpus is in existence; for example:

- What linguistic features in the target language do the learners in question use significantly more often ('overuse') or less often ('underuse') than native speakers do?
- How far is the target language behaviour of the learners influenced by their native language (NL transfer)?
- In which areas do they tend to use 'avoidance strategies', failing to exploit the full range of the target language's expressive possibilities?
- In which areas do they appear to achieve native-like or non-native-like performance?
- What (in order of frequency) are the chief areas of non-native-like linguistic performance which learners in country A suffer from and need particular help with?

To some extent, teacher X's interest in such questions may be directed towards improving her own teaching practices: for example, she will be able to save time where the students experience no difficulty, and concentrate remedial work on areas where more help is patently needed. In other words, she will be able to tailor teaching to need. To some extent, however, her interest will also be directed towards a more collaborative mode of research with teachers and researchers in other institutions and in other countries, who are collecting the data of their students, just as she is collecting the data of hers. Such a collaboration is needed if we are to answer more generic questions such as:

- What are the particular areas of overuse, underuse and error which native speakers of language A are prone to in learning target language T, as contrasted with native speakers of languages B, C, D . . . ?
- What, in general, is the proportion of non-native target language behaviour (overuse, underuse, error) peculiar to native speakers of language A, as opposed to such behaviour which is shared by all learners of the language, whatever their mother tongue?

It appears odd that SLA research has not yet provided a clear answer to these questions, especially to the second one, which concerns the influence of the native language on learning, and which has obvious implications for how languages should be successfully learned. The study of learner corpora for the first time provides for a research programme which will lead to its being answered.

There are many refinements and elaborations of such a research programme which can be envisaged – such as the collection of corpora of the same students at different stages of learning (a longitudinal learner corpus, in fact), or the collection of a (preferably longitudinal) corpus of the data derived from individual learners rather than from a homogeneous group. These refinements lie largely in the future. But, to answer questions such as those above, for the time being, we may look forward to the success of an international learner corpus programme which entails collecting comparable data from comparable learner groups, each of which consists of speakers of a different native language: e.g. a corpus of English produced by NSs (native speakers) of French, a similar corpus produced by NSs of Chinese, a similar corpus produced by NSs of Polish, and so on. To complete the international corpus design we also need a comparable corpus, insofar as it can be obtained, of NSs of the target language, English, as a standard of comparison, or norm, against which to measure the characteristics of the learner corpora. This is indeed the design of the International Corpus of Learner English (ICLE), founded and coordinated by Sylviane Granger, the editor of this volume.

Much of this book is devoted to the first fruits of the ICLE project, which is already beginning to yield findings of considerable interest. We should also mention the role of other large learner corpus projects now coming to fruition: the 10-million-word Longman Learners' Corpus, rich in variety of mother tongues and levels of learner attainment, on which Gillard and Gadsby report in Chapter 12; also the homogeneous corpus of 10 million words (all from Chinese-speaking learners) collected in the HKUST project on which Milton reports in Chapter 14.

The background: corpus research and research into language learning

Rather dramatically, we may claim that the concept of a learner corpus is an idea 'whose hour has come'. Corpus linguistics (which nowadays means 'computer corpus linguistics') is a relatively new branch of linguistics which has been gathering momentum over the past 30 years, as computers have grown enormously in storage and processing ability. Its influence has spread into many branches of language research, but has been rather slow to gain a foothold in the educational sphere, for two reasons, one practical and the other theoretical. The first reason is that computers cost money, and computer-based research requires a concentration of human resources and equipment which is not easily available to those working in areas such as English language teaching (ELT) and second language acquisition (SLA), where resources are scarce. Education is the Cinderella of the academic world, particularly in language learning, where research projects are usually funded inadequately, if they are funded at all.

The second reason is that the intellectual climate current in applied linguistics over the past 20 years has not lent itself to the kinds of empirical methods that corpus linguistics fosters. If, to dramatise again, we characterise the theme of this book as 'SLA meets corpus linguistics', this is not likely to be a meeting of unalloyed joy and goodwill. Rather, it may well be an encounter marked by some suspicion and misunderstanding. Why this is so is not immediately evident. It might seem that a large and carefully compiled database of learner's language is going to be a useful resource for anyone wanting to find out how people learn languages, and how they can be helped to learn them better. After all, the notion of interlanguage (IL) research rests on the principle that understanding language learning means understanding the intermediate approximative language systems which learners, as learners, progressively acquire. And how, it may be asked, could we better study such interlanguage knowledge than by studying the language which learners produce? Surely this is the only really hard evidence we have of what progress learners are making or failing to make?

What may seem an eminently sensible course of action to a layperson does not necessarily commend itself to the academic world. Two mutually opposed intellectual currents have taken the focus of attention away from the practical linguistic study of what learners speak and write. One is the emphasis on communicative teaching and learning as a process rather than a product (see Kaszubski in Chapter 13 of this volume). This has inevitably steered people away from the precise study of the product: what learners write and say. The other current is the mentalistic tendency to regard SLA as a process taking place in the human mind, an acquisition of competence, with only an indirect connection with the observable performance of the learner.

If the learner corpus is characterised as an idea 'whose hour has come', then this is partly due to the feeling that it is time that some balance was restored in the pursuit of SLA paradigms of research, with more attention being paid to the data that the language learners produce more or less naturalistically – in non-test, non-classroom conditions. In the 1960s and 1970s, studies in error analysis (EA) followed this data-oriented approach, and the negative attitudes to EA inherited from that period have coloured many people's thinking ever since. But today, the computer, with its ability to store and process language, provides the means to investigate learner language in a way unimaginable 20 years ago. Moreover, the precedent of EA should not be dwelt upon since the learner corpus is a new phenomenon: it enables us to investigate the non-native speaking learners' language (in relation to the native speaker's) not only from a negative point of view (what did the learner get wrong?) but from a positive one (what did the learner get right?). For the first time it also allows a systematic and detailed study of the learner's linguistic behaviour from the point of view of 'overuse' (what linguistic features does the learner use more than a native speaker?) and 'underuse' (what features does the learner use less than a native speaker?).

Some potential limitations of corpus-based research

However, it would be misleading to paint too rosy a picture of the new field of learner corpus research, promising though it is. We have to consider some of its possible drawbacks.

The first thing to observe is true of corpus linguistics generally: a great deal of spadework has to be done before the research results can be harvested. A major task, for which we must remain grateful to many pioneer researchers represented in this book, is the compilation of learner corpora in the first place. Only those who have first-hand knowledge of this work can fully appreciate that the compilation of a corpus (with proper attention to quality, design criteria and so on) always takes twice as long as one thought, and sometimes ten times as much effort. Further, if the corpus is to be fully used for the extraction of linguistic information, different kinds of annotation (e.g. part of speech tagging, error tagging, parsing) can be added, either manually or with the help of computer annotation tools: these are also time-consuming tasks. Ironically, before it comes to be optimally useful, perhaps after 20 or more years, a corpus may be felt to be out of date. An alternative approach is to discard the concept of a static corpus of a given length, and to continue to collect and store corpus data indefinitely into the future – clearly a recipe for a hard life and a late retirement! Contributors to the present book are continually aware of this problem, and more than once note that their present findings are provisional, full results requiring further research over a longer period.

In addition to this, one must also consider the types of linguistic information which may be practicably retrieved from a learner corpus. Before the annotation of corpora has taken place, automatic searches are bound to be limited to those features of language which are easily observable in the electronic record of the text, corresponding in most cases to the orthographic record. Initial stages of annotation of texts (e.g. by automatic tagging) are also likely to be restricted to relatively superficial linguistic features. In spite of the restriction on the levels of linguistic analysis that may be practicably undertaken, this volume illustrates quite a range of levels of information extraction, from word-based vocabulary studies to grammatical studies, to phraseological studies based on word combinations, and to studies of style and discoursal phenomena.

Another aspect of learner corpus research which may strike the applied linguist as retrograde is a tendency to concentrate on written rather than spoken language. This tendency has dogged corpus linguistics from the start: the truth is that whereas humans are built primarily to process speech, computers are built primarily for the written word. As far as speech is concerned, for practical reasons, the only spoken discourse that can be collected in a corpus is discourse that has been transcribed into the written form – and transcription is a slow, time-consuming process. Yet this limitation should not be overemphasised; after all, writing is an exceedingly important skill for most foreign language learners, and well deserves the expenditure of effort to collect corpora of written learner language. It was natural, if not inevitable, that the first priority of the ICLE initiative should be to develop corpora of written language production. But it is also encouraging that this limitation is now being addressed, through the compilation of comparable native and non-native (NNS) corpora of spoken discourse, as reported by De Cock et al. in Chapter 5 of this book.

At present, most, if not all, learner corpus studies tend to be studies of groups of learners, which means they are able to contribute little to the predominant theme of current SLA research, which is the process by which the individual learner acquires target language competence. However, through the coding of speaker/writer identity in the corpus header information, the productions of individuals can be retrieved from a corpus and compared. As corpora are enlarged in the future, it is likely that this aspect will be developed further, particularly in a longitudinal dimension. Furthermore, it can be argued that the collective attainment of learner groups is a facet of SLA research which has been unduly neglected, and should benefit from a comeback, enabling, for example, the influence of NL on language learning to be more systematically studied.

Moving on to more philosophical issues, one frequently-raised objection to corpus linguistics is that a corpus is a finite sample of an (in principle) infinite population: we cannot easily extrapolate from what is found in a corpus to what is true of the language or language variety it supposedly 'represents'. This thorny issue of 'representativeness' may affect learner corpus research as follows. The methodology associated with learner corpora is to isolate a variable in terms of which two otherwise comparable corpora differ: particularly the variable of the learners' native language. But it is very difficult to be sure that what the two corpora represent differs only with respect to this variable: for example, two English learner corpora of native languages X and Y may provide evidence that differences in English language performance are due to the NLs concerned. But it is conceivable that particular observed effects may be due to other factors, such as differences in cultural context, or in educational institutions and practices. The conclusion is that we have to be cautious in drawing general inferences from the results of a corpus analysis, and alert to the influence of hidden variables implicit in the way we collected or sampled the data.

Lastly, we may take note of the temptation to confuse description and prescription in learner corpus research. The conventional prescriptive view has been that the goal of foreign language learning is to approximate closer and closer to the performance of native speakers. Yet which native speakers? American, Australian, British or Caribbean? Highly educated or less so? Old or young? Such questions as these cause difficulties, although in practice teachers probably have covert answers to them. The problem becomes more noticeable when we compare learner corpora with a native-speaker 'reference corpus', like the LOCNESS corpus mentioned in Chapter 1. Native-speaking students do not necessarily provide models that everyone would want to imitate. And, when we come to examine a reference corpus of native-speaker speech, the less admirable features of the native speaker's performance can show up especially clearly. In Chapter 5, it is pointed out that in two corresponding spoken corpora, one of NSs and the other of NNSs, the natives made much more frequent use of 'vagueness tags' such as *and things, and stuff like that*, and *or something*. Although the non-natives can be technically described as 'underusing' such vague expressions, this term 'underuse' and the contrasting 'overuse' should be not used in a judgemental spirit. They should be interpreted, to my mind, not prescriptively but descriptively, as a convenient shorthand for 'significantly more/less frequent use by NNSs than by NSs'. Prescription comes into the picture only when we ask how such corpus findings are to be interpreted for pedagogical purposes. It is a matter for debate as to whether a finding such as that above should feed into the development of teaching materials on 'how to be vague in spoken English'.

Conclusion

Like any healthily active and developing field of inquiry, learner corpus research has to continue to face challenges both material and intellectual before it wins a secure and accepted place in the discipline of applied linguistics. It is my belief that this book will make a significant contribution in paving the way to that acceptance. In particular, the book encourages the different research communities of corpus linguistics and SLA/ELT studies to look at one another's work, in a world where divergent, rather than convergent, trends in research thinking are all too common. This can be seen, for example, in the extensive bibliography, which combines major works of the two fields. On a more practical level, the book sets out a whole range of methodologies that researchers can apply to their own material, thus stimulating, hopefully, much new research in this area of growing interest.

Introduction

Sylviane Granger

Computer learner corpus (CLC) research is still in its infancy. With roots both in corpus linguistics and second language acquisition (SLA) studies, it uses the methods and tools of corpus linguistics to gain better insights into authentic learner language. This volume is intended to open up a new field of research to a wider audience and includes articles on all aspects of computer learner corpus research, from the initial stage of corpus compilation to the final stage of pedagogical application. Although the main focus of the book is English as a Foreign Language, the approach could easily be applied to other foreign languages.

The book is divided into three main parts. Part I is a general outline of learner corpus design and analysis. In the opening chapter, I first discuss the place of learner corpus research within corpus linguistics, SLA and ELT, and then outline the basic principles underlying learner corpus compilation and computer-aided linguistic analysis of learner data. In the second chapter, Fanny Meunier presents the major linguistic software tools, focusing in particular on their relevance for interlanguage studies.

In Part II, the principles outlined in the first part of the book are put into practice through a series of case studies examining various aspects of learner lexis, discourse and grammar. The first three chapters analyse learner lexis from a variety of angles: high-frequency words (Håkan Ringbom), adjective intensification (Gunter Lorenz) and recurrent word combinations (Sylvie De Cock et al.). The following three chapters focus on discourse phenomena: connectors (Bengt Altenberg and Marie Tapper), questions (Tuija Virtanen) and features of reader/writer visibility (Stephanie Petch-Tyson). The research in the last two chapters is carried out on tagged corpora and highlights aspects of learner grammar on the basis of the frequencies of individual tags (Sylviane Granger and Paul Rayson) and tag sequences (Jan Aarts and Sylviane Granger).

Part III shows how CLC-based studies can help improve pedagogical tools: EFL grammars (Doug Biber and Randi Reppen), dictionaries (Patrick Gillard and Adam Gadsby), writing textbooks (Przemysław Kaszubski) and electronic tools (John Milton). Implications for classroom methodology are highlighted in the last chapter (Sylviane Granger and Christopher Tribble).

Interest in learner corpora is growing fast, with both SLA specialists and ELT practitioners beginning to recognize their theoretical and practical value. There is no doubt in my mind that we are on the verge of a learner corpus boom. This volume will serve its purpose if it helps would-be learner corpus builders and analysts to get started in a field of research which is certain to make an important contribution to foreign language learning and teaching.

Part I

Learner Corpus Design and Analysis

CHAPTER ONE

The computer learner corpus: a versatile new source of data for SLA research

Sylviane Granger

1 Corpus linguistics and English studies

Since making its first appearance in the 1960s, the computer corpus has infiltrated all fields of language-related research, from lexicography to literary criticism through artificial intelligence and language teaching. This widespread use of the computer corpus has led to the development of a new discipline which has come to be called 'corpus linguistics', a term which refers not just to a new computer-based methodology, but as Leech (1992: 106) puts it, to a 'new research enterprise', a new way of thinking about language, which is challenging some of our most deeply-rooted ideas about language. With its focus on performance (rather than competence), description (rather than universals) and quantitative as well as qualitative analysis, it can be seen as contrasting sharply with the Chomskyan approach and indeed is presented as such by Leech (1992: 107). The two approaches are not mutually exclusive however. Comparing the respective merits of corpus linguistics and what he ironically calls 'armchair linguistics', Fillmore (1992: 35) comes to the conclusion that 'the two kinds of linguists need each other. Or better, that the two kinds of linguists, wherever possible, should exist in the same body.'

The computer plays a central role in corpus linguistics. A first major advantage of computerization is that it liberates language analysts 'from drudgery and empowers [them] to focus their creative energies on doing what machines cannot do' (Rundell and Stock 1992: 14). More fundamental, however, is the heuristic power of automated linguistic analysis, i.e. its power to uncover totally new facts about language. It is this aspect, rather than 'the mirroring of intuitive categories of description' (Sinclair 1986: 202), that is the most novel and exciting contribution of corpus linguistics.

English is undoubtedly the language which has been analysed most from a corpus linguistics perspective. Indeed the first computer corpus to be compiled was the Brown corpus, a corpus of American English.

Since then English corpora have grown and diversified. At the time, the 1 million words contained in the Brown and the LOB were considered to be perfectly ample for research purposes, but they now appear microscopic in comparison to the 100 million words of the British National Corpus or the 200 million words of the Bank of English. This growth in corpus size over the years has been accompanied by a huge diversification of corpus types to cover a wide range of varieties: diachronic, stylistic (spoken vs. written; general vs. technical) and regional (British, American, Australian, Indian, etc.) (for a recent survey of English corpora, see McEnery and Wilson 1996).

Until very recently however, no attempt had been made to collect corpora of learner English, a strange omission given the number of people who speak English as a foreign language throughout the world. It was not until the early 1990s that academics, EFL specialists and publishing houses alike began to recognize the theoretical and practical potential of computer learner corpora and several projects were launched, among which the following three figure prominently: the International Corpus of Learner English (ICLE), a corpus of learner English from several mother tongue backgrounds and the result of international academic collaboration, the Longman Learners' Corpus (LLC), which also contains learner English from several mother tongue backgrounds and the Hong Kong University of Science and Technology (HKUST) Learner Corpus, which is made up of the English of Chinese learners.

2 Learner corpus data and SLA research

2.1 *Empirical data in SLA research*

The main goal of Second Language Acquisition (SLA)[1] research is to uncover the principles that govern the process of learning a foreign/second language. As this process is mental and therefore not directly observable, it has to be accessed via the product, i.e. learner performance data. Ellis (1994: 670) distinguishes three main data types: (1) language use data, which 'reflect learners' attempts to use the L2 in either comprehension or production'; (2) metalingual judgements, which tap learners' intuitions about the L2, for instance by asking them to judge the grammaticality of sentences; and (3) self-report data, which explore learners' strategies via questionnaires or think-aloud tasks. Language use data is said to be 'natural' if no control is exerted on the learners' performance and 'elicited' if it results from a controlled experiment.

Current SLA research is mainly based on introspective data (i.e. Ellis's types 2 and 3) and language use data of the elicited type. People have preferred not to use natural language use data for a variety of reasons. One has to do with the infrequency of some language features, i.e. the fact that 'certain properties happen to occur very rarely or not at all unless specifically elicited' (Yip 1995: 9). Secondly, as variables affecting language use are not controlled, the effect of these variables cannot be investigated systematically. Finally, natural language use data fails to reveal the entire linguistic repertoire of learners because 'they [learners] will use only those aspects in which they have the most confidence. They will avoid the troublesome aspects through circumlocution or some other device' (Larsen-Freeman and Long 1991: 26).

Introspective and elicited data also have their limitations, however, and their validity, particularly that of elicited data, has been put into question. The artificiality of an experimental language situation may lead learners to produce language which differs widely from the type of language they would use naturally. Also, because of the constraints of experimental elicitation, SLA specialists regularly rely on a very narrow empirical base, often no more than a handful of informants, something which severely restricts the generalizability of the results. There is clearly a need for more, and better quality, data and this is particularly acute in the case of natural language data. In this context, learner corpora which, as will be shown in the following section, answer most of the criticisms levelled at natural language use data, are a valuable addition to current SLA data sources. Undeniably however, all types of SLA data have their strengths and weaknesses and one can but agree with Ellis (1994: 676) that 'Good research is research that makes use of multiple sources of data.'

2.2 *Contribution of learner corpora to SLA research*

The ancestor of the learner corpus can be traced back to the Error Analysis (EA) era. However, learner corpora in those days bore little resemblance to current ones. First, they were usually very small, sometimes no more than 2,000 words from a dozen or so learners. Some corpora, such as the one used in the Danish PIF (Project in Foreign Language Pedagogy) project (see Faerch et al. 1984) were much bigger, though how much bigger is difficult to know as the exact size of the early learner corpora was generally not mentioned. This was quite simply because the compilers usually had no idea themselves. As the corpora were not computerized, counting the number of words had to be done manually, an impossible task if the corpus was relatively big. At best, it would sometimes have been possible to make a rough estimate of the size on the basis of the number of informants used and the average length of their assignments.

A further limitation is the heterogeneity of the learner data. In this connection, Ellis (1994: 49) comments that, in collecting samples of learner language, EA researchers have not paid enough attention to the variety of factors that can influence learner output, with the result that 'EA studies are difficult to interpret and almost impossible to replicate'. Results of EA studies and in fact a number of SLA studies have been inconclusive, and on occasion contradictory, because these factors have not been attended to. In his book on transfer, Odlin (1989: 151) notes 'considerable variation in the number of subjects, in the backgrounds of the subjects, and in the empirical data, which come from tape-recorded samples of speech, from student writing, from various types of tests, and from other sources' and concludes that 'improvements in data gathering would be highly desirable'.

Yet another weakness of many early learner corpora is that they were not really exploited as corpora in their own right, but merely served as depositories of errors, only to be discarded after the relevant errors had been extracted from them. EA researchers focused on decontextualized errors and disregarded the rest of the learner's performance. As a result, they 'were denied access to the whole picture' (Larsen-Freeman and Long 1991: 61) and failed to capture phenomena such as avoidance, which does not lead to errors, but to under-representation of words or structures in L2 use (Van Els et al. 1984: 63).

Current learner corpora stand in sharp contrast to what are in effect proto-corpora. For one thing, they are much bigger and therefore lend themselves to the analysis of most language features, including infrequent ones, thereby answering one of the criticisms levelled at natural language use data (see section 2.1). Secondly, there is a tendency for compilers of the current computer learner corpora (CLCs), learning by mistakes made in the past, to adopt much stricter design criteria, thus allowing for investigations of the different variables affecting learner output. Last but not least, they are computerized. As a consequence, large amounts of data can be submitted to a whole range of linguistic software tools, thus providing a quantitative approach to learner language, a hitherto largely unexplored area. Comparing the frequency of words/structures in learner and native corpora makes it possible to study phenomena such as avoidance which were never addressed in the era of EA. Unlike previous error corpora, CLCs give us access not only to errors but to learners' total interlanguage.

2.3 *Learner corpus data and ELT*

The fact that CLCs are a fairly recent development does not mean that there was no previous link between corpus linguistics and the ELT world. Over the last few years, native English corpora have increasingly been used in ELT materials design. It was Collins Cobuild who set this trend and their pioneering dictionary project gave rise to a whole range of EFL tools based on authentic data. Underlying the approach was the firm belief that better descriptions of authentic native English would lead to better EFL tools and indeed, studies which have compared materials based on authentic data with traditional intuition-based materials have found this to be true. In the field of vocabulary, for example, Ljung (1991) has found that traditional textbooks tend to over-represent concrete words to the detriment of abstract and societal terms and therefore fail to prepare students for a variety of tasks, such as reading quality newspapers and report-writing. The conclusion is clear: textbooks are more useful when they are based on authentic native English.

However much of an advance they were, native corpora cannot ensure fully effective EFL learning and teaching, mainly because they contain no indication of the degree of difficulty of words and structures for learners. It is paradoxical that although it is claimed that ELT materials should be based on solid, corpus-based descriptions of native English, materials designers are content with a very fuzzy, intuitive, non-corpus-based view of the needs of an archetypal learner. There is no doubt that the efficiency of EFL tools could be improved if materials designers had access not only to authentic native data but also to authentic learner data, with the NS (native speaker) data giving information about what is typical in English, and the NNS (non-native speaker) data highlighting what is difficult for learners in general and for specific groups of learners. As a result, a new generation of CLC-informed EFL tools is beginning to emerge. Milton's (Chapter 14, this volume) *Electronic Language Learning and Production Environment* is an electronic pedagogical tool which specifically addresses errors and patterns of over- and underuse typical of Cantonese learners of English, as attested by the HKUST Learner Corpus. In the lexicographical field, the *Longman Essential Activator* is the first learner's dictionary to incorporate CLC data (see Gillard and Gadsby, Chapter 12, this volume). In addition, use of CLC data could also give rise to new developments in ELT methodology (see Granger and Tribble, Chapter 15, this volume) and curriculum development (Mark 1996) within the framework of data-driven learning and form-focused instruction.

3 Learner corpus compilation

3.1 Learner corpus design criteria

'A corpus is a body of text assembled according to explicit design criteria for a specific purpose' (Atkins and Clear 1992: 5). It follows from this definition that a corpus needs to be carefully compiled. As pointed out by Sinclair (1991: 9) 'the results are only as good as the corpus': in other words the quality of the investigation is directly related to the quality of the data. It is especially important to have clear design criteria in the case of learner language, which is a very heterogeneous variety: there are many different types of learners and learning situations.

Table 1.1: Learner corpus design criteria

Language	Learner
Medium	Age
Genre	Sex
Topic	Mother tongue
Technicality	Region
Task setting	Other foreign languages
	Level
	Learning context
	Practical experience

Not all features singled out by Atkins and Clear are relevant to learner corpus compilation. This is because a learner corpus is a 'special corpus', a category in which Sinclair (1995: 24) also includes the language of children, geriatrics, users of extreme dialects and very specialized areas of communication. Table 1.1 lists some of the main features which are relevant to learner corpus building.

Following Ellis (1994: 49) I distinguish between the features that pertain to the language situation and those that characterize the learner. The language attributes are fairly similar to those used in native corpus compilation. Medium distinguishes between written and spoken corpora. Within each medium several genres can be distinguished: for example, argumentative vs. narrative writing or spontaneous conversation vs. informal interview. It is very important to record this attribute because learner output has been shown to vary according to the task type. The topic is also a relevant factor because it affects lexical choice, while the degree of technicality affects both the lexis and the grammar (frequency of the passive, complexity of noun phrases, etc.). Task setting refers to features such as the degree of preparedness (timed vs. untimed), whether the task was part of an exam or not and whether the learners had access to ELT tools when performing the task and if so, which.

Apart from age and sex, all the attributes pertaining to the learner are proper to learner corpora. Because of the influence of the mother tongue on L2 output, it is essential to separate learners with different L1s. In addition, it is useful to record the region the learner comes from, in order to distinguish between the regional varieties of one and the same language, such as the differences in the French spoken in Belgium and in France. Learners may also be influenced in their English by other foreign languages and it is useful to be aware of these other possible influences. Whilst proficiency level is obviously of primary importance, it is also a somewhat subjective notion: people use terms such as 'intermediate' to refer to very different degrees of proficiency. For this variable – as for many others – the wisest course is to resort to 'external criteria', i.e. criteria which 'are all founded upon extra-linguistic features of texts' rather than 'internal features', which are essentially linguistic (Atkins and Clear 1992: 5). In practice, this means that the level of proficiency is defined by referring to the teaching level (primary/secondary/university) and/or the number of hours/years of English the learners have had. After this initial selection, it will be the researcher's task to characterize learners' proficiency in terms of internal evidence.

The learning context distinguishes between English as a Second Language (ESL) and English as a Foreign Language (EFL), according to whether English is learnt in an English-speaking country or not, a crucial distinction which is too often disregarded in SLA studies. Other variables which affect learner output are subsumed under the umbrella term 'practical experience' which covers the number of years of English teaching, the ELT materials used and the period of time, if any, spent in an English-speaking country.

This list, by no means exhaustive, can of course be adapted according to research goals. The main thing is to have clear criteria so as to achieve 'soundly based conclusions, making it not only possible but indeed legitimate to make comparisons between different studies' (Engwall 1994: 49).

3.2 *ICLE design criteria*

To illustrate how these criteria can be applied in practice, I will briefly describe the principles that have governed the compilation of the International Corpus of Learner English. As appears from Table 1.2, the criteria are of two kinds: some are common to all the subcorpora of ICLE and some are variable.

The subjects who have contributed data to ICLE share the following attributes. They are young adults (c. 20 years old), who are studying

Table 1.2: ICLE design criteria

Shared features	**Variable features**
Age	Sex
Learning context	Mother tongue
Level	Region
Medium	Other foreign languages
Genre	Practical experience
Technicality	Topic
	Task setting

English in a non-English-speaking environment, i.e. they are EFL, not ESL learners. Their level of proficiency is 'advanced', a notion which is defined on the following external ground: they are university undergraduates in English Language and Literature in their third or fourth year.

ICLE consists exclusively of written productions,[2] which all represent the same genre, namely essay writing.[3] These essays, which are approximately 500 words long, are unabridged and so lend themselves to analyses of cohesion and coherence, two areas which are of particular interest in advanced learner writing. Although the essays cover a variety of topics, the content is similar in so far as the topics are all non-technical and argumentative (rather than narrative, for instance).[4]

Several of the variable attributes relate to the learner. The first is sex: the corpus contains writing by both male and female learners. The second is the learner's mother tongue background. With the years, ICLE has grown from just one national variety to 14 (French, German, Dutch, Spanish, Swedish, Finnish, Polish, Czech, Bulgarian, Russian, Italian, Hebrew, Japanese and Chinese) and the corpus keeps expanding, with new varieties being added regularly. Some of the national varieties are subdivided regionally. The Dutch subcorpus, for example, includes data from learners living in the Netherlands and in Belgium. There are variables relating to the amount/type of practical experience and others relating to the task: the essays cover a variety of topics; they can be timed or untimed, part of an exam or not; they may or may not have involved the use of ELT tools.

These variables are recorded via a learner profile questionnaire filled in by all learners (for a copy of the questionnaire, see Granger 1993).[5]

3.3 *Corpus size*

'The whole point of assembling a corpus is to gather data in quantity' (Sinclair 1995: 21). However, Sinclair hastens to add that 'In practice the size of a component tends to reflect the ease or difficulty of acquiring the material.' Is learner data easy to acquire? The answer is definitely 'no'. Even in the most favourable environment, i.e. technically advanced countries like Hong Kong, where learners are expected to word-process their assignments, learner corpus compilation is a painstaking process (see Milton 1996: 235 for a description of these difficulties and useful advice on how to address them). As a result, one can hardly expect learner corpora to reach the gigantic sizes of native corpora.

One factor which has a direct influence on the size of learner corpora is the degree of control exerted on the variables described in the preceding section and this in turn depends on the analyst's objectives. If the researcher is an SLA specialist who wants to assess the part played by individual learner variables such as age, sex or task type, or if he wants to be in a position to carry out both cross-sectional and longitudinal studies, then he should give priority to the quality rather than the quantity of the data. This is not to say that size is not a consideration. As de Haan (1992) demonstrates, optimum corpus size depends on the specific linguistic investigation to be undertaken: for some linguistic studies, for instance those involving high-frequency words or structures, relatively small samples of c. 20,000 words may be sufficient, while for others much larger samples are needed. In ICLE we have opted for a size of 200,000 words per national subcorpus. This is obviously very small in comparison with current NS corpora, but is nevertheless a real improvement over the narrow empirical foundation of most SLA studies.

Things are very different, however, if the researcher works within an ELT framework. A learner corpus compiled by an ELT publisher with a view to improving ELT tools, such as a learner's dictionary, for example, needs to be very large because it is supposed to be representative of a whole learner population. The 10-million-word Longman Learners' Corpus, where the level of detail on learner attributes is kept to a minimum, is a good illustration of this type of corpus.

3.4 *Data capture, mark-up and documentation*

Data capture, mark-up and documentation are to a large extent similar for learner corpora and native corpora. As these stages are well documented in the literature (see in particular Barnbrook's 1996 excellent introductory textbook), I will limit myself in this section to a few practical hints for the would-be learner corpus builder.

Of the three methods of data capture – downloading of electronic data, scanning and keyboarding – it is keyboarding that currently seems to be most common in the field of learner corpora. Indeed it is the only method for learners' handwritten texts.[6] Fortunately the fast-growing number of computers at students' disposal both at home and on school/university premises is improving this situation and researchers can expect to get a higher proportion of material on disk in the near future.

Both keyboarded and scanned texts contain errors and therefore require significant proofreading. In the case of learner corpora this stage presents special difficulties. The proofreader has to make sure he edits out the errors introduced during keyboarding or scanning but leaves the errors that were present in the learner text, a tricky and time-consuming task. One useful way of starting the process is to run the learner texts through a spellchecker. Highlighted forms can then be compared to the original texts and eliminated or retained as the case may be. Because of the limitations of the spellchecker, this process will only eradicate erroneous word-forms. Other errors such as omissions, additions or homonyms (*their/there, it's/its*) can only be spotted by careful manual editing. In any case, as errors can escape the attention of even the most careful of proofreaders, it is advisable to keep original texts for future reference.

Using a standard mark-up scheme called SGML (Standard Generalized Markup Language), it is possible to record textual features of the original data, such as special fonts, paragraphs, sentence boundaries, quotations, etc. Markup insertion is a very time-consuming process and researchers should aim for 'a level of mark-up which maximizes the utility value of the text without incurring unacceptable penalties in the cost and time required to capture the data' (Atkins and Clear 1992: 9). In the case of learner corpora, which tend to contain few special textual features, this stage can be kept to a minimum[7], although it should not be bypassed. For some types of analysis it would be highly advantageous to have textual features such as quotations, bold or underlining marked up in the learner corpus.

In order to be maximally useful, a corpus must be accompanied by relevant documentation. Full details about the attributes described in section 3.1. must be recorded for each text and made accessible to the analyst either in the form of an SGML file header included in the text files[8] or stored separately from the text file but linked to it by a reference system.[9] Both methods enable linguists to create their own tailor-made subcorpora, by selecting texts which match a set of predefined attributes, and focus their linguistic search on them. On this basis, learner corpus analysts are able to carry out a wide range of comparisons: female vs. male learners, French learners vs. Chinese learners, writing vs. speech, intermediate vs. advanced, etc.

4 Computer-aided linguistic analysis

4.1 Contrastive Interlanguage Analysis

A learner corpus based on clear design criteria lends itself particularly well to a contrastive approach. Not a contrastive approach in the traditional sense of CA (Contrastive Analysis), which compares different languages, but in the totally new sense of 'comparing/contrasting what non-native and native speakers of a language do in a comparable situation' (Pery-Woodley 1990: 143). This new approach, which Selinker (1989: 285) calls a 'new type of CA' and which I refer to as CIA – Contrastive Interlanguage Analysis – lies at the heart of CLC-based studies. James (1994: 14) sees this new type of comparison as a particularly apt basis for a 'quantificational contrastive typology of a number of English ILs.'

CIA involves two major types of comparison:

(1) NL vs. IL, i.e. comparison of native language and interlanguage;
(2) IL vs. IL, i.e. comparison of different interlanguages.

As the two types of comparison have different objectives, it is useful to examine them separately.

NL/IL comparisons aim to uncover the features of non-nativeness of learner language. At all levels of proficiency, but especially at the most advanced ones, these features will not only involve plain errors, but differences in the frequency of use of certain words, phrases or structures, some being overused, others underused. Before CLCs became available, work on learner production data had focused mainly on errors, but now SLA specialists can also investigate quantitatively distinctive features of interlanguage (i.e. overuse/underuse), a brand new field of study which has important implications for language teaching. To take just one example, writing textbooks and electronic tools such as grammar checkers, even those designed for non-native speakers, advise learners against using the passive and suggest using the active instead. A recent study of the passive in native and learner corpora (see Granger forthcoming a) however, shows that learners underuse the passive and that they are thus not in need of this type of inappropriate advice.

NL/IL comparisons require a control corpus of native English and as clearly appears from section 1, there is no lack of them. A corpus such as ICE (International Corpus of English) even provides a choice of standards: British, American, Australian, Canadian, etc. One factor which analysts should never lose sight of, however, is the comparability of text type. As many language features are style-sensitive, it is essential to use control corpora of the same genre. As demonstrated in Granger and Tyson (1996: 23), a comparison of the frequency of three connectors – *therefore, thus* and *however* – in the LOB, a corpus covering a variety of text types, and ICLE, which only includes argumentative essay writing, leads to a completely distorted view: it fails to bring out the underuse of these connectors by learners which clearly appears when a comparable corpus of native speaker argumentative essays is used instead. The corpus used in this case was the LOCNESS (Louvain Corpus of Native English Essays), a 300,000-word corpus of essays written by British and American university students. Whilst this corpus has the advantage of being directly comparable to ICLE, it has the disadvantage of being relatively small and containing student, i.e. non-professional writing. Criticisms can be levelled against most control corpora.[10] Each has its limitations and the important thing is to be aware of them and make an informed choice based on the type of investigation to be carried out.

The second type of comparison – IL vs. IL – may involve comparing ILs of the same language or of different languages. As the focus of this volume is on English interlanguages, I shall, in this section, deal exclusively with the former type. The main objective of IL/IL comparisons is to gain a better insight into the nature of interlanguage. By comparing learner corpora or subcorpora covering different varieties of English (different in terms of age, proficiency level, L1 background, task type, learning setting, medium, etc.), it is possible to evaluate the effect of these variables on learner output. Lorenz (Chapter 4, this volume), for example, draws interesting conclusions on the effect of age/proficiency on written output by comparing German learners of English from two different age groups with a matched corpus of native English students. On the other hand, the influence of the learner's mother tongue can be studied on the basis of corpora such as ICLE or LLC, which cover a high number of L1 backgrounds. In the field of grammar, the underuse[11] of passives mentioned above has been found to characterize the writing of advanced learners from three different mother tongue backgrounds – Swedish, Finnish and French – which might indicate that it is more of a cross-linguistic invariant than a transfer-related feature, as I would intuitively have thought on the basis of the French learner data only. Note, however, that for transfer to be unambiguously established, the researcher has to have access to good contrastive descriptions of the languages involved. Lack of reliable CA data casts doubt on the reliability of results of previous interlanguage investigations (see Kamimoto et al.'s 1992 criticism of Schachter's influential paper on avoidance). In other words, if we wish to be able to make firm pronouncements about transfer-related phenomena, it is essential to combine CA and CIA approaches.[12]

4.2 *Automated linguistic analysis*

4.2.1 LINGUISTIC SOFTWARE TOOLS

One of the main advantages of computer learner corpora is that they can be analysed with a wide range of linguistic software tools, from simple ones, which merely search, count and display, to the most advanced ones, which provide sophisticated syntactic and/or semantic analysis of the data. These programs can be applied to large amounts of data, thus allowing for a degree of empirical validation that has never been available to SLA researchers before.

Text retrieval programs – commonly referred to as 'concordancers' – are almost certainly the most widely used linguistic software tools. Initially quite rudimentary, they have undergone tremendous improvement over the last few years and the most recent programs, such as *WordSmith*, for example, have reached a high degree of sophistication, enabling researchers to carry out searches which they could never hope to do manually. They can count words, word partials and sequences of words and sort them in a variety of ways. They also provide information on how words combine with each other in the text. Finally, they can also carry out comparisons of entities in two corpora and bring out statistically significant differences, a valuable facility for CIA-type research. Gillard and Gadsby (Chapter 12, this volume) illustrate well how CLC-based concordances can be used to discover patterns of error, which in turn can be converted into useful hints for learners in ELT dictionaries or grammars.

The value of computerization, however, goes far beyond that of quick and efficient manipulation of data. Using the appropriate electronic tools, SLA researchers can also enrich the original corpus data with linguistic annotations of their choice. This type of annotation can be incorporated in three different ways: automatically, semi-automatically or manually.

Part-of-speech (POS) tagging is a good example of fully automatic annotation. POS taggers assign a tag to each word in a corpus, which indicates its word-class membership. The interest of this sort of annotation for SLA researchers is obvious: it enables them to conduct selective searches of particular parts of speech in learner productions.

Semi-automatic annotation tools enable researchers to introduce linguistic annotations interactively, using the categories and templates provided or by loading their own categories (see Meunier, Chapter 2, this volume).

If software does not exist for a particular type of annotation, researchers can always develop and insert their own annotations manually. This is the case for error tagging. Once an error taxonomy has been drawn up and error tags inserted into the text files, the learner corpus can be queried automatically and comprehensive lists of specific error types can be produced (see Milton and Chowdhury 1994, Milton, Chapter 14, this volume and Dagneaux et al. forthcoming).

The corpus linguistics literature contains many good introductory surveys to linguistic software (see Barnbrook 1996 and McEnery and Wilson 1996 for a general survey, and Meunier, Chapter 2, this volume, for a review of software tools for interlanguage analysis). Rather than duplicating these surveys, I will devote the final section of this article to some general methodological issues.

4.2.2 CLC METHODOLOGY

One issue of importance in CLC methodology is how to approach learner corpora. Research can be hypothesis-based or hypothesis-finding. Using the traditional hypothesis-based approach, the analyst starts from a hypothesis based on the literature on SLA research and uses the learner corpus to test his hypothesis. The advantage of this approach is that the researcher knows where he is going, which greatly facilitates interpretation of the results. The disadvantage is that the scope of the research is limited by the scope of the research question.

The other approach is defined as follows by Scholfield (1995: 24): 'in more exploratory, "hypothesis-finding" research, the researcher may simply decide to gather data, e.g. of language activity in the classroom, and quantify everything he or she can think of just to see what emerges'.

This type of approach is particularly well suited to CLCs, since the analyst simply has to feed the data into a text analysis program and wait to see what comes out. This approach is potentially very powerful since it can help us gain totally new insights into learner language. However, it is potentially a very dangerous one. SLA specialists should avoid falling prey to what I would call the 'so what?' syndrome, which unfortunately affects a number of corpus linguistics studies. With no particular hypothesis in mind, the corpus linguist may limit his investigation to frequency counts and publish the 'results' without providing any interpretation for them. 'So what?' are the words that immediately come to mind when one reads such articles.

There is no way however, in which one approach is better, in absolute terms, than the other. Depending on the topic and the availability of appropriate software, the analyst will opt for one or the other or combine the two. Moreover, as rightly pointed out by Stubbs (1996: 47) 'The linguist always approaches data with hypotheses and hunches, however vague.' What matters then is that the CLC enables SLA researchers to approach learner data with a mere hunch and let the computer do the rest.

Another important methodological issue is the role of the statistical-quantitative approach in computer-aided analysis. Figures and linguists can be an explosive mixture and the cry of 'it's statistically significant' is heard all too often in contexts where it has no real meaning. Scholfield's (1995) book *Quantifying Language* aims to heighten linguists' awareness of the principles underlying a field he calls 'linguometry'. He warns them that 'No investigation, however clever the design or complex the statistical analysis, is any use if the "grassroots" measurement of the variables involved is unsatisfactory in some way' (ibid.: 29). But in the field of learner corpora, the notion of statistical significance should be weighed against that of pedagogical significance. A teacher analysing his learners' output with the help of computer techniques may well come up with highly interesting new insights based on quantitative information which may in itself not be statistically significant but which nevertheless has value within a pedagogical framework. A much greater danger than not being 'statistically significant', in my opinion, is to consider figures as an end in themselves rather than a means to an end.

Lastly, a computerized approach has linguistic limitations. It is better suited to some aspects of language than others and SLA researchers should resist the temptation of limiting their investigations to what the computer can do. Ideally suited for the analysis of lexis and to some extent grammar, it is much less useful for discourse studies: 'many textual and discoursal phenomena of interest are harder to get at with the help of existing software, and a manual analysis of the texts then seems the only possibility' (Virtanen 1996: 162). SLA researchers should never hesitate to adopt a manual approach in lieu of, or to complement, a computer-based approach. As Ball (1994: 295) remarks, 'given the present state of the art, automated methods and manual methods for text analysis must go hand in hand'.

5 Conclusion

By offering more accurate descriptions of learner language than have ever been available before, computer learner corpora will help researchers to get more of the facts right. They will contribute to SLA theory by providing answers to some yet unresolved questions such as the exact role of transfer. And in a more practical way, they will help to develop new pedagogical tools and classroom practices which target more accurately the needs of the learner.

Notes

1 I use 'SLA' as a general term referring both to the description of learner language and the explanation of its characteristics. This stands in sharp contrast to the more restricted UG (Universal Grammar)-centred approach to SLA.

2 We have started compiling a corpus of informal interviews. At present only the French learner variety is covered, but there are plans to extend it to other national varieties (see De Cock et al., Chapter 5, this volume).

3 Free compositions have a somewhat ambiguous status in SLA data typology. Though considered as elicited data, they are usually classified at the lower extreme of the +/– control continuum. They are different from clearly experimental data in that learners are free to write what they like rather than having to produce items the investigator is interested in. For this reason they represent a special category of elicitation which Ellis (1994: 672) calls 'clinical elicitation' as opposed to 'experimental elicitation'.

4 The corpus also contains a small proportion of literature exam papers.

5 In one section of the questionnaire, students are requested to give their permission for the data to be used for research purposes.

6 For the transcription of spoken material, see Edwards (1992) and Crowdy (1994).

7 Going against an earlier decision (see Granger 1993: 62), it was later decided not to use mark-up to normalize any errors in the ICLE learner corpus because of the high degree of subjectivity involved.

8 See Johansson (1994) for detailed encoding guidelines.

9 Though both methods are valid, the latter is often preferred by corpus users because SGML-sensitive text retrieval software is not widely available (however, see Bradley 1996 and Porter and Quinn 1996 for recent developments in this field).

10 A good candidate, however, would be a corpus of newspaper editorials, a text type which combines the advantages of being argumentative in nature and written by professionals.

11 In my terminology 'underuse' is a neutral term, which merely reflects the fact that a word/structure is less used, while 'avoidance' implies a conscious learner strategy.

12 For a description of the Integrated Contrastive Model, which combines CA and CIA, see Granger (1996a).

CHAPTER TWO

Computer tools for the analysis of learner corpora

Fanny Meunier

Introduction

One frequently-cited advantage of corpus linguistics is that it makes it possible to conduct large-scale and accurate quantitative analyses that have not previously been feasible. This chapter focuses on the linguistic aspects of quantification in non-native production data. Special emphasis is laid on the potential of automatic and quantitative analysis to reveal features of non-nativeness and to pave the way for more qualitative analysis.

1 Raw and annotated data

Corpus linguists work on a variety of corpus formats. They work on raw, i.e. unannotated, corpora but also, and preferably, on elaborately annotated data. A brief description of the various corpus formats follows.

A **raw corpus** is a corpus of machine-readable plain texts (written or spoken) with no extra features added. Corpora can also be annotated, or **tagged**, for various linguistic aspects. Leech (1993: 275) defines corpus annotation as 'the practice of adding interpretative (especially linguistic) information to an existing corpus of spoken and/or written language by some kind of coding attached, or interspersed with, the electronic representation of the language material itself'. In what follows we will focus on the annotation of written rather than spoken corpora and concentrate on part-of-speech, syntactic, semantic, discoursal and error tagging.

1.1 Part-of-speech (or POS) tagging

POS tagging is a process of attaching a word category tag – often complemented with a series of attributes – to each word in a text. Figure 2.1 displays a sentence tagged with the *TOSCA* tagger (for details of this and other software tools featured in this chapter see the list of software at the end of this volume).

<ICLE-FIN-JYV-0001.1>	IGN(left)
We	PRON(pers,plu)
in	PREP(ge)
Finland	N(prop,sing)
are	AUX(prog,pres)
just	ADV(excl)
getting	V(montr,ingp)
a	ART(indef)
law	N(com,sing)
that	CONJUNC(subord)
also	ADV(add)
women	N(com,plu)
can	AUX(modal,pres)
do	V(cxtr,infin)
military	ADJ
service	N(com,sing)
as	PREP(ge)
volunteers	N(com,plu)
.	PUNC(per)

Figure 2.1 Sentence tagged with the *TOSCA* tagger

POS taggers are either rule-based (*ENGCG*), probabilistic (the *Birmingham Tagger*, *CLAWS*) or 'mixed', i.e. both rule-based and probabilistic in nature (*TOSCA*). They are all fully automatic, easily available (some are freely accessible on the web[1]) and on the whole, very successful. The average success rate is about 95 per cent.[2]

At first sight all the well-known and commonly used taggers look fairly similar (accessibility and success rate). However, one crucial aspect which has to be taken into account in the choice of a tagger – and which will inevitably determine the precision of further analysis – is not primarily the type of tagger itself (probabilistic, rule-based, etc.) but rather the complexity or refinement of the tagset.[3] The number of tags, including punctuation tags, varies greatly from one tagger to another: from less than 50 to more than 250 tags (*Birmingham Tagger*: 48 tags, *TOSCA*: 270 tags). The more refined the tagset, the more refined the analysis. Some taggers distinguish verbs and modal auxiliaries. Others differentiate verbs, primary auxiliaries (*do*, *have* and *be*) and modal auxiliaries. Other systems include tags for modal auxiliaries, semi-auxiliaries, *do* auxiliaries, passive auxiliaries, perfect auxiliaries and progressive auxiliaries. What this means is that a concrete analysis such as the fully automatic retrieval of passive verbs[4] could not be performed on corpora tagged with a minimal tagset. If the required tags are not included in the system, the search process would be extremely laboured and would probably lead to both low recall and extremely low precision (cf. Ball 1994). There is thus a clear link between the refinement of the tagset and the precision of the analysis to be carried out.

When it comes to tagging interlanguage, one is faced with the methodological question of whether it is necessary to use a specific tagger adapted to 'learner' language. When the tagger is used on more advanced data, research has shown that there is no need for a specific tagger for interlanguage (cf. Meunier 1995). A comparative study carried out by the TOSCA research group even showed that the success rate was sometimes slightly higher for learner language, probably because the learners' language was on the whole structurally less complex (see section 2.1). However when the language under analysis differs widely from the native speaker (NS) norm, i.e. structurally unknown varieties, children, early beginners, anomalous and pathological language, the only solution seems to be to start from the text to derive the grammar, i.e. in this case designing a specific tagger for what is viewed as a 'different' language (see Pieneman 1992: Jagtman 1994).

The best way of finding the best tagger for a particular corpus type and analysis is to run several taggers on a small representative sample of the text (5,000 words) to check their respective success rates and potential refinement.

1.2 *Syntactic tagging or 'parsing'*

Parsing is the process of marking and analysing the syntactic constituents of a text (noun phrase, verb phrase, adverb phrase, prepositional phrase, etc.). POS tagging is a prerequisite for parsing. Syntactic functions (subject, verb, object, etc.) are sometimes automatically assigned (*ENGCG*, see Figure 2.3). Figures 2.2 and 2.3 illustrate one sentence parsed with the *TOSCA* parser and one with the *ENGCG* parser.

As Barnbrook suggests (1996: 117), 'the automation of the parsing process tends to be rather more complex than the automation of tagging. The automatic parser which is capable of dealing accurately and unambiguously with completely unrestricted texts has not yet been developed.' Despite the problem of full automation, some systems provide an accurate and refined syntactic analysis. Some systems (e.g. *TOSCA*) require the manual introduction of syntactic markers with the help of a built-in editor. The analyst must bracket complex constituents (noun phrases with heavy pre- and postmodification, series of coordinated structures, etc.) in order to facilitate automatic syntactic analysis and to allow for a restricted number of possible structures in the output analysis. The obvious drawback of that method is that it is time-consuming but on the other hand it offers very refined syntactic analysis (see Figure 2.2). Other parsers such as the *ENGCG* are fully automatic. Each word is assigned all of its potential syntactic functions and constraints are then used to reduce ambiguities (for a complete description see Karlsson et al. 1995). The obvious advantage of using the *ENGCG* parser is that

```
#
NOFU,TXTU()
 UTT,S(act,decl,indic,motr,pres,unm)
  A,PP()
   P,PREP(){Through}
   PC,NP()
     NPPR,COORD()
       CJ,AJP(attru)
         AJHD,ADJ(attru){political}
       COOR,CONJN(coord){and}
       CJ,AJP(attru)
        AJHD,ADJ(attru){economical}
       NPHD,N(com,plu){difficulties}
       PUNC,PM(dash){-}
       NPPO,PP()
        P,PREP(){like}
        PC,COORD()
        CJ,NP()
         NPHD,N(com,plu){revolutions}
        COOR,CONJN(coord){or}
        CJ,NP()
         NPPR,AJP(attru)
         AJHD,ADJ(attru){natural}
        NPHD,N(com,plu){disasters}
PUNC,PM(dash){-}
SU,NP()
  DT,DTP()
   DTPS,PN(plu,quant){many}
 NPHD,N(com,plu){people}
NOFU,COORD(act,decl,indic,motr,pres)
 CJ,CONJ(act,decl,indic,motr,pres)
  V,VP(act,indic,motr,perf,pres)
   OP,AUX(indic,perf,pres){have}
   MVB,LV(indic,motr,pastp){left}
   OD,NP()
    DT,DTP()
     DTCE,PN(plu,poss){their}
    NPPR,AJP(attru)
     AJHD,ADJ(attru){native}
    NPHD,N(com,plu){countries}
COOR,CONJN(coord){and}
CJ,CONJ(act,decl,indic,intr,pres)
 V,VP(act,indic,intr,perf,pres)
 MVB,LV(indic,intr,pastp){gone}
A,PP()
 P,PREP(){to}
 PC,NP()
  DT,DTP()
   DTCE,ART(def){the}
  NPHD,N(com,plu){Western countries}
  NPPO,CL(act,indic,intens,past,rel,unm)
   SU,NP()
    NPHD,PN(rel){which}
```

```
  A,AVP(gen)
   AVHD,ADV(gen){often}
  V,VP(act,indic,intens,past)
   MVB,LV(indic,intens,past){seemed}
  A,PP()
   P,PREP(){to}
   PC,NP()
    NPHD,PN(pers,plu)[them}
  CS,PP()
   P,PREP(){like}
   PC,NP()
    NPHD,N(com,sing){paradise}
PUNC,PM(decl,per){.}
```

Figure 2.2 Sentence parsed with the *TOSCA* parser

```
"<*through>"
        "through" <*> PREP @ADVL
"<political>"
        "political" A ABS @AN>
"<and>"
        "and" CC @CC
"<economical>"
        "economical" A ABS @ AN>
"<difficulties>"
        "difficulty" N NOM PL @SUBJ @<P
"<$->"
"<like>"
        "like" <**CLB> CS @CS
        "like" PREP @ ADVL
        "like" V IMP VFIN @+FMAINV
        "like" V PRES -SG3 VFIN @+FMAINV
"revolutions>"
        "revolution" N NOM PL @SUBJ @<P
"<or>"
        "or" CC @CC
"<natural>"
        "natural" A ABS @AN>
"<disasters>"
        "disaster" N NOM PL @SUBJ @<P
"<$->"
"<many>"
        "many" <Quant> PRON ABS PL @PCOMEL-O @<P @APP
        "many" <Quant> DET POST ABS PL @QN>
"<people>"
        "people" N NOM SG/PL @SUBJ
"<have>"
        "have" V PRES -SG3 VFIN @+FAUXV
        "have" V IMP VFIN @+FMAINV
"<left>"
        "leave" PCP2 @-FMAINV
        "left" <Nominal> A ABS @OBJ
```

```
"<their>"
        "they" PRON PERS GEN PL3 @GN>
"<native>"
        "native" A ABS @AN>
"<countries>"
        "country" N NOM PL @SUBJ @OBJ @PCOMPL-O
"<and>"
        "and" CC @CC
"<have>"
        "have" V PRES -SG3 VFIN @+FAUXV
"<gone>"
        "go" PCP2 @-FMAINV
"<to>"
        "to" PREP @ADVL
"<the>"
        "the" DET CENTRAL ART SG/PL @DN>
"<*western>"
        "western" <*> <Nominal> A ABS @AN>
"<countries>"
        "country" N NOM PL @<P
"<which>"
        "which" PRON WH NOM SG/PL @SUBJ @OBJ
"<often>"
        "often" ADV ADVL @ADVL
"<seemed>"
        "seem" V PAST VFIN @+FMAINV
"<to>"
        "to" PREP @ADVL
"<them>"
        "they" PRON PERS ACC PL3 @<P
"<like>"
        "like" PREP @ADVL
        "like" V PRES -SG3 VFIN @+FMAINV
"<a>"
        "a" <Indef> DET CENTRAL ART SG @DN>
"<paradise>"
        "paradise" N NOM SG @<P
"<$.>"
```

Figure 2.3 Sentence parsed with the *ENGCG* parser

it is fully automatic. The logical drawback of full automation is that the output is less refined (Hutchinson and Barnett 1996; Van Halteren 1996). Some words remain ambiguous: they are not only assigned multiple tags (see *like* in Figure 2.3) but also multiple syntactic functions (see the first occurrence of *countries* in Figure 2.3).

As an alternative to 'full' parsing, 'skeleton' parsers and 'partial' parsers are being developed. The approach behind skeleton parsers is that they should be able to assign macro-structures to a sentence (e.g. NP–VP–NP) but need not necessarily analyse the macro-constituents into their further sub-constituents (see Leech and Garside 1991; Garside 1993). Partial parsers, on the other hand, provide a micro-analysis of one specific constituent only (e.g. noun phrases only) into its further sub-constituents. These tools are not widely available on the market and many of them are still being developed, improved or adapted.

1.3 Semantic tagging

Although semantic tagging is at a very early stage of development, researchers are carrying out a great deal of interesting work. An automatic content analyser has been developed in Lancaster. Wilson and Rayson (1993: 216) state that:

> content analysis is concerned with the statistical analysis of primarily the semantic features of texts. In practice this means using a given set of content categories . . . into which the words in the text are classified. . . . This means that hypotheses about the semantic content of texts can be generated and tested with reference to standard text norms in a way which is not possible with traditional qualitative research.

Their system contains 21 major categories and automatically assigns a semantic tag to words. Antonymy is indicated by +/− markers, multiple semantic tags can be given. A higher level of linguistic processing is applied to simple frequency counts in order to provide finely-tuned analysis such as linking the adjective and the noun it modifies (e.g. 'John-angry', 'Ruth-attractive'), modifiers and adjectives (e.g. *sensible* vs. *very sensible*), negation of items (e.g. *clever* vs. *not clever*).

This type of semantic/content analysis offers great potential for the analysis of learner language. It could help detect areas of lexical poverty such as the expression of 'belief', and the use of boosters, maximizers and minimizers.

1.4 Discoursal tagging

The development of software for marking discourse features is also in an early phase and there are no fully automatic systems. Recent developments include the software *Xanadu* (Lancaster) which is used to mark cohesive relationships (see Garside 1993 and Fligelstone 1992 for more details). Research on the automatic annotation of discourse elements is also being carried out in Nijmegen where Aarts and Oostdijk are adapting the grammar that underlies the *TOSCA* parser to deal with the language of dialogue in fiction (see Aarts and Oostdijk in preparation for a complete description of the system).

1.5 *Error tagging*

It might seem reasonable to assume that existing style and grammar checkers could, as their names suggest, be used to pinpoint grammatical and stylistic errors. The automatic flagging of errors would greatly facilitate the error annotation of learner corpora. But research carried out on these programs, which are usually developed for native speakers of the language, has shown results to be very poor (for more details see Bolt 1992 and Granger and Meunier 1994). However, the spellchecking function of these programs (also available on most wordprocessors) has turned out to be a powerful feature for interlanguage analysis. It enables the corrector to detect a variety of errors which result in non-English spelling, such as formal spelling errors (*it did not *ocur*) but also derivational errors (*he was *unconsistent*), inflectional errors (*he *gived it to me*), word coinages (*John was *overenjoyed*) and blends (*the *scientifics were proud of their vaccine*).

Error tagging is currently a manual process and therefore very time-consuming. Very few corpora have been annotated for errors and those that have are not usually made available. The French component of the International Corpus of Learner English (ICLE) is partly error-tagged (for details see Dagneaux et al. forthcoming) and Milton and Chowdhury (1994) report on an error-tagged corpus of Chinese learners of English. If large error-tagged corpora – using comparable error tagsets – were made available, it would be possible to use POS and error-tagged corpora to automatically retrieve recurring error patterns which could then lead to partial automation of the error-tagging procedure (cf. Milton and Chowdhury 1994). The analysis of error-tagged corpora will improve current pedagogical tools – dictionaries, grammar books, writing books and style and grammar checkers.

As one can see, there are quite a number of tools available for annotating many linguistic aspects of language, but annotating the corpus is only half the story. Linguists also need computer tools to support corpus analysis and this is the topic of section 2.

2 Working with software tools to analyse interlanguage

This section presents a variety of automatic approaches to statistical, lexical, grammatical and syntactic analyses of learner language. Only currently available tools and corpus formats (raw, POS tagged, etc.) are taken into account and no further mention will be made of semantic, discourse and error analysis.

2.1 *General statistics*

Wordprocessors, grammar checkers and text retrieval software provide the user with a series of general statistics.

1 Consider hyphen (except at start and end) to be part of a word: **NO** 2 Consider apostrophe (except at start and end) as part of a word: **YES** 3 Consider digits (except at start) as part of a word: **YES** 4 Consider digits at start as part of a word: **NO** 5 Count all words (if NO, exclude words in stop file): **YES** 6 Count possessive ('s) forms (if NO, add to total for form w/o's): **YES**

Figure 2.4 Default parameters of the *WORDS* program

2.1.1 WORD COUNTING

Word counting is often considered a trivial task, easily performed by the computer, but a closer look shows that it is not as easy as it may seem. Word counts of one and the same text performed by various software programs (including a wordprocessor) can yield different results: in fact a specific test using five different pieces of software[5] gave five different results, with a difference of up to 10 per cent. These differences are due to the fact that the programs have different default parameters. The user usually has no access to these parameters and does not know what the program considers to be a 'word'. Consequently, the results of statistical tests can sometimes be flawed. Researchers should therefore not use different tools to count words in different corpora. To solve these problems, Johnson (1995) has recently developed a word counting program called *WORDS* which clearly lays out the default parameters set for the task. These parameters, except for two designed for the layout and presentation of the data (alphabetical sorting and case sensitivity), are illustrated in Figure 2.4.

2.1.2 WORD/SENTENCE STATISTICS

Several word/sentence statistics are produced by text retrieval software and grammar checkers: number of sentences, average number of words per sentence, number of short and long sentences,[6] number of sentences ending with '?' or '!', average number of syllables per word, average number of letters per word, etc.

Mean sentence length (MSL) has often been used to describe the syntactic complexity or maturity of a text, but it has also been criticized for several reasons, one of which is that run-on sentences are not at all representative of syntactic maturity. To improve the notion of MSL, Hunt (1970) developed a more accurate index, the mean T-unit length (MTUL). Hunt (1970: 4) defines the T-unit as 'one main clause plus any subordinate clause or non-clausal structure that is attached to it or embedded within it'. Several studies (O'Donnell 1974; Francis and Kučera 1982; Ball 1994) have shown the advantage of MTUL over MSL but the main problem with MTUL is that unlike MSL, it cannot be computed automatically.[7]

Table 2.1: Sentence length analysis

	MSL (words/sentence)	**short sentences (<12 words) (%)**	**long sentences (>30 words) (%)**
E2F1 intermediate	17.25	50	7
E2F1 advanced	19.08	39	11
E2D1 advanced	17.59	40	8
E1 American	18.26	27.5	18
E1 British	22.36	25	20

Abbreviations:
E2F1 intermediate: first year university students, EFL learners, L1 French.
E2F1 advanced: third and fourth year university students, EFL learners, L1 French.
E2D1 advanced: third and fourth year university students, EFL learners, L1 Dutch.
E1 American: university students, L1 American English.
E1 British: university students, L1 British English.

Even though MSL does not seem to be the ideal measure to use, it can nevertheless reveal interesting features of syntactic development in interlanguage production data, especially when combined with other statistics such as the number of short and long sentences (see also Schills and de Haan 1993). A study I carried out on five similar-sized[8] corpora, each of approximately 100,000 words, revealed that there was a tendency for the MSL gradually to increase from intermediate to advanced learners and from advanced learners to native speakers. However, the most interesting feature revealed by the study was that the ratios of short to long sentences vary a great deal from non-native to native corpora (see Table 2.1). Non-native speakers use a high proportion of short sentences (40–50 per cent) and an extremely low proportion of long sentences (7–11 per cent). Native speakers, on the other hand, use both a reasonable amount of short (25–27.5 per cent) and long (18–20 per cent) sentences. These figures clearly show that native speakers tend to vary the length of their sentences much more than learners.

2.2 *Lexical analysis*

Automatic lexical analysis is performed with the help of a 'concordancer' or 'text retrieval software' which provides much more than simple retrieval functions. Concordancers are used for frequency analysis, context analysis and analysis of lexical variation.

2.2.1 FREQUENCY ANALYSIS

Wordlists (and corresponding frequencies) in various sorting formats (e.g. frequency sorting, alphabetical sorting) can be displayed. These lists are particularly useful for comparison with similar native language data. Working with raw frequencies enables the analyst to discover statistically significant overuse/underuse[9] of words or lemmas[10] and constitutes the first step towards more qualitative research.

Distribution or dispersion graphs give the distribution or dispersion of the item under analysis and show whether it is (un)evenly represented in the corpus, a measure which is particularly useful for comparison of corpora. They provide frequencies of the word (single word or combination of words) divided into *x* times *x* per cent (to be defined by the user). These frequencies are given in graph format. A study of the distribution of the word *indeed* carried out on a 200,000-word corpus made up of 100,000 words of French learner argumentative essays (0–50 per cent) and 100,000 of Dutch learner argumentative essays (51–100 per cent) illustrates the usefulness of the dispersion graphs (see Figure 2.5 – software used: *TACT*).

Figure 2.5 shows that the number of *indeed* forms is much higher in the first part of the corpus (first 50 per cent, L1 French) than in the second part (L1 Dutch learners). The difference here can be explained by the fact that French learners establish an erroneous one-to-one

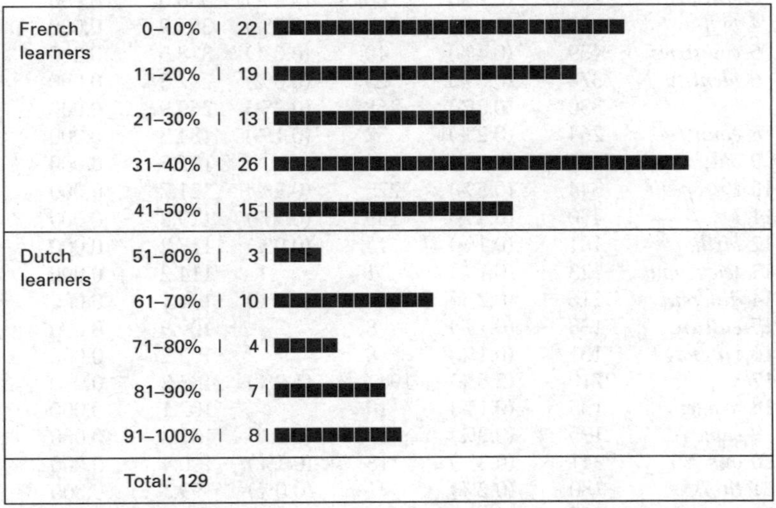

Figure 2.5 *TACT*'s distribution graph

equivalence between *indeed* and the French *en effet*, a frequent connector in French argumentative essay writing.

Comparison of wordlists. This facility, provided in *WordSmith*, compares all the words in two files and reports on all those which appear significantly more often in one than the other, including those which appear more than a minimum number of times in one file even if they do not appear at all in the other. This facility is intended to support stylistic comparison, such as comparisons of several versions or translations of the same story, or of texts on the same topic. The first and second columns of the display show the frequency in the first file (with per cent if frequency of word in file is > 0.01 per cent), the third and fourth give the frequency in the second file (again with per cent if frequency of word in file is > 0.01 per cent) and then there is the chi-square (column 5) and *p* values[11] (column 6). The words are sorted by chi-square values. Table 2.2 illustrates the output display.

Table 2.2: *WordSmith*'s 'compare lists' feature

Corpus 1: fr100.lst
Corpus 2: locness.lst

WORD	Freq. corp.1	% corp.1	Freq. corp.2	% corp.2	Chi-square	sort: key-ness
1 *ü*	755	(0.7%)	77	(0.1%)	531.0	0.000
2 *nation*	455	(0.4%)	26	(0.0%)	367.8	0.000
3 *europe*	794	(0.7%)	186	(0.2%)	358.0	0.000
4 *will*	1065	(1.0%)	337	(0.3%)	355.9	0.000
5 *countries*	439	(0.4%)	40	(0.0%)	318.5	0.000
6 *identity*	374	(0.3%)	23	(0.0%)	297.8	0.000
7 *we*	830	(0.8%)	268	(0.3%)	269.9	0.000
8 *country*	264	(0.2%)	52	(0.1%)	134.3	0.000
9 *cultural*	151	(0.1%)	6		127.5	0.000
10 *European*	544	(0.5%)	225	(0.2%)	121.7	0.000
11 *I*	430	(0.4%)	155	(0.1%)	119.8	0.000
12 *birth*	161	(0.1%)	14	(0.0%)	117.2	0.000
13 *television*	123	(0.1%)	1		114.2	0.000
14 *different*	216	(0.2%)	40	(0.0%)	114.1	0.000
15 *culture*	138	(0.1%)	8		109.9	0.000
16 *language*	131	(0.1%)	8		103.2	0.000
17 *a*	2710	(2.5%)	1947	(1.9%)	103.2	0.000
18 *women*	135	(0.1%)	10		102.1	0.000
19 *same*	195	(0.2%)	37	(0.0%)	101.3	0.000
20 *our*	341	(0.3%)	118	(0.1%)	100.4	0.000
21 *think*	180	(0.2%)	31	(0.0%)	99.1	0.000
22 *are*	847	(0.8%)	466	(0.4%)	98.5	0.000

2.2.2 CONTEXT ANALYSIS

Concordances display word tokens in context, with possible adaptation of the context size and various sorting facilities (alphabetical, ascending and descending frequencies, left- and right-hand sorting, etc.). Several types of queries can be performed. A distinction could be made between single-item queries (SIQ) and multiple-items queries (MIQ). SIQs could be described as queries based on one specific item, be it a word-token (e.g. *several*) or a lemma. MIQs involve word combinations (e.g. *on the contrary*).

It is also possible to use wildcard symbols in the queries, i.e. symbols which have the value of representing an unspecified character or sequence of characters. This allows the user to search for:

word partials:[12] /discover*/ will pick up *discover, discovers, discovered, discovering, discovery, discoveries* but also potential words such as **discoverate* or **discoverys* which are sometimes produced by learners. Stoplists, i.e. lists containing items to be excluded in the search procedure, can also be used. People interested in the lemma *argue* may search for /argu*/ but they will want to exclude 'argum*' (for argument, arguments, argumentative, . . .) and 'argua*' (for arguable and arguably).

word combinations including blanks: the /the * of/ search string will pick up all the three-word expressions starting with *the* and ending in *of*; the /on the * hand/ string will pick up *on the one hand, on the other hand*, etc.

Collocation facilities. Some software programs can estimate the lexical collocability of words on the basis of their lexical co-occurrences. *TACT*'s collocate display[13] shows all the words that occur in the neighbourhood of the selected words in the text (e.g. within five words on each side). The word types are organised by their Z-scores. The Z-score takes the observed frequency of a word in the mini-text and compares it with a theoretical frequency of occurrence within that same mini-text. Basically, a higher Z-score means that the co-occurrence has greater significance in a statistical sense. For a detailed explanation see Barnbrook (1996: 95–7).

Another powerful feature of some concordance programs is the collocation generator which can find strings of text (from two to *n* words) which are repeated at least twice. The user has to set the parameters and the output is a list of strings plus frequencies. This is a purely mechanical technique and of course not very interesting strings, such as *of an* or *will be a* and also all the topic-related strings, will be given along with more interesting combinations. A comparison of two 100,000-word corpora of argumentative essays on similar topics written by advanced learners of English (L1 French) and native American students reveals that some word sequences are used repeatedly by non-native speakers and not even used once in the native corpus. Some of these are: *a kind of, as a matter of fact, we can say that* and *with regard to*. Some other strings such as *more and more, as far as, in order to, I think that* and *on the other hand* were also produced by native speakers but they were statistically overused by the non-native speakers ($\chi^2 > 7.88$, $p > 0.005$ per cent). This confirms the findings of an earlier study conducted by Granger et al. (1994).

2.2.3 LEXICAL VARIATION ANALYSIS

Lexical variation (or diversity) is measured by the type/token ratio of the words in a text (i.e. the number of types divided by the number of occurrences, or tokens), and is computed by concordancers and some style and grammar checkers. A high type/token ratio results from the use of many different words in a text, and therefore implies that there is little repetition.

One of the problems one faces when analysing lexical variation, however, is that of text length. The shorter the text, the higher the type/token ratio. A 1,000-word essay may have a type/token ratio of about 40 per cent, whereas a 100,000-word corpus of essays may have a type/token ratio of about 10 per cent. It is therefore essential to compare texts of the same length, because the relation between the number of types and the total number of words in a text is not linear and a large number of the words used in the first 100 words of a text are likely to be repeated in the rest of the text. When dealing with texts of various lengths a different measure can also be used: the mean type/token ratio. *WordSmith*, for example, calculates the ratio for the first 1,000 running words, then again for the next 1,000 words, and so on till the end of the corpus. A running average is then computed, which means that the average ratio is based on consecutive 1,000-word chunks of text.

But just how reliable is the type/token ratio in differentiating native and non-native language in terms of variety, or richness, of vocabulary? In a study of mean type/token ratio (hereafter MTTR) from intermediate EFL, advanced EFL and native speaker (British and American) corpora, I found the advanced learners' MTTR to be only slightly higher than the intermediate and, more surprisingly, that the two native corpora had a lower MTTR than the intermediate learners. See Table 2.3.

Type/token ratio thus seems not to be a discriminating feature between NS and non-native speaker (NNS) writers and furthermore, a lexically rich essay seems not necessarily to be a good quality one.[14] Advanced learners' lexical problems are not due to a lack of vocabulary but rather to the inappropriate use they make of the words they know.

Table 2.3: Mean type/token ratio computed with *WordSmith*

	E2F1 intermediate ICLE	E2F1 advanced ICLE	E1 British	E1 American
No. of words	84,173	107,370	103,892	112,861
Type/token ratio (mean)	40.24%	40.74%	39.60%	39.76%

Abbreviations:
E2F1 intermediate: first year university students, EFL learners, L1 French.
E2F1 advanced: third and fourth year university students, EFL learners, L1 French.
E1 British: university students, L1 British English.
E1 American: university students, L1 American English.

The possible correlation between the individual type/token ratio and the marks students get is an interesting question which should be analysed more thoroughly in future research.

2.2.4 OTHER LEXICAL MEASURES

Lexical density (LD) measures the percentage of lexical words – or content words – as opposed to grammatical or function words (i.e. auxiliaries, articles, prepositions, etc.) in the total number of words. The higher the percentage, the higher the lexical density.

As McCarthy argues (1990: 72), LD is a statistical measure determined by text-type and is largely independent of text length. Interesting differences can be observed in the vocabulary loads of different texts: spoken, written, various genres, etc. (see Ure 1971; McCarthy 1990; Biber 1988).

LD counts are not automatically computed by current software. Two semi-automatic methods can however be used to calculate the lexical density of texts. Work on **raw corpora** requires the creation of a stoplist containing all the function words of the language under analysis. The total frequency of all the lexical words, i.e. those which are not in the stoplist, can then be computed and compared to the total number of words. Another way of computing LD is to use a **tagged corpus** and add up the frequencies of 'lexical tags' (number of ADJ tags + number of V tags + etc.) and then calculate the ratio of the total number of lexical tags to the total number of words.

Lexical sophistication. Software does not automatically measure lexical sophistication of texts but this measure can be obtained by comparing a text against core vocabulary lists to see what words in the text are and are not in the lists, and to see what percentage of the items in the text are covered by the lists. *VocabProfile* is a program which compares the words in a text with the words in three base lists. The first list includes the most frequent 1,000 word families in English, the second list includes the second 1,000 most frequent word families and the third list includes words which are frequent in upper secondary school and university texts across a wide range of subjects. Similar work can also be achieved by using the 'compare files' feature of *WordSmith* in which the user can create his own 'base lists'.

Lexical sophistication can also be computed on the basis of word lengths, on the hypothesis that long words are usually more sophisticated than short ones. *WordSmith*, for instance, provides the user with the exact number of *x*-letter words (from 3- to 14-letter words).

2.3 *Grammatical analysis*

Most retrieval facilities and frequency counts described in the lexical analysis section can be applied to grammatical analysis and will therefore not be rediscussed here (cf. sections 2.1 and 2.2). Instead, some types of grammatical analysis which can be performed on interlanguage data will be illustrated.

Frequencies of single tags can easily be accessed and analysed (frequency of connectors, modal auxiliaries, etc.) and results will show whether the analysed word category is equally used, overused or underused by learners and how evenly it is distributed across the corpus (see Granger and Rayson, Chapter 9, this volume).

Analyses of combinations of lexical and grammatical categories. Work on tagged corpora is much more informative and precise than work carried out on raw corpora. In a study of anaphoric reference, for instance, it is obviously convenient to have the demonstrative *that* separated from the relative *that*. The following command line 'that | PN | dem' in the concordance menu of *TACT* will pick up all instances of demonstrative *that*. The concordances can also be left- or right-hand sorted. 'That | PN | dem |>' will output right-hand sorted concordances. Another example is the analysis of phrasal verbs: a search on 'take | * | (ADV,part)' will pick up all the 'take' phrasal verbs in the corpus.

Tag sequences. Analysis of the frequency, distribution and representation of sequences of tags can provide new insights into learner language (see Aarts and Granger, Chapter 10, this volume). The analysis of erroneous or unusual tag sequences might also lead to the discovery of errors in interlanguage (Atwell and Elliott 1987).

Using text retrieval programs[15] on POS tagged corpora enhances the power of grammatical analysis a great deal. These programs offer a wide range of possibilities and are now available at very reasonable prices. It is surprising that very few articles dealing with interlanguage analysis based on POS tagged corpora have yet been published.

2.4 *Syntactic analysis*

As shown in section 1, syntactic analysis has not yet been fully automated. Some syntactically analysed corpora are available (the Penn Treebank, the Nijmegen corpus) but they are few and far between.

To compensate for this, a number of intelligent editors have been designed specifically for work on parsed corpora. They help the user in his syntactic analysis and once the corpus is analysed, they can be used to perform structural queries based on a higher level of linguistic analysis. A concrete example of such a system is the *TOSCA Tree Editor* which helps the user to build new tree structures from raw text, to edit material which has already been POS tagged and to work on partial syntactic annotations produced by an (automatic/semi-automatic) parser. The system can also query syntactically analysed sentences and output frequency of structures (how many prepositional phrases?), combination of structures (how many adverb phrases are followed by noun phrases?) or internal organisation of structures (how many noun phrases have adjective premodifiers and relative clause postmodifiers?).

The automatic characterization of language involves work on words, tags and combinations of both, but this is not enough. Linguists also need insight into the syntactic structures of language. There are few quantitative or qualitative studies of syntactic structures in the literature. Oostdijk and de Haan (1994: 41) point out that even though frequency counts of syntactic structures are obviously useful, very few studies have been done. Biber's (1988) study of variation in spoken and written English combined frequency counts of *items* (indefinite pronouns, demonstratives, *seem/appear*, etc.) and of *structures* (e.g. subordinator-*that* deletion as a form of syntactic reduction, agentless passives, WH relatives). Such automated studies are very rare and, if they are long over-due for native English, they are virtually non-existent for ESL or EFL.

The results of such studies would improve the description of learner language a great deal. Even if English is 'syntactically' a very flexible language and if at an advanced level very few structures are really erroneous, the overuse or underuse of some structures and the internal complexity or simplicity of some other structures could reveal interesting features of interlanguage (Meunier in preparation).

Conclusion

In conclusion I shall focus on four major issues raised by this study.

Firstly, many user-friendly software tools for language analysis are available nowadays. They provide the user with easily accessible search facilities and generate quantitative measures automatically. These tools should be used in full awareness not only of their possibilities and options (what kind of type/token ratio do they give? which word classes does the system include? etc.) but also of their limitations and drawbacks. The tools may be limited but progress in the field is extremely rapid. At the same time, it is essential to report on their drawbacks because this is the main means by which they can be improved.

Secondly, we are fortunate to have various text 'formats' (raw, tagged, parsed) at our disposal nowadays. The choice of the right text format is an essential prerequisite for research. Task, tool and text choice should always be correctly matched. Short, manual pilot studies are sometimes worth carrying out in order to determine the feasibility, accuracy and reliability of automatic analysis (see Granger forthcoming a).

Another important point is that quantitative measures are essential in language analysis but they are not sufficient. Surface differences – or similarities – between aspects of native and non-native language always require further qualitative investigation.

Finally I would like to plead for more investigation into the syntactic structure of interlanguage, which is certain to reveal many interesting features of non-nativeness which are as yet undiscovered.

Notes

1 Freely available on the web are: the *Brill Tagger* (anonymous ftp blaze.cs.jhu.edu/pub/brill/Programs), the *Xerox Tagger* (http://www.xerox.com/lexdemo/xlt-overview.html). A free limited tagger service is also available for the *ENGCG* tagger (engcg-info@ling.helsinki.fi).

2 This overall percentage does not mean that all word classes are equally correctly assigned. The user should be aware that some very frequent and unambiguous word classes are always assigned correctly. More problematic tags are sometimes assigned with a much lower success rate (e.g. adverbial particles vs. prepositions). It should also be noted that some taggers do not always disambiguate multiple tags, i.e. in ambiguous contexts all the possible word classes of a word remain, which skews the overall success rate.

3 The tagset is the list of all the POS tags and their attributes.

4 The analysis of passive forms is potentially very useful for the description of learner language (see Granger forthcoming a).

5 A wordprocessor (*WordPerfect 5.1*), a text retrieval program (*TACT*), two spell, grammar and style checkers (*Grammatik* and *Correct Grammar*) and a word counting program (*WORDS*).

6 The default settings for length of short and long sentences in *Grammatik* are < 12 and > 30 respectively. These defaults can be changed by the user.

7 It could potentially be computed on parsed texts if the syntactic description was refined enough and if length-counting devices were included in the system.

8 In a comparison of two (or more) corpora it is advisable to work on similar-sized corpora. The results of some statistical tests can be flawed if the sizes are too dissimilar. Note also that frequencies cannot be extrapolated from small to large corpora.

9 Significant statistical overuse and underuse of items (words, lemmas, structures, etc.) are usually computed with the help of the chi-square (χ^2) test. For an introduction to the χ^2 test see McEnery and Wilson (1996: 69–71).

10 Some concordancers have a (semi-automatic) lemmatizer facility included. Most of the time the user has to group all the entries of one and the same lemma together (e.g. *go, goes, going, went, gone* = lemma 'go'). Automatic searches can then be performed on lemmatized entries (e.g.: 'go').

11 See note 9.

12 Work with word partials can sometimes be used as one way of lemmatizing word entries, depending on the (ir)regularity of the word morphology.

13 A similar feature in *WordSmith* is the 'key-word links' function.

14 Linnarud (1975: 19ff), in an investigation of compositions written in English by Swedish university students, showed that texts with high lexical variation did not necessarily receive good marks. What was true, however, was that all writers evaluated as above average had at least an average figure for lexical variation.

15 Some programs cannot work on POS tagged corpora.

Part II

Studies of Learner Grammar, Lexis and Discouse

CHAPTER THREE

Vocabulary frequencies in advanced learner English: a cross-linguistic approach

Håkan Ringbom

1 Introduction

The emergence of a corpus of advanced learner English (see Granger, Chapter 1, this volume) has made possible a new, more concrete approach to the lexical features of learner language. Opinions about how learner language actually differs from native speaker (NS) language frequently occur in the literature. So far, however, they have not been substantiated by concrete evidence from larger collections of texts. There are some small-scale studies comparing learners of one particular L1 with NSs (e.g. Linnarud 1986), but for more information we need large numbers of texts of the same type produced by speakers of many different language groups. When these are compared with each other and with similar NS productions a wider perspective can be achieved.

This is an exploratory study where I will try to show how vocabulary frequencies may reveal interesting cross-linguistic differences. I have made use of seven western European learner corpora from the International Corpus of Learner English (ICLE) database (771,278 words altogether) comparing them with each other and with the LOCNESS native speaker (British and American) corpus of argumentative essays. The essays are all argumentative (the literature exam papers in some of the corpora have been excluded), but they deal with a variety of topics.[1]

2 Overall vocabulary patterns

In this study I have worked with percentages per 10,000 words. The raw figures are easily calculable from the given percentage and the size of each corpus. Quantitative terms, overuse and underuse, will be used, but no statistical significance tests have been made to back them up. This is mainly because the present state of the ICLE corpus is incomplete and even minor changes in the form of texts added to the

Table 3.1: The 100 most frequent words out of total vocabulary (%)

	NS	FRE	SPA	FIN	FINSW	SWE	DUTCH	GERM
1 (the)	6.6	5.9	6.1	5.6	5.2	5.0	6.1	5.1
1–10	25.6	25.7	26.3	25.1	24.9	24.8	24.9	23.8
1–30	37.2	39.2	39.7	37.9	38.9	38.2	37.6	36.8
1–50	42.8	46.2	46.7	44.6	46.0	44.9	44.4	43.6
1–70	46.8	52.4	51.7	49.4	50.8	49.6	48.6	48.3
1–100	51.3	57.3	56.2	54.2	56.0	54.6	53.0	52.9

subcorpora will affect the frequencies to some extent. Still, since the words examined are those with the highest frequencies in English and thus in most cases occur well over 100 times in all, or nearly all corpora, most differences commented upon should have a general significance even without a supporting statistical apparatus.

Since the vocabulary of non-native speakers (NNSs) is smaller than that of NSs of a comparable educational level, a reasonable hypothesis is that the overused words would be primarily those word forms that occur most frequently in the texts. In other words, many high-frequency words would have consistently higher frequencies in NNS texts than in texts written by NSs. But whether such overused high-frequency words would be found in the top 10, the top 50 or the top 100 words is not clear. Some elucidation is provided by Table 3.1, which shows the percentage of the most frequent words of the total vocabulary used in the corpora. The topmost row shows the frequency of the commonest word in the language, the definite article. The next row gives the percentage for the ten most frequent words in the language, where, apart from *the*, the words *to, of, is, and, in, a* and *that* are always included. Row 3 shows the percentage of the 30 most frequent words in the language, the following row for the 50 most frequent words, and so on.

In all corpora, the ten most frequent words account for about a quarter of the total vocabulary of a text: some a little more, others a little less. In the last three rows, however, a difference is developing between the NS corpus and the learner corpora in that the figures for NSs are consistently lower than for learner groups. Table 3.1 shows that it is words in the frequency bands from 30 to 100, rather than those among the top ten, which tend to be overused by learners.

3 High-frequency verbs

If the words commonly used by learners are found especially in the frequency bands 30–100, can special categories of overused words be discerned? It is clear that most of the top 100 words are function words

Table 3.2: Occurrences of the most frequent verbs per 10,000 words (lemmas)

Word	NS	FRE	SPA	FIN	FINSW	SWE	DUTCH	GERM
be	467	484	506	533	537	460	503	489
have	110	133	153	163	158	159	145	133
do	50	55	75	76	85	72	72	84
can	55	65	72	78	81	53	68	64
Total	682	737	806	850	861	744	788	770

with grammatical rather than lexical meaning. If we consider the different word classes, verbs will here be more interesting than nouns, which tend to indicate content rather than language or style. Table 3.2 lists the lemmatized forms, including contracted forms such as *don't* and *isn't*, of the high-frequency verbs *be, have, do* and *can,* which are mostly used as auxiliaries. (The other tables in this chapter list non-lemmatized word forms.)

The exception from the general pattern of learners overusing these auxiliary verbs is provided by the Swedes, who use both *be* and *can* less than other nationalities do, even less than the natives.

As far as the most frequent main verbs are concerned, NSs show not only a smaller number of high-frequency verbs used more than once in 1,000 words, but also a distribution different from that of the learners. *Make* is the most frequent verb form (14 occurrences per 10,000 words) in NS, followed by *use* (13), *believe* (10) and *feel* (10). These are the only verb forms with a frequency of ten or more. NNSs, on the other hand, also favour *make,* but tend to use some other verbs, especially *think* and *get,* even more frequently. *Find, want* and *know* are other favourites with learners. Table 3.3 shows that the figures for high-frequency verbs are nearly always higher for learners than for NSs. Swedish speakers in particular are very fond of monosyllabic high-frequency verbs, and in the choice of these verbs there is a strikingly high correspondence between Swedish and Finland-Swedish learners, which is not paralleled in the use of auxiliaries.

In this context we may note Granger's (1996b: 118) conclusion, based on two 10,000-word corpora of French and NS ICLE essays on the same topic, that 'French learners do not overuse Romance words to the detriment of Germanic words (at least in formal writing); on the contrary, they seem to overuse Germanic words'. Overuse of Germanic high-frequency verbs is an even more conspicuous feature in learners with a Germanic language as L1 (cf. Källkvist 1993, who makes the point that Swedish learners overuse common verbs such as *do, make* and *get).*

Table 3.3: High-frequency main verb forms: occurrences per 10,000 words

Word	NS	FRE	SPA	FIN	FINSW	SWE	DUTCH	GERM
think	6	21	21	22	30	30	16	22
get	6	7	18	18	16	16	14	19
make	14	12	16	15	17	17	12	10
become	8	14	7	13	9	9	13	5
want	6	11	11	9	14	12	11	14
take	9	10	6	9	11	12	8	11
find	5	9	7	7	11	11	6	10
know	4	7	9	9	11	11	9	10
use	13	4	13	9	9	11	6	6
go	5	8	7	8	10	8	12	12
live	3	11	12	6	8	11	6	10

The most conspicuous overuse by learners occurs with the verb *think*, and the reason is not hard to find. It has often been pointed out that learners, including advanced learners, overuse the phrase *I think*, and Table 3.4 shows that this is the case also in the ICLE corpora:

Table 3.4: *I think*: frequencies per 10,000 words

NS	FRE	SPA	FIN	FINSW	SWE	DUTCH	GERM
3	10	5	7	16	16	6	9

In particular, learners with Swedish as their L1 show a predilection for this phrase. Like Finnish learners, they also overuse the verb *get*. The use of *get* illustrates what is one of the main shortcomings of ICLE learners: a lack of collocational competence in that a word is used in contexts where native speakers would normally choose some other word (*to get their own opinion* pro *to form their own opinion*). However, this Nordic overuse is more conspicuous in some contexts than others.

There are four main uses of the verb *get:* with a direct object, with a past participle or adjective, with an adverb forming a phrasal verb, and with an infinitive. Nordic (and Spanish) learners overuse *get* especially when it takes a direct object (*get an education*), not to the same extent when it is followed by a participle, and not at all when it is followed by an adverb. This can be seen from Table 3.5.

Table 3.5: Different uses of *get*: frequencies per 10,000 words

	NS	FRE	SPA	FIN	FINSW	SWE	DUTCH	GERM
Get + obj	2	3	11	9	10	9	6	8
Get + PP/adj	1	2	6	5	3	3	4	4
Get + adv	3	2	2	3	3	3	3	5
Get + inf	0	0	0	0	0	1	1	2

4 Top word forms

Table 3.6 contains a list of the most frequent words in the different subcorpora. Since the topics of the essays tend to cluster in different nationalities, there has to be some principle to exclude such words as are central to the content of the essays but reveal little about their

Table 3.6: Frequencies per 10,000 words

Word	NS	FRE	SPA	FIN	FINSW	SWE	DUTCH	GERM
the	662	591	616	556	519	503	614	513
of	357	373	382	322	301	299	309	267
to	323	337	302	308	322	357	301	338
and	227	235	269	276	262	302	274	273
a	211	262	217	218	241	217	242	243
is	203	192	210	221	231	189	180	179
in	197	193	226	205	212	212	212	187
that	179	143	163	157	157	161	142	135
be	102	115	81	109	100	95	86	86
it	97	116	126	142	121	122	114	115
this	95	82	87	55	62	68	74	63
for	95	87	79	97	87	91	100	97
as	88	79	72	74	79	75	64	72
not	81	87	96	86	103	87	82	86
are	77	96	121	108	116	95	102	97
they	66	77	86	63	68	65	107	75
by	60	38	45	32	49	34	51	43
with	59	53	55	48	58	58	59	61
on	59	55	42	53	58	47	63	53
have	56	77	88	88	92	99	74	67
their	55	60	58	50	41	54	62	55
will	49	88	27	26	47	46	34	25
would	46	34	28	43	44	38	25	26
an	45	39	40	38	36	32	36	34
or	42	52	62	56	63	50	46	59
from	39	34	26	29	28	37	32	28

continued overleaf

Table 3.6: (cont'd)

Word	NS	FRE	SPA	FIN	FINSW	SWE	DUTCH	GERM
one	37	42	32	38	41	32	35	44
has	37	39	46	56	54	43	40	33
but	36	66	70	57	55	58	64	67
people	35	62	63	71	63	65	70	57
we	34	81	98	65	121	120	34	41
more	32	42	40	42	37	35	37	33
there	32	26	35	53	53	40	41	45
if	32	34	38	45	49	40	25	36
can	30	38	47	50	54	33	43	38
these	30	20	28	19	20	20	22	17
many	30	19	21	22	22	23	17	20
which	29	42	46	29	25	28	42	30
because	28	23	43	21	16	15	30	28
all	28	48	53	47	43	43	47	36
at	27	35	30	25	34	36	36	44
was	27	26	25	24	25	21	57	42
he	26	20	24	24	26	14	42	38
I	25	45	36	52	94	88	41	136
also	25	29	16	28	20	25	27	20
our	25	37	60	33	55	67	14	27
should	24	25	15	26	21	23	17	25
other	24	28	30	30	28	33	25	26
who	24	19	32	32	31	22	36	38
what	23	29	30	35	36	39	24	26
about	23	19	26	28	23	31	25	30
only	23	25	28	23	27	21	27	34
his	23	18	15	14	21	12	24	28
no	22	20	14	28	26	22	17	24
when	22	17	27	25	27	28	32	28
been	20	18	23	27	23	24	18	13
life	20	19	32	25	28	17	17	32
do	20	27	37	34	45	40	29	38
its	19	30	15	17	5	10	16	6
such	18	18	13	11	10	9	9	11
could	17	16	18	17	16	11	15	12
some	17	30	33	37	27	25	26	24
how	17	11	13	16	18	21	11	14
were	17	13	20	13	13	14	35	17
any	16	11	12	13	10	10	9	12
does	16	12	11	14	16	11	11	13
out	16	10	8	12	12	13	18	20
so	16	27	33	30	27	26	31	31
being	16	11	15	13	11	13	11	18

Table 3.6: (cont'd)

Word	NS	FRE	SPA	FIN	FINSW	SWE	DUTCH	GERM
most	15	16	21	20	19	17	19	16
into	15	9	8	11	14	14	12	14
them	15	27	34	19	19	22	27	28
very	14	22	31	25	24	16	28	24
those	14	11	16	14	13	9	14	9
make	14	12	16	15	17	17	12	10
time	14	18	25	20	19	23	19	23
even	14	18	15	29	24	17	19	18
than	13	17	15	19	20	17	17	16
way	13	17	26	24	24	24	20	17
up	13	13	10	12	16	15	18	18
new	13	21	14	12	11	22	10	10
own	13	17	6	11	14	15	10	11
children	12	10	12	13	19	16	13	16
society	12	17	21	20	25	24	18	12
like	12	13	18	17	21	19	21	25
then	11	7	8	9	11	10	10	10
had	11	10	11	14	15	12	26	23
much	11	10	13	15	14	14	12	14
just	10	8	8	17	10	11	12	14
example	10	12	12	16	10	10	12	6
first	10	15	10	6	6	8	16	12
important	9	12	18	14	12	14	11	13
different	9	18	15	15	13	18	10	9
still	9	12	7	13	18	9	17	12
us	9	17	27	22	26	25	8	12
world	8	27	34	42	26	31	20	16
you	8	33	33	34	49	31	46	72
want	7	11	11	9	14	12	11	14
good	7	9	15	15	14	12	12	11
same	7	17	11	13	14	12	9	8
think	6	23	21	22	30	30	16	22
get	6	8	18	18	16	16	14	19
where	6	10	8	9	15	10	12	12
without	6	10	13	11	8	10	9	12
too	6	10	9	12	10	10	12	11
women	6	10	13	20	14	5	13	11
television	5	25	28	38	11	4	30	3
countries	5	35	12	17	14	18	9	4
always	4	11	10	11	11	8	10	11
things	4	6	16	13	9	18	12	12
money	4	12	45	27	14	8	16	8

language and style. I have only included in Table 3.6 those words which occur at least once in 1,000 words in most of the subcorpora (five out of eight). Words excluded because they reach this frequency in only one or two subcorpora, but not in the others are, for example *imagination* (SWE, SPA), *nature* (FINSW, FRE), *language* (FIN), *sovereignty* (NS), *European* (FRE, NS). Often these words occur in the title of the essay. A consistent selection procedure excluding words essential to the content of the essay reduces topic sensitivity, which will to some extent be present whenever word frequency patterns are established for texts with different content.

The frequencies of the top ten words or so do not show conspicuous divergences in the corpora. *The* and *that* seem to be somewhat more used by native speakers than by learners, while *and* is used less.

As Hofland and Johansson (1982: 22) point out, a high frequency of *an* indicates a high proportion of Latinate vocabulary. For Germanic learners it is therefore not surprising that contrary to *a*, which NSs use less than all learners, *an* has a lower frequency in all learner corpora than in NS. French and Spanish learners use *an* more than Germanic learners, but less than NSs. That the French group does not use *an* more is especially interesting against the background that they use *a* more than any other group. Granger's statement quoted above about French learners overusing Germanic rather than Romance words, thus receives further support.

Among words overused by all learner groups are auxiliaries (*are, have, can, do*), personal pronouns (*we, I, you*), negations (*not*) and conjunctions (*or, but, if*). Underused words, which are fewer in number, are, for example, the demonstratives *this* and *these*, and the prepositions *by* and *from*.

While many high-frequency words have consistently lower frequencies in all varieties of learner language, there are naturally also words which show great variation: some learner groups overuse them, whereas others underuse them. The underused words, in particular, may show a clear relation to the structure of the L1. For instance, Finns tend to underuse prepositions, especially multifunctional prepositions (see frequencies for *with, by, at*). This must be seen against the background of the Finnish language: in Finnish the relationships expressed by prepositions in the Germanic languages are normally indicated by case endings, which, however, have several other functions as well.

5 Conclusion

Study of word frequencies in ICLE can shed more light on the characteristics of advanced learner English and, at any rate indirectly, on the role of L1-transfer. At least in the Finnish, Finland-Swedish and Swedish corpora errors clearly attributable to L1-transfer are relatively few.

While such overt transfer, as manifested in errors, relies closely on forms and patterns perceived to be similar in L1 and L2, we also have to reckon with covert transfer, where L1-based procedures are being used in the absence of appropriate L2-procedures being available, for instance in discourse. Contrary to overt transfer errors, cross-linguistic formal similarity is largely irrelevant to covert transfer (see Ringbom 1992; cf. Kellerman 1995; Jarvis forthcoming). And even though transfer-based grammatical or lexical errors are not especially common in ICLE, this does not mean that the L1 plays an insignificant part in the form the texts have taken. It rather means that transfer is manifested in other, more subtle ways than the obvious errors made by learners at earlier stages. Most clearly this can be seen in learner groups whose L1 is structurally different from English. Evidence of covert transfer is manifested by avoidance or underuse rather than overuse: L2-constructions without direct equivalents in the L1 tend to be avoided or underused. If a particular English category or structure is missing in the L1 it is generally underused even by advanced learners.[2]

The frequency tables above show that the English of advanced learners from different countries with a relatively limited variation of cultural and educational background factors shares a number of features which make it differ from NS language. A frequently voiced view is that learner language is vague and stereotyped. This would be a natural consequence of its vocabulary being more limited than that of native speakers. However, concrete evidence of exactly what constitutes this vagueness has been hard to come by.

High-frequency words in ICLE may provide concrete support for the labelling of advanced learner language as 'vague'. Table 3.6 shows that there are especially two vague words that are much overused by all seven learner categories: *people* and *things*.

It may, however, be relevant to note a different view about vagueness and learner language, even though it refers to spoken, not written production. Channell (1994: 21) states: 'It is often noticed by teachers that the English of advanced students, while grammatically, phonologically and lexically correct, may sound rather bookish and pedantic to a native speaker. This results in part from an *inability to use appropriate vague expressions*' (my italics). Unfortunately Channell does not say what particular expressions she is referring to. The impression of bookishness and pedantry may result from many other stylistic features, often from the use of an inappropriate stylistic register.

It seems, however, reasonable to suggest that advanced learner language is in some respects more, in others less, vague than NS language. The ICLE frequency lists given here provide some examples of overuse of vague words. Table 3.6 thus reveals that high-frequency vague, i.e. non-numerical, quantifiers occur more often in learner texts than in NS texts. The frequencies for *more, all, other, some* and *very* are all lowest in the NS corpus, while exceptions from this trend are provided by *many* and *any*, which occur more often in NS than in any learner corpus. *Very* has been characterized by Granger (forthcoming c) as *the* all-round amplifier *par excellence* which is significantly overused by learners (see also Lorenz 1996 and this volume for German overuse of *very*). Granger refers only to French-speaking learners, but Table 3.6 shows that all other learner groups except the Swedes overuse *very* even more than the French. While a frequency table of the top words gives an indication of what words are overused by groups of learners, evidence of underuse, which would mostly occur with low-frequency words, must be sought elsewhere, for example by analysing frequency lists of near-synonyms in large corpora.

The limited vocabulary that advanced learners have in comparison with NSs is a main reason for the general impression of learner language as dull, repetitive and unimaginative, with many undeveloped themes. Often they also give an impression of verbosity in that many words are, strictly speaking, unnecessary in their contexts. One of the few researchers producing concrete evidence for this is Altenberg (1996), who analysed the Swedish subcorpus of ICLE, showing the ways in which Swedes in their argumentative essays produce a language close to fiction and informal talk (see also Granger and Rayson, Chapter 9, this volume). The subject of their sentences mostly consists of a single head without modifiers (especially pronouns) and their lexical density is lower than for NSs: they use a higher proportion of verbs and a lower proportion of nouns and non-Germanic words. To some extent this can be deduced from the tables above. These features have the effect of diluting the information content (for a discussion of NNS writers' tendency to focus on interpersonal involvement at the expense of information content, see Petch-Tyson, Chapter 8, this volume). Frequency lists show that while a few common words are underused by learners, many more are overused, regardless of the learners' L1. Table 3.6 shows that learner groups in general overuse some core nouns (*time, way, society, people, things*), core verbs (*think, get*), auxiliaries (*be, do, have, can*) and most vague quantifiers (*all, some, very*). Conjunctions are another type of words where learners show higher frequencies than NSs: *but* and *or* are consistently overused. As for the less frequent connective devices, the choice of favourites seems largely to depend on which ones have close equivalents in the L1 (see Granger and Tyson 1996 for French-speaking learners).

The high-frequency words and phrases used by learners are at times unnecessary or could easily be supplanted by e.g. adverbial constructions. Frequency tables provide support for learners sticking to what Hasselgren (1994) has aptly termed 'the teddy bear principle' in connection with Norwegian learners: learners depend on what is familiar and clutch for the words they feel safe with. But we must not forget the inevitable variation existing not only across different L1-groups but also between individuals of the same group, between teaching traditions, educational systems and different topics treated in the texts. Sufficiently large corpora reduce this variation, but it is still better to talk only about tendencies rather than making categorical statements. What we can say is that learners with a particular L1 *tend to* use a particular word or phrase more or less frequently than both other learner groups and native speakers.

Jarvis (forthcoming) has pointed out that imprecise form-concept associations account for a large proportion of learner errors, also at advanced stages. He draws on the theory of experientialism and points to the reluctance of learners to modify their conceptual L1-based systems when learning another language. His is a promising approach to elucidating lexical differences existing between NS and advanced learner language. However, it requires detailed study of the contexts of the errors, which will be feasible only when ICLE has been error-tagged. And it seems that the non-native features of the ICLE essays are less due to errors than to an insufficient and imprecise, though not necessarily erroneous, use of the resources available in English (cf. Ringbom 1993).

Sensible use of existing corpora like ICLE, LOB and Brown can dispel stereotyped views about 'correct' and 'incorrect' usage that many, if not most students have when they enter university. If students make use of existing corpora where they can look up authentic data this can indeed prove 'a valuable eye-opener to the wider linguistic issues of frequency, acceptability, collocability and style in current language' (Svartvik 1993: 19).

Work on learner corpora has only just begun. This chapter has tried to show that a seemingly simple word frequency count may provide a useful starting point for many interesting small-scale projects where the general characteristics of advanced learner language as well as the relative importance of transfer and universal features can be further explored.

Acknowledgements

I am grateful to Signe-Anita Lindgren, Anthony Johnson and Tuija Virtanen-Ulfhielm for much valuable practical help, and to Sylviane Granger for constructive criticism of this chapter.

Notes

1 The sizes of these subcorpora are as follows:
NS = native speaker corpus, 82,329 words

FRE = French (Belgian) learner corpus, 129,549 words
SPA = Spanish learner corpus 60,487 words
FIN = Finnish learner corpus, 119,928 words
FINSW = Finland-Swedish learner corpus, 55,333 words
SWE = Swedish learner corpus, 100,863 words
DUTCH = Dutch learner corpus, 111,597 words
GERM = German learner corpus, 111,192 words

2 Underuse, or avoidance, of phrasal verbs has been treated by Sjöholm (1995). Learners generally tend to avoid phrasal verbs: more so, if phrasal verbs are not found in their L1 (as in Finnish), and less so in advanced learners. Cf. Hulstijn and Marchena (1989), Laufer and Eliasson (1993).

CHAPTER FOUR

Overstatement in advanced learners' writing: stylistic aspects of adjective intensification[1]

Gunter Lorenz

Advanced learners are typically 'advanced' by virtue of having mastered the basic rules of syntax and morphology. Where they do deviate from the norm, their deviations usually – in written production at least – concern rather finer points of lexico-grammar and style. These are difficult to pinpoint individually, yet in their accumulated effect tend to generate an impression of 'non-nativeness' or 'lack of idiomaticity'. This report attempts to identify such peculiarities in German learners' intensification of adjectives.

1 The issue

Although syntactically marginal, adjective intensification plays a major role in spoken and written interaction. By amplifying and downtoning adjectival qualities, as in *crucially important* or *hardly significant*, we express assertion or caution, emphasis or doubt, and we take a committed or a non-committal stance towards the message in question. More than their mere denotation would suggest, intensifiers therefore convey speaker-stance, in some cases even to the point of creating a sense of identity and group membership.[2] It is this interpersonal function – and the resulting need for continual innovation (Partington 1993) – which makes intensifiers sensitive to style, and presumably also to non-native versus native usage.

The present report is based on the results of a more detailed learner corpus study (Lorenz 1997) in which adjective intensification is examined from a functional perspective. More specifically, the investigation aimed at contrasting the ways in which native and non-native writers deal with the problem of 'how to scale an adjectival quality'. For this purpose, it would not have been sufficient to search and retrieve a set of previously identified intensifiers. To take stock, the non-native and native inventories of adjective intensification were recorded as comprehensively as possible, rather than checking the corpora for a pre-defined finite set. The target data therefore includes *any* lexical item or phrase which was found to focus on an adjective and which had an intensifying function.

2 The corpora

The corpus searches were effected on two native and two non-native corpora containing argumentative essays from the following sources:

+ **German teenagers (16–18)**. Citations from this corpus are marked **'BWF'** below; the acronym stands for the *Bundeswettbewerb Fremdsprachen*, Germany's national foreign language competition.
+ **German university students of English (20–25)**; corpus citations marked **'UNI'**.
+ **British teenagers (15–18)**; corpus citations marked **'GCE'**.[3]
+ **British undergraduates (19–23)**; corpus citations marked **'LOCNESS'**, the ICLE reference corpus of native argumentative writing.

These four corpora contain around 100,000 words each. While the corpus structure was originally designed for learner/native speaker comparisons of different age groups (BWF vs. GCE and UNI vs. LOCNESS), it also enables developmental comparisons within either population (BWF vs. UNI and GCE vs. LOCNESS), or between them (BWF + GCE vs. UNI + LOCNESS). Furthermore, it should be interesting to see how the four sub-corpora inter-relate with respect to linguistic proficiency.

3 The search results

The corpus searches have produced three sets of results, concerning (a) the non-native/native differences in the actual *inventories* of adjective intensification, i.e. their lexical resources and their distribution across the four corpora, (b) the individual non-native *deviations*, and (c) several *stylistic* aspects of adjective intensification, as become apparent in the overall numerical patterns. This report solely concentrates on some of the implications of (b) and (c).

The most immediate difference between learners' and native speakers' usage lies in the overall intensifier counts, as can be seen in Table 4.1.

Table 4.1: Sum total of all adj-int instances[4]

	BWF	UNI	GCE	LOC
adj - int (raw)	910	463	358	393
adj - int (SF)	696	643	522	427

The figures indicate that the German learners use far more intensifiers than the native speakers. Taking the two sub-corpora of each group together, the non-native speakers (NNS) have a standardized total of 1,339, compared with the native speakers' (NS) 949. Although this represents an NNS overuse of 41.1 per cent, and one which is extremely significant statistically (the chi-square is as high as 62.9), there is also a marked *stylistic* significance: the figures lie on a decreasing cline from the least proficient corpus – that of the younger learners – to the most proficient one, namely that of the older native speakers' group.[5] Thanks to the linguistic grading within the four corpora, this finding actually brings out a stylistic *tendency* and provides an intuitive appeal which is not afforded by a simple 'learners versus native speakers' contrast.

In the present case, the frequency pattern seems to imply that low adjective intensifier counts correlate with linguistic maturity and native-like argumentative writing. Yet this finding alone is not of any pedagogical value. (It would simply be too crude to advise learners to go easy on adjective intensification; after all, native speakers do use it, and use it effectively at that.) It is therefore necessary to find out exactly why and in what respect German learners tend to over-intensify.

4 Hypothesis 1: the function of adjective intensification

In trying to find an explanation for the NNS overuse, it seemed advisable first to consider what *kinds* of adjectives were most frequently intensified by the learners and the native speakers. It might be assumed that intensification had an entirely different function for the two groups. But the results were rather baffling (Table 4.2).

Table 4.2: Top ten NNS and NS intensified adjectives

NNS (BWF + UNI)		NS (GCE + LOC)	
important	62.6	***important***	29.1
good	35.8	***good***	25.5
different	32.9	*successful*	14.2
interested	32.4	***different***	13.2
interesting	31.0	***high***	11.7
difficult	26.0	*aware*	10.9
hard	17.9	***difficult***	9.8
high	15.8	***bad***	8.4
easy	15.3	***hard***	8.0
bad	14.3	*ambiguous*	7.6

Note that no less than seven out of the top ten intensified adjectives are the same; note also that the top two, i.e. the most prominent ones, are identical. This lexical accordance, of course, becomes fuzzier in the lower frequencies, but even for those it can be shown that the items still share their most important semantic categories (Lorenz 1997, Chapter 4). By highlighting the same kinds of adjectives, learners and native speakers therefore seem to be doing the same thing – at least semantically. Intensification 'means' the same for both populations.

In by far the majority of instances, both groups tend to intensify (a) adjectives that depict what the writers consider to be *important, different, interesting* – in short, relevant and worth reading, or (b) 'nuclear' or 'core' adjectives such as *good, bad, high, hard* (Carter 1987; Stubbs 1986). The chief adj-int functions hence seem to be (a) one of attracting and channelling the reader's attention, and (b) one of differentiating and enhancing the meaning of a very general adjective. Yet as both learners and native speakers share this preference, there cannot be a purely functional explanation to the numerical differences.

5 Hypothesis 2: cross-cultural differences

Another plausible interpretation of the figures would be a cross-cultural one: it is inviting to assume that the German learners were culturally more 'given' to overstating an issue, and therefore to overusing emphatic devices. By the same token, the opposite would be true for the native speakers of British English, who are, after all, well known for their *under*stating tendencies. To verify or falsify the relevance of these widespread cultural stereotypes, the Quirkian intensifier categories come into play.

Quirk et al. (1985: 589ff) have proposed a set of scalar intensifier categories which are defined according to the respective degree they express:[6]

Amplifiers:	Ma**X**imizers (*completely, absolutely* etc.)
	Boosters (*very, highly, immensely* etc.)
Downtoners:	**A**pproximators (*nearly, virtually* etc.)
	Compromisers (*fairly, pretty, rather* etc.)
	Diminishers (*slightly, a little* etc.)
	Mi**N**imizers (*hardly, scarcely* etc.)

If the above hypothesis was correct, i.e. if there was a cultural bias for overstatement among German learners, the NNS overuse should pertain to those devices which express positive emphasis, as opposed to those which express caution. Consider Table 4.3.

As Table 4.3 shows, and contrary to the 'cultural overstatement hypothesis', the German learners overused all the individual scalar

Table 4.3: Scalar category counts

Scalar category	NNS (SF)	NS (SF)	χ^2	NNS overuse (%)
X	163.1	126.7	4.7	28.7
B	858.6	580.2	53.7	48.0
Σ amplifiers	1021.7	706.9	57.1	44.5
A	35.5	29.4	0.6	20.8
C	157.7	116.3	6.3	35.6
D	25.6	15.6	2.4	64.1
N	98.4	81.1	1.7	21.3
Σ downtoners	317.2	242.5	10.0	30.8
Σ all	1338.9	949.3	66.0	41.0

intensifier categories – even those which are more commonly associated with *under*statement. This is particularly surprising for the 'compromiser', 'diminisher' and 'minimizer' categories: compromisers and diminishers are habitually used as hedged ways of boosting a quality, compare *pretty vicious* <GCE> and *rather horrific* <LOCNESS>, as well as diminishing *a little outrageous* <GCE>, where the strong adjective collocate – even out of context – makes it perfectly clear that the writer is downplaying the intensification for rhetorical effect. A similar mechanism is at work in minimizer collocations such as *hardly surprising* <GCE>, *not exactly high* <GCE> and *not very popular* <LOCNESS>, which are used as hedged ways of actually negating the qualities in question. (By saying *hardly surprising*, for example, we normally express something like 'not at all surprising', but in a more hedged way.)

It is through the habitual use of such understatement that the semantic distinction between compromisers/diminishers and boosters on the one hand and minimizers and emphatic negation on the other becomes blurred. And while this finding is by no means a new one (cf. Spitzbardt 1965: 351), it is quite surprising to note that German advanced learners appear to have mastered this mechanism and use it to the same effect. Their collocations include *pretty terrified* <BWF>, *rather thrilling* <BWF> and *a little shocked* <BWF>, as well as *not really perfect* <BWF>, *not that ultra-strong* <UNI> and *not very pleased* <UNI>. In context, all these co-occurrences were used in an understating way. There thus does not seem to be a fundamental difference in the way the German and the British writers achieve understatement through intensification.

To reiterate, the frequency counts indicate that, compared to native speakers, the learners tend to over-indulge in all degrees of adj-int devices, mitigating as well as enhancing, overstating as well as playing down adjectival qualities. In stylistic terms, the learners overuse the devices of both *litotes* and *hyperbole*. The 'cultural difference hypothesis' as sketched above is hence too crude to be of any descriptive value here. It can certainly not account for the way advanced German learners feel compelled to overuse all degrees of adjective intensifiers.

6 Hypothesis 3: lack of lexical differentiation

In view of the above, it seems logical enough to seek to explain deviances in non-native written style in terms which reflect the specific conditions of EFL production. Although adjective intensification has been shown to have the same function for the two groups of informants (see section 4), non-native writers must still feel a greater *need* to resort to its conceptual and pragmatic potential. To recap briefly, the main two functions apparent were (a) to focus the reader's attention, and (b) to specify and enhance the meaning of an otherwise vague and colourless adjective.

Concentrating on the second of these chief functions for the moment, it is conceivable that, for want of a native-like command of the vocabulary, non-native speakers often have to make do with an 'INT + ADJ' combination where native speakers would simply use a single suitable adjective. In other words, the NNS surplus in intensifiers would have been used to cover up lexical insufficiencies. And some learners' citations do bear every sign of such a coping strategy:

01 *Ladies and Gentlemen, you have to admit that the use of TLH is* ***absolutely easy****, isn't it?* <BWF>

02 *But I think that the ending is really good because it shows how* ***absolutely silly*** *it is to keep trying to get better weapons and to have newer inventions than the others.* <BWF>

In cases such as citations 01 and 02, one does indeed get the impression that the writers rated the adjectives too weak for their argumentative purposes. In both cases they chose to intensify them by *absolutely* – an unwise choice, perhaps, given that both *easy* and *silly* are middle-of-the-range, gradable adjectives and do not tend to collocate with maximizers.[7] Yet it would be rash to draw conclusions from such singular occurrences.

If intensification were used to compensate for learners' lexical weaknesses on a systematic, numerically significant scale, then these weaknesses would have to be reflected in the NNS and NS adjective resources. One could, consequently, expect the native speakers' inventory of adjectives – *all* adjectives, not just the intensified ones – to contain a greater variety of lexical items along a given semantic dimension. In order to express the concept of [SIZE], for example, the native corpora should contain more *big-small* variants than the learners'.

This hypothesis was tested by manually sifting all adjective tags from all four corpora. Yet surprisingly, the finding contravened the above expectations: the learners used many more conceptual synonyms of *big* and *small*, including *minute, tiny, enormous, giant, gigantic, huge, massive, vast* etc. And furthermore, they even made use of one differentiating device that the native speakers did not employ at all – that of affixation: it was the NNS corpora exclusively which yielded 'intensifying word-formations' such as *grey**ish**, **ultra**-strong, **super**-cool* or ***hyper**-developed*.

It should become clear that these are not the symptoms of lexical helplessness on a larger scale. For the learners, intensification is only one device – albeit an important one – for upgrading and focusing adjectival meaning. They do not appear to overuse intensification out of necessity, but rather for conscious effect.

7 Non-native style and perceived over-zealousness

It appears as if the preceding hypotheses have been somewhat too general. In search of a more wholly plausible explanation of the NNS adj-int excess, one might reconsider what has been identified as 'function (a)' in section 4. The most prominent adj-int function for both populations lies in intensifying qualities which are meta-linguistic, i.e. which mark off those parts of the text that the writer believes to be particularly *important*, *different* and *interesting*. The reader, in turn, will treat these expressions as 'sign-posts' through the text and will expect the respective passages to contain the vital points. Given the importance of such pragmatic signals, and given the massive non-native overuse in this field (see, e.g. Table 4.2: intensified *important* – NNS 62.6 vs. NS 29.1), it is easy to see the potential for irritation and frustration on the part of the reader. At best, the effect is likely to be that of a markedly non-native style, perceived as overly eager to impress.

One can but speculate as to the source of this over-keen pragmatic sign-posting on the part of the German learners. It could, for example, have to do with a certain insecurity among non-native speakers regarding the effectiveness of their own writing. Anxious to make an impression and conscious of the limitations of their linguistic repertoire, they might feel a greater need than native speakers to stress the importance – and the relevance – of what they have to say. This attitude may even partly be induced by writing classes which teach the students to 'be interesting': NNS *very important* and *very interesting* are by far the most frequent adj-int combinations of the whole data.[8]

8 Scalar incompatability and too much effort

It would appear that hypotheses such as the above are somewhat too general, too global to explain the numerical NNS/NS differences. For pedagogical purposes, however, there is no real need for a hard and fast rationale, or for trying to paraphrase the psychology of the non-native adj-int overuse. Yet it remains to be seen how the stylistic tendencies feature in the actual syntactic contexts. Consider the following learners' citations:

03 *It is possible to create any kind of baby – either **very intelligent** or **absolutely stupid**, either superior or inferior.* <BWF>

04 *They put this **extremely huge** and heavy glass-mug filled with dark beer in front of me.* <UNI>

05 *Soon I experienced that in England you can have **very delicious** food – in Indian, Chinese or Mexican restaurants, where you can fully trust in the cooks.* <UNI>

06 *For people living in the city centre on a warm summer day it's **really impossible** to open the window because no whiff of fresh air will come in.* <UNI>

Sentences 03–06 illustrate the learners' tendency towards hyperbolic expression. In all four cases the intensifiers are not essential to the argument – on the contrary, they potentially even distract from the main points. In 03, for example, the emphasis is misdirected and immaterial to the writer's concern about genetic engineering. In 04, *huge and heavy* alone, with its emphatic alliteration, would be quite expressive enough to illustrate the social pressures of drinking alcohol. And 05 and 06 are likewise typical of a wordiness often to be found in non-native writing.

The four citations originally became noted, among others, through the fact that they share an important characteristic: they each contain an adj-int collocation with a gradational irregularity. As was the case for 01 and 02, *stupid* in 03 is a gradable adjective and thus more likely to be intensified by a booster such as *extremely*. In 04–06, on the other hand, the adjectives are ungradable and would normally call for a maximizer such as *absolutely*. These scalar incompatibilities, while bringing out the intensifiers' incongruity, would hardly be classed as 'mistakes' in the conventional sense of the term. As informal tests have shown, they would not even necessarily be picked out by native-speaker assessors. It is only by looking at a substantial amount of corpus data that the deviating pattern becomes apparent. And whereas some of the co-occurrences would be less unusual in informal spoken usage, they are simply not very likely to occur in native argumentative writing.[9] In the present context, the infelicities have been helpful in identifying verbosity in NNS expression. Once brought into focus, it becomes easier to spot unwarranted intensification:

07 *It is possible to produce more than 90 **totally equal** babies or to create a **totally new** race with the available genes.* <BWF>

08 *To travel is wonderful in order to get new friends, to see **absolutely new** places and to discover our unique planet.* <BWF>

09 *Then you are **very intelligent** and when you enter the university no teacher can surprise you with a **completely new** thing and you will get into a certain 'routine' so you can cope with all the studying.* <BWF>

Sentences 07–09 display a wordiness similar to 03–06. Although here the intensifiers are appropriately graded, they appear stylistically out of place. The impression is one of bookishness and of overstatement – in the sense of 'too much communicative effort'. And as these qualities are often cited as typical of non-native style, a fair share of the numerical adj-int overuse can certainly be accounted for in this way.

9 Packed themes and information overcharge

Some of the aforesaid is, admittedly, difficult to put to pedagogical use. While the issue of scalar compatibility could – and probably should – be fruitfully applied to teaching, there does not seem to be any regularity in the superfluous adj-int instances. Exploring further, however, the general tendency becomes manifest in another very distinct pattern of non-native usage.

To understand this pattern, recourse must be taken to the most common principle of structuring information in English writing. It has frequently been observed (Halliday 1985; Quirk et al. 1985; Fries 1994, among others) that there is a habitual connection between the 'givenness' of information and thematic (clause-initial) position on the one hand, and 'newness' and rhematic (clause-final) position on the other. According to Fries (1994: 233), this correlation is 'most prominent in formal written English', which makes it particularly relevant to the present material. As Mauranen (1996) furthermore shows, thematic structuring can be a sensitive area for non-native writing, and it hence deserves special attention in the current context.

It has already been established above that the main adj-int function lies in highlighting what is interesting, relevant and new to the reader; intensification is consequently most likely to occur in the 'new' range of the clause, i.e. in rhematic position. Moreover, it would seem to be most effectively put to use when solely and unequivocally focused on an adjective, as in the case of predicative adjectives. Most typically, then, adjective intensification can be expected to be found in predicative constructions and rhematic position.

In view of these considerations, the 2,124 (raw) adj-int occurrences were checked for predicative versus attributive use. The rounded standardized totals are shown in Table 4.4.

The figures in Table 4.4 conform to the expectations worded here: around 75 per cent of all adj-int instances occur in predicative position. While this is the case for learners and native speakers alike, it is the

Table 4.4: Predicative vs. attributive adj-int instances

	BWF	UNI	GCE	LOC
pred. (SF)	524	469	372	333
attr. (SF)	171	174	150	95
attr. (%)	24.6	27.0	28.8	22.1

tendencies which are of interest here. Note that in native writing development, from GCE to LOCNESS, attributive usage decreases with linguistic maturity. This 6.7 per cent decrease (in absolute terms even 57.9 per cent) makes the feature seem stylistically undesirable in fully proficient native writing. In the learner data, on the other hand, the evolution from BWF to UNI seems to go in the reverse direction. The relative increase is, admittedly, only one of 2.4 per cent, and even smaller in absolute terms (1.8 per cent), but the point is not so much the rate of this development. Didactically, it is simply disturbing to note that it is not going the right way.

Advanced German learners appear to have problems with regard to structuring their information within the clause. As the concepts of 'given/new' and 'theme/rheme' are not as easy to pinpoint as the attributive-predicative distinction,[10] it would be too optimistic to try to obtain similar figures for the former two as for the latter. For this reason, the non-native tendencies may here be illustrated in several typical contexts:

10 *A **highly specified** and specialized training for journalists is for that reason one demand.* <BWF>

11 *A **really visible** reason for the emancipated woman being alive is the high rate of unmarried or divorced women.* <UNI>

12 *A **very difficult** question is whether one should have a hero at all, as I don't think that there is any person in the whole, wide world to whom one should look up admiringly.* <UNI>

13 *I thought that my **absolutely authentic** Rock music should hit the charts in seconds.* <UNI>

14 ***Absolutely laden** tramways toddle through the lanes ringing not because of cars standing on the rails but because of children hopping there.* <UNI>

In each of these citations the subject noun complex is made unnaturally 'heavy', and the intensifiers contribute enormously to that effect. The adj-int complex is not placed in the rheme, where one would expect to find the elements that are new, relevant and noteworthy enough to be intensified. On the contrary, by pre-modifying an adjective which in turn pre-modifies the subject noun, the writers put too much weight into the clause's theme. Such 'packed themes' present the reader with more information and emphasis than the reader would normally anticipate. This violation of the 'principle of end-weight' makes for awkward and unnatural reading. (Note how some of the sentences – cf. 10 and 11 – literally beg to be restructured.) Native speakers' attributive adj-int usage would more typically resemble the following:

15 *Shoplifting is a* ***reasonably common*** *occurrence in Britain, and it is usually lack of money or the hatred of rejection which will cause such crimes.* <GCE>
16 *Aids is also a* ***very taboo*** *subject in Britain and little is known about it, so that it should also be taught along with sex education.* <GCE>
17 *In fact [De Gaulle's] veto of Britain's entry into the EEC in 1962 was a* ***purely personal*** *decision (it did not enjoy the unanimous support of his ministers).* <LOCNESS>
18 *Kahn is a* ***very intelligent*** *man, his mind is artificial.* <GCE>
19 *When he was being generous it was to make him feel good about himself; people thought he was a* ***very magnanimous*** *person.* <LOCNESS>

Two observations need to be made about these citations: first, and more evidently, the intensified adjective is always placed in the 'new' range of the clause, modifying the subject complement in a simple theme/rheme sequence. Secondly, what is particularly striking semantically is the redundancy in NS style. In each case, the complement noun is a lexical superordinate of the subject and does not add any new information. Without the adj-int complex, grammatically no more than the noun's modification, the clauses would be tautological: shoplifting, of course, is an occurrence (15), Aids is a subject (16), De Gaulle's 1962 veto was a decision (17) etc. Such nouns have been termed 'general nouns' (Halliday and Hasan 1976), 'anaphoric labels' (Francis 1986, 1994) or 'carrier nouns' (Ivanič 1991), and their cohesive function has been explored from various angles. In the present case, it appears as if they were meant to couch the adjective and its intensifier, thereby giving them more 'space' and affording them more time to dwell on the reader's mind. That way, although the 'INT + ADJ + NOUN' construction is semantically almost equivalent to a simple intensified predicative adjective, its emphasis is actually even greater, as well as more reader-friendly.

To conclude this glance at information structure, the German learners' style is much more 'packed' than that of the native speakers. While both groups numerically prefer predicative over attributive intensification by about three to one, their developmental trends point in converse directions: the steep decline of NS attributive intensification makes it seem stylistically less desirable, a stance which is not quite shared by the non-native speakers; the more mature learners used it even more than the younger ones.

Besides this quantitative evidence, however, the qualitative findings show a marked difference in the *kind* of attributive intensification employed. When the native speakers did intensify adjectives inside noun phrases, they were almost exclusively in rhematic position, i.e. precisely where one would expect a new and emphatic load to be. And moreover, native speakers would invariably alleviate the condensed effect of such noun phrases by inserting an 'empty' head, a carrier noun that does not add any new information to the proposition. On the learners' side, however, there is no such alleviation. Their typical attributive intensification is (a) placed in thematic position, and (b) in no way semantically redundant. The combined effect of these features is one of information 'overcharge' and one of pragmatic signposting which is misleading to the reader.

10 Pedagogical conclusions

Advanced German learners of English have been found to overuse the lexico-grammatical function of adjective intensification. This overuse does not seem to be derived (a) from a fundamentally different understanding of the function as a whole, (b) from a cultural propensity for overstatement, or (c) from a lack of lexical differentiation in the learner language. What appears to differ between the two populations are the principles that govern emphasis and the presentation of new information. The learners not only use more intensification, they also use it in places where it is semantically incompatible, communicatively unnecessary or syntactically undesirable. It transpires that the impression of overstatement is not automatically generated by the numerical excess, but by genuine misapplication.

Stylistically, it is difficult to gauge exactly how much damage is caused by such patterns of non-nativeness, but they certainly make for highly unnatural, hyperbolic pieces of communication. Didactically, it is worrying to note that some of the infelicities are actually on the increase in the writing of the more mature learners. What seems to be at fault, then, is the whole writing attitude; EFL student writing appears to be more geared towards creating an impression than towards arguing a case. It is small wonder that – with the weaker students at least – this may lead to wordiness and overstatement.

Teaching must stress that emphasis is not a good thing per se, but that it must be instrumental to the coherence of an overall argument. It would be naive to try and simply restrict the number of intensifying devices; instead, the students need to develop a sensibility for the economy of information: not every noun needs to be premodified by an adjective, and not every adjective in turn needs to be intensified. Unlike in German, perhaps, the important points in English writing do not tend to be made 'in passing', and 'good style' is very sensitive towards excessive embellishment. For non-native writers of English, this may mean that improving the structuring of information could go a long way towards a more natural style of writing.

As regards the merits of learner corpus methodology, the NNS patterns reported here reflect stylistic deviations which would hardly have been detected in more traditional error analysis. The greatest strength of the approach probably lies in utilising large numbers to detect tendencies, and then homing in on individual citations to understand them. The present material affords the additional luxury of yielding developmental data; in this way, trends become apparent for both native and non-native writing style and give us a clearer idea of both the standard and the learners' progress. By following such analytical procedures in what is likely to be a long and laborious process, we may eventually learn more about what it means to use English naturally and idiomatically.

Notes

1 This is the revised version of a paper presented at the computer learner corpus symposium at AILA 1996 in Jyväskylä, Finland.

2 Note how every generation of teenagers coins its own set of expressions like *ab fab* (*absolutely fabulous*), *bloody brill* (*brilliant*), *dead ace* or *well wicked*. And just as these are noted by outsiders and begin to be adopted on a wider scale, they are 'out' and obsolete in their in-group function.

3 For reasons of convenience with regard to DOS-file management, the abbreviations each contain three capital letters. GCE, incidentally, stands for the now obsolete General Certificate of Education.

4 The abbreviation 'adj-int' is here used to refer to *adjective intensification*; the frequency table contains both the actual corpus totals as retrieved by the searches ('raw'), as well as in rounded standardized form ('SF'), arithmetically normalized per 100,000 words. Because of the variation in corpus size, only the latter, of course, can be directly compared.

5 While it can be taken as axiomatic that young learners (BWF) are linguistically less mature than older native speakers (LOCNESS), the case is not nearly as clear for the two groups in the middle, namely the older learners of UNI and the younger native speakers of GCE. Interestingly, however, the full-length study showed that there is indeed a *proficiency cline* within the four sub-corpora (see Lorenz 1997, Chapters 5, 7 and 9): wherever a given linguistic feature was of any stylistic interest, its respective corpus frequencies either continually rose or fell with linguistic proficiency (BWF→ UNI→GCE→LOCNESS).

6 Note that the term 'intensification' is not restricted to items which enhance the meaning of their focus ('amplifiers'), but also extends to those which have a restricting function ('downtoners').

7 This violation of collocational principles has been termed 'scalar incompatibility' (Lorenz 1997, section 8.2.4); see further below.

8 It should also be added here that, according to mechanically assigned word-class tags for all four corpora, the learners were also found to use 8.6 per cent more adjectives than their native-speaking counterparts (NNS 14,324 vs. NS 13,188 per 200,000 words). This fits in well with writing directives which aim for 'lively' and 'colourful' written production. What is particularly worrying is that the overuse was found to aggravate as the learners get older: there is an 8.7 per cent rise in adjectives from BWF 6,865 SF to UNI 7,459 SF. In this respect, the learners' style therefore increasingly diverges from native-like behaviour.

9 Citations 01–06 are by no means the only examples of scalar incompatibility in the learners' corpora – other combinations include *?not quite exciting, ?totally damaged, ?very horrible* and *?not too fine; very delicious* alone, for example, appeared three times. The problem is not a well-documented one and not part of the descriptions of adjective intensification in the standard grammars.

10 Rather than being hard-and-fast grammatical concepts, 'given/new' and 'theme/rheme' depend on the vague notions of context and shared knowledge. But see Halliday (1985: 59f).

CHAPTER FIVE

An automated approach to the phrasicon of EFL learners

Sylvie De Cock, Sylviane Granger, Geoffrey Leech and Tony McEnery

1 Introduction

Many researchers now believe that prefabricated or prepatterned expressions rather than words have a predominant role in the production of both written and spoken language (Altenberg 1993). Prefabs (as they have been called) play a major part in spontaneous spoken interaction, where they 'can be said to act as a kind of "autopilot" which the speaker can switch on to gain time for the creative and social aspects of the speech process' (Altenberg and Eeg-Olofsson 1990: 2). Reliance on such prefabs thus allows speakers to play for time, enabling them to speak without too much hesitation or too many pauses (Aijmer 1996: 9) and consequently to avoid too much non-fluency.

The recognition that speakers mainly operate on what Sinclair (1991) calls the 'idiom principle' rather than the 'open-choice principle' has, over the last two decades, led to growing interest in the study of the phrasicon (Fillmore 1978), i.e. the study of the various ready-made expressions. This phraseological trend has not failed to reach the sphere of second language acquisition (SLA) and of the analysis of learner language.

This article is a first step towards a corpus-based study of the spoken phrasicon of adult advanced EFL learners of French mother tongue, which will, amongst other things, try to test the validity of Kjellmer's hypothesis (1991: 124) that learners' foreign-soundingness may be due to the fact that '[their] building material is individual bricks rather than prefabricated sections.' The approach adopted here is contrastive: the analysis of the phraseological competence of learners will be based on a comparison of a corpus of non-native speaker (NNS) and a corpus of native speaker (NS) speech. The study of the phrasicon in its entirety, however, lies well beyond the scope of this chapter. Our focus will be on only one of its subsets: formulae or formulaic expressions, i.e. frequently used multi-word units that perform pragmatic or discourse structuring functions.[1] Formulae will be examined on the basis of recurrent word combinations, i.e. 'any continuous string of words occurring more than once in identical form' (Altenberg forthcoming), which are automatically extracted from the corpora using retrieval software (*Tuples* and *Combinator*) especially designed by Tony McEnery for the purpose of this analysis.

First of all, we will briefly review some of the literature on formulae in SLA. The corpora and the software used in the study will be described in a second section. In the third, we will then focus upon the recurrent word combinations in the NS and NNS data, before focusing, in the final section, on a series of formulaic word combinations that have been referred to as 'vagueness tags'.

2 Formulaic expressions in SLA

Previous work on formulae in SLA has mainly concentrated on the speech of children or adult beginners learning ESL in naturalistic settings (children: Hakuta 1974; Huang and Hatch 1978; Wong-Fillmore 1979; Vihman 1982; Bahns et al. 1986; adults: Hanania and Gradman 1977). These studies are usually limited in scope, as they focus on a very limited number of learners. One of the main concerns of most of these case studies is to try to provide an answer to the question as to 'whether the use of formulaic language is a learning strategy, . . . [contributing to] analysis and rule formation, often considered the "real" task of language learning' (Weinert 1995: 186). There have been comparatively few studies involving advanced adult learners. Yorio (1989) and Granger (forthcoming c) have analysed the written productions of adult ESL and EFL learners respectively. Scarcella (1979) studied the spoken formulae of 30 advanced adult ESL learners on the basis of what she calls 'routine tests', which are in fact very similar to the discourse control tasks used in pragmatic research. For a good review of the literature on formulaic language in SLA, see Weinert (1995).

This study is unique in that it sets out to analyse the formulaic competence of advanced adult EFL learners on the basis of recurrent word combinations automatically extracted from corpora of informal speech, an approach that has so far only been used to investigate the phrasicon of native speakers (Altenberg and Eeg-Olofsson 1990; Altenberg 1990, 1993, forthcoming; Renouf 1992). In the present case, the EFL learners were speakers of French as a mother tongue, and their productions were compared to those of a comparable set of native speakers of English.

3 Methodology

3.1 Description of the corpora

Two comparable corpora were used in the analysis: (i) a 62,975-word corpus of 25 informal interviews with advanced[2] EFL learners of French mother tongue collected at the Université Catholique de Louvain (henceforth referred to as the NNS corpus or NNSC); (ii) an 80,448-word corpus of 25 informal interviews with native speakers of British English collected at the University of Lancaster (henceforth the NS corpus or NSC). Both NS and NNS informants are young adult university students and are aged between 19 and 25. The proportion of males to females is the same in both corpora: 6 males to 19 females. The informal interviews, which were not recorded surreptitiously, follow the same set pattern and are of similar length. For detailed information on the informants and the interview format, see De Cock (1996).

3.2 *Description of the software*

Due to the lack of availability of suitable corpus analysis tools, software for the extraction of word combinations for this study was specially developed at Lancaster. The *WordSmith* program, which became available during development, is able to do some word combination extraction. However, since it does not have the desired level of statistical functionality, and is not SGML aware (the speaker turns in NSC and NNSC are SGML delimited), it was not used for our study.

The most important statistics we decided to incorporate were chi-square as a measure of significance in differences, and a slightly modified version of Juilland's numeric dispersion measure[3] as an indication of how well a particular word combination is spread throughout the corpus. This dispersion measure ranges from 1 (occurring equally in each section) and 0 (occurring in one section only); for how it is calculated, see Lyne (1985: 102–3).

Two programs were developed for studying word-combinations in the NS and NNS corpora: *Tuples* and *Combinator*. Each is discussed briefly below.

Tuples extracts word combinations from corpus texts. The user specifies what size of word combination should be extracted, and the program proceeds to generate a frequency list of all word combinations of the specified size in the corpus. The user can set a frequency threshold, below which word combinations are not reported. The program respects SGML delimited sections of text in the corpus. Thus, if it is the language of only one of the speakers in the interview that is of interest, the user simply identifies for the program which SGML markers delimit the areas to be analysed, and then the program ignores text outside those regions. So for example, in this study, the program is told to look only at regions delimited <B> . . . </B>, resulting in an analysis of the turns of speaker 'B' only (i.e. NS and NNS interviewees only, ignoring the contributions of the interviewer).

The output from the *Tuple* program is a frequency-ordered list of word combinations. Below, by way of an example, is an output from the

NS corpus: the program was instructed to extract three-word combinations which occurred more than forty times in interviewee data only:

85 I don't know
77 a lot of
47 and it was

If the user wishes, the program can also generate output files in which the dispersion of each word combination is calculated on the basis of the number of occurrences in each interview or in arbitrarily sized chunks of the corpus. Below is an example giving dispersion values (D) by interview:

85	I don't know	D = 0.825998
77	a lot of	D = 0.833474
47	and it was	D = 0.687843

In this example, we have a view of how well dispersed across the interviews each word combination is in the corpus. If required, the number of occurrences of the word combinations in each interview is also available, allowing users to assess the impact of individual speakers/interviews on the dispersion value yielded by the program.

Combinator is capable of comparing the use of word combinations across a range of files. An example output from a comparison of the three-word combinations above in the NS and NNS corpora is given below:

D = 0.625000 Chi2 = 38.250000 Yule = –0.375000 0 = 85.000000
1 = 187.000000 I don't know
D = 0.777778 Chi2 = 6.222222 Yule = 0.222222 0 = 77.000000
1 = 49.000000 a lot of
D = 1.000000 Chi2 = 0.000000 Yule = 0.000000 0 = 47.000000
1 = 47.000000 and it was

For each word combination, *Combinator*'s output lists 'D', the dispersion measure across the two files, 'Chi2' (chi-square), a measure of the significance of any difference in frequency of occurrences, 'Yule', a difference coefficient (cf. Hofland and Johansson 1982: 14), the number of occurrences in each of the files, and the word combination itself.

4 Recurrent word combinations in EFL speech

4.1 *Automatic extraction*

As stated above, formulaic expressions have been investigated on the basis of automatically extracted recurrent word combinations. This focus on word combinations is justified because formulae have been defined as 'multi-word units'. It ought to be pointed out, however, that such an approach causes our analysis to be restricted to continuous formulae only, i.e. formulae that consist of unbroken sequences of words (Nattinger and DeCarrico 1992: 38). Discontinuous formulaic expressions will not be considered here.

We chose to examine formulae consisting of two to five words and used *Tuples* to retrieve the recurrent word combinations of corresponding lengths from the speech of the interviewees in the NS and NNS corpora. Yet, in view of the mass of the material yielded by the program, it was decided to limit the investigation to two-three-four- and five-word combinations that occur with a frequency greater than 9, 4, 3, and 2 respectively. These frequency thresholds were adopted bearing in mind that the length of recurrent word combinations is inversely related to their frequency.[4] In addition to reducing the material to a manageable size, these somewhat arbitrary frequency thresholds can also be regarded as giving 'at least some guarantee that the selected word combinations have some currency in spoken discourse and that they are of some interest from that point of view' (Altenberg forthcoming). In other words, emphasis is laid on the routine nature of formulae.

We decided not to eliminate hesitation features such as *erm* and *er* from the text, but to consider them as word units. This approach is different from, for example, that adopted by Renouf (1992) in her study on longer sequences of words in spoken discourse. She explains that she removed these features from her corpus 'because they generally function as interpolations within otherwise unbroken strings' (ibid.: 302). This assumption is not necessarily valid. The prefabricated nature of formulae and recurrent word combinations in general makes it at least equally valid to assume that their production may not be interrupted by extraneous hesitation features.

4.2 *Overall quantitative comparison between NS and NNS speech*

The application of *Tuples* to NS and NNS yields fundamental data on recurring combinations in these corpora. It is useful, at this stage, to define word-combination-oriented notions of type and token: each different word combination is considered a different type and each occurrence of a word combination a different token. The number of tokens and types in Tables 5.1 and 5.2 are relative frequencies based on 50,000 words[5] per variety. The asterisked figures indicate statistically significant differences.[6]

The information contained in Tables 5.1 and 5.2 confirms the observation made earlier about the relationship between the length and frequency of recurrent word combinations: they are inversely related, and thus, as word combination length increases, the number of recurrent

Table 5.1: Recurrent word combinations in NSC and NNSC

	Tokens NSC	Types NSC	Log T/t ratio† NSC	Tokens NNSC	Types NNSC	Log T/t ratio NNSC
Two-word recurrent combinations	31,866	5,432	83.15	32,087	5,476	82.63
Three-word recurrent combinations	12,289	3,753	87.58	12,678†*	3,900	87.25
Four-word recurrent combinations	3,252	1,305	88.89	3,296	1,271	87.94
Five-word recurrent combinations	733	338	88.50	703	302	86.68

T/t = type/token

† We have used a logarithmic type/token ratio here for the following reason. Type/token ratio in general changes with the size of the sample of a text, and therefore cannot be used in comparisons of texts or corpora of substantially different sizes. However, as Herdan (1960: 26) points out: 'The logarithmic type/token ratio, i.e. the log type/token, remains . . . constant for samples of different size from a given . . . text, and is, therefore suitable to serve as a style characteristic.' In the present case, however, it is worth mentioning that roughly the same difference between the type/token ratio characteristics of the two corpora would also have been evident, had we chosen the ordinary type/token ratio rather than the logarithmic one. The results were multiplied by 100 for the sake of readability.

word combination tokens and types decreases.[7] This relationship holds for both NSC and NNSC.

A closer look at Tables 5.1 and 5.2 reveals that, overall, the number of recurrent word combination tokens in NNSC is either similar to or slightly higher than that in NSC. It is particularly striking that the number of longer word combination tokens above frequency threshold (four- and five-word recurrent combinations) is significantly higher in NNS. Milton and Freeman (1996) and Milton (Chapter 14, this volume) came to similar conclusions for the writing of Chinese learners of English: they report that learners use word sequences, especially longer ones, with higher frequency than NSs.

For shorter word combinations, Tables 5.1 and 5.2 show that the log type/token ratio tends to be comparable in both corpora. However, for longer word combinations, the log type/token ratio in NNSC is lower than that in NSC (cf. Table 5.2: five-word recurrent combinations above frequency threshold: 75.67 vs. 70.77).

The observations made above allow us to draw the following tentative conclusion with regard to learners and the idiom principle: contrary to Kjellmer's hypothesis, learners do use prefabs. Nevertheless, they

Table 5.2: Recurrent word combinations above frequency threshold in NSC and NNSC

	Tokens NSC	Types NSC	Log T/t ratio NSC	Tokens NNSC	Types NNSC	Log T/t ratio NNSC
Two-word recurrent combinations above frequency threshold (>9)	16,338	588	66.19	16,525	606	65.24
Three-word recurrent combinations above frequency threshold (>4)	4,591	512	74.39	4,634	508	73.17
Four-word recurrent combinations above frequency threshold (>3)	681	119	73.80	872+***	149	73.11
Five-word recurrent combinations above frequency threshold (>2)	134	39	75.67	186+***	43	70.77

seem to differ from NSs in that they show a tendency to repeat some prefabs more often. In other words, learners appear to make a more routine use of prefabs, at least of longer ones, than NSs.

4.3 *Top ten two-word combinations in NS and NNS speech*

The top ten NS and NNS two-word combinations listed in Table 5.3 give us an indication of the type of result that arises from the automatic extraction of word combinations.

When considering formulae, not all the items in Table 5.3 are equally relevant. Both the NS and NNS top tens contain what Altenberg (1990: 137) calls 'phrase or clause fragments', whose frequency is due in a large measure to the very high frequency of the words which compose them, the best example being *in the*. Yet, some interesting observations can be made. Learners seem to resort more often to repetitions (*the the*, *to to* and *I I*) and filled pauses (*and er*). This tendency towards a greater frequency of hesitation phenomena is confirmed in longer sequences.

There are a number of word combinations in both lists that could be labelled formulae as we have defined them. There are five such combinations in the NS top ten (*you know*, *sort of*, *I mean*, *I think* and *and then*) and a maximum of three[8] in the NNS (*and er*, *I think* and *in fact*), the only

Table 5.3: Relative frequencies of the top ten two-word combinations in NSC and NNSC based on 50,000 words per variety

NSC		NNSC	
it was	376	*it was*	502
you know	284	*I don't*	330
sort of	278	*and er*	262
I mean	222	*I think*	253
I was	214	*don't know*	239
I think	190	*in the*	201
in the	189	*to to*	193
and I	171	*I I*	184
I don't	161	*the the*	162
and then	140	*in fact*	157

Table 5.4: NS and NNS relative frequencies of those formulae which are not common to both NS and NNS top tens

Formulae	NS	NNS
you know	284	74
sort of	278	27
I mean	222	81
and then	140	110
in fact	3	157
and er	52	262

one common to both being *I think*. Table 5.4 gives the NS and NNS relative frequencies of those NS and NNS formulae which are not common to both NS and NNS top tens.

Tables 5.3 and 5.4 point to a possible underuse of formulae by learners, potentially compensated for by the use of more repetition and filled pauses. In other words, these features may be a sign of higher dysfluency in learner speech.

5 Vagueness tags in learner speech

We will now focus on a series of formulaic expressions that have been dealt with under the heading of 'vagueness tags' (Altenberg forthcoming), 'vagueness category identifiers' (Channell 1994) and 'set-marking tags' (Dines 1980). Altenberg's term will be used here. Examples of vagueness tags include *and things like that* as in *I'm supposed to read er the Guardian and things like that* (in NSC) and *or whatever* in the example *they only had sort of thirty members or whatever* (in NSC). According to Nikula (1996: 52), these expressions 'signal quite explicitly either speakers' . . . uncertainty towards their message or their willingness to leave their message vague'. The identification of vagueness tags amongst the automatically extracted word combinations requires a considerable degree of filtering.

5.1 *Filtering the data*

The frequency lists of recurrent word combinations yielded by *Tuples* are by no means to be equated with lists of formulae as defined in section 1 above. Indeed, simple frequency of occurrence is not in itself grounds to believe that a word combination is a formula. These lists are clearly preliminary in nature and hence they serve as a starting point for further analysis. The filtering process required for the identification of formulaic expressions, and hence vagueness tags, is manual and to an extent subjective. It includes the following three steps:

1. The first part of this process is essentially formal in nature and consists of:

- the elimination of non-fluencies such as unintentional repetitions and stutterings, e.g. *the the, I I, it was it was.*
- the elimination of most combinations of closed-class items that are only phrase or clause fragments, e.g. *in the,* and *it and.*
- the subjective elimination of those word combinations which are fragmentary in nature, e.g. *are a lot of, don't know if you.*

2. The next phase of the filtering process is an assessment of whether the remaining candidate formulae have the potential to serve any pragmatic or discourse functions.

3. The list of formulae resulting from the application of the first two steps of the filtering process to the data is a frequency list of 'potential' formulae. This means that, to take a concrete example, not all 284 instances of the potential formula *you know* (in NSC) actually occur formulaically as units in their own right. Some of these instances occur as part of larger sequences such as *do you know what I mean* (*Tuples* does not automatically eliminate from the lists all the word combinations subsumed in larger sequences) or with no particular pragmatic meaning at all, as in *this bloke said oh you shouldn't do that don't you know there are lots of scorpions all around here.* Refined frequency counts of 'actual' formulae are thus called for. The production of a list of actual formulae is the purpose of the final stage of the filtering process, where each occurrence of a potential formula is examined in context.

5.2 *Potential vagueness tags in NSC and NNSC*

Table 5.5 lists the 'potential' vagueness tags that occur with a frequency above the thresholds set above in either NSC and/or NNSC. These 'potential' vagueness tags were chosen from the word combinations remaining after the application of the first two filtering steps to *Combinator*'s output.

Before we can draw any hard and fast conclusions about the relative usage of vagueness tags by NSs and NNSs, we have to subject this potential list to the third step of the filtering process. Word combinations which are subsumed by longer ones and those which are deemed to lack a specific pragmatic function are discarded. For example, when occurring in the word combination *or something like that*, *or something* is discounted, as is the following instance of *and so on*: *and so on the twentieth of of May there is a festival which is international* (taken from NNSC).

Problems arose when a particular word combination was preceded by or followed by an unclear passage (transcribed in the data as '<X>' '<XX>' or '<XXX>' according to the perceived length of the unclear passage), making it uncertain whether it was a unit on its own or part

Table 5.5: Absolute frequencies of 'potential' vagueness tags in NSC and NNSC

Vagueness tags	**NSC**	**NNSC**
and all	17	7^{-*}
and everything	25	5^{-***}
and so on	2	19
and stuff	28	0
and stuff like that	15	0
and that	31	7^{-***}
and that sort of thing	3	0
and things	49	5^{-***}
and things like that	14	3
or anything	17	0
or something	38	11^{-***}
or something like that	8	8
or whatever	11	1
something like that	12	13
sort of thing	14	0
stuff like that	20	0
that sort of thing	5	0
things like that	26	11^{-*}
Total	335	90^{-***}

of a larger sequence. In such cases, the word combination was considered to be delimited by the unclear passage and was counted as a unit in its own right. An example is the following occurrence of *or something*: *slave labour . yeah they're on like two pound an hour* <u>*or something*</u> <X> (NSC).

5.3 *Learner underuse*

Table 5.6 lists the number of word combinations that are actually used as vagueness tags in NSC and NNSC:

Table 5.6: Absolute frequencies of 'actual' vagueness tags in NSC and NNSC

Vagueness tags	NSC	NNSC
and all	0	0
and everything	21	4
and so on	2	18
and stuff	12	0
and stuff like that	15	0
and that	2	0
and that sort of thing	3	0
and things	31	1
and things like that	14	3
or anything	14	0
or something	30	4
or something like that	8	8
or whatever	11	1
something like that	1	4
sort of thing	5	0
stuff like that	4	0
that sort of thing	1	0
things like that	7	4
Total	181	47–***

The figures in Table 5.6 reveal, from a statistical point of view, a highly significant underuse of vagueness tags by NNSs: even accepting that the NS corpus is slightly larger than the NNS corpus, NSs use almost four times as many vagueness tags as learners. That said, learners also overuse some vagueness tags. The figures for *and so on* are particularly striking; it is used almost ten times as often by NNSs as by NSs.

Learners' underuse of vagueness tags may have a significant impact on how they are perceived by native speakers. Channell (1994: 21) notes that learners 'while grammatically, phonologically, and lexically correct, may sound rather bookish and pedantic to a native speaker'. Given Crystal and Davy's (1975: 111) suggestion that 'lack of precision is one of the most important features of the vocabulary of informal conversation', the underuse of vagueness tags by learners that we have observed in informal interviews may go some way towards explaining this impression of 'bookishness'.

It is worth noting that tags are not the only devices by which vagueness can be expressed. Markers such as *sort of* and *kind of* introduce imprecision too. Interestingly, these markers also show systematic differences in the way they are used by NSs and NNSs. Not only are they underused by learners (the absolute unfiltered frequencies are: *kind of* 58 in NSC vs. 31 in NNSC; *sort of* 321 in NS vs. 22 in NNSC), but, whereas NSs follow these markers with verb phrases 30–35 per cent of the time, NNSs almost exclusively combine them with noun phrases, in a way that is characteristic of written English. Furthermore, learners sometimes employ these vagueness markers to fulfil unique pragmatic functions. This is for instance the case when they use *sort of* or *kind of* followed by a word borrowed from French (e.g. *sort of braderie* or *sort of vapeur*) to bridge gaps in their English vocabulary.

The apparent inability of advanced EFL learners to master the use of vagueness expressions has at least three possible causes: systematic differences in the way vagueness is expressed in their French mother tongue and in English; shortfalls in teaching (the use of vague language in the classroom may be stigmatised); and finally, lack of contact with native speakers, a particular problem for EFL learners.

6 Conclusion

These first results show that advanced learners use prefabs, and in some cases even more prefabs than NSs. Consequently, they can be said to apply the idiom principle, but the chunks they use (1) are not necessarily the same as those used by NSs, (2) are not used with the same frequency, (3) have different syntactic uses, and (4) fulfil different pragmatic functions. We are aware that we have only touched upon a largely unexplored territory, but we hope that this first study will act as a spur for further research in this promising field.

Acknowledgements

This chapter was written within the framework of the Louvain-Lancaster Academic Collaboration Programme funded by the Commissariat Général aux Relations Internationales, the British Council and the

Fonds National de la Recherche Scientifique who also fund Sylvie De Cock's research post as a 'Collaborateur Scientifique'.

Notes

1 Formulaic expressions are essentially the same as Aijmer's (1996) 'conversational routines' except that the latter term also includes single words.
2 The advanced learners were third and fourth year students studying English language at university.
3 See Lyne (1985) for an excellent discussion of a variety of dispersion measures, in which Juilland's dispersion measure is shown to be the most reliable. The measure that was used here was slightly modified to allow it to be used with a corpus split into uneven sections.
4 The same observation was made by Altenberg (1990: 135) concerning the relationship between recurrent word combination length and frequency in the London-Lund Corpus.
5 This figure was chosen as an 'idealised' size, because it is a convenient value lying between the sizes of the two corpora ('B' or interviewee turns only): NSC = 57,097 words; NNSC = 40,957 words.
6 * = chi-square with $p \leq 0.05$; ** = chi-square with $p \leq 0.01$; *** = chi-square with $p \leq 0.005$. The plus and minus signs indicate overuse and underuse respectively.
7 Although Zipf's, law according to which 'there is an inverse relationship between the length of a word and its frequency' (Crystal 1987: 87), was formulated for single words, it is interesting that it applies equally to word-sequences.
8 To dismiss *and er* as a conjunction + hesitation feature may be oversimplified. De Cock (1996: 88–91) shows that such combinations can be seen to exhibit a number of pragmatic and discourse functions (e.g. turn-yielding device, summariser).

CHAPTER SIX

The use of adverbial connectors in advanced Swedish learners' written English

Bengt Altenberg and Marie Tapper

1 Introduction

Effective communication requires coherence and clarity. One way of achieving this is to signal logical or semantic relations between units of discourse by means of connectors such as *but* (to indicate a contrast), *because* (reason), *therefore* (result), *in addition* (listing), *for instance* (exemplification), etc. Connectors can be said to function as cohesive 'signposts' in discourse (Leech and Svartvik 1994: 177), helping the listener or reader to relate successive units to each other and thus making sense of the text. Several studies have also attempted to demonstrate that connectors contribute to a better understanding of spoken and written discourse. Although the results of these studies have been contradictory and rather inconclusive, the prevailing opinion among researchers and language teachers seems to be that, appropriately used, connectors have a positive effect on the clarity and comprehensibility of discourse (see e.g. Mauranen 1993: 163ff; Tyler 1994; Flowerdew and Tauroza 1995).

At the same time, a number of studies have shown that the use of connectors is problematic for language learners, in particular foreign language learners (see e.g. Crewe 1990). One reason for this is that connectors are not always needed and that they have to be used with discrimination. Their main function is to facilitate the interpretation of underlying relations in discourse and to resolve potential ambiguities. Relations that can be inferred from the text do not have to be marked explicitly, which means that a high frequency of connectors in a text does not necessarily improve its cohesive quality (cf. Crewe 1990). On the other hand, underuse and misuse of connectors are likely to reduce the comprehensibility of the text.

A second problem for learners is that the use of connectors is sensitive to register and discourse type. For example, the connectors used in conversation differ a great deal from those used in expository prose (cf. Altenberg 1984, 1986). This means that learning to use connectors appropriately is closely linked with learning to produce different types of discourse. In other words, connector usage is dependent on the development of the learner's communicative competence and how language is taught.

A problem that is particularly relevant for foreign language learners is that the use of connectors tends to vary from one language and culture to another. Languages do not provide identical sets of connectors, and some cultures do not seem to require overt marking of textual relations to the same extent as others. For example, Finnish writers of academic prose have been shown to use explicit connectors less than Anglo-American writers (Mauranen 1993: 168ff).

In this study we will be concerned with the use of connectors by advanced Swedish EFL learners. Swedish and English are closely related languages with many basic similarities and, although no contrastive research has been carried out on connector usage in the two languages, there is little reason to suspect that Swedes should have serious problems with English connectors. Yet, our experience tells us that even advanced Swedish learners tend to misuse as well as underuse connectors. This impression is supported by a study of expository essays written in Swedish and English by university students at Stockholm University, in which Wikborg and Björk (1989) found that underuse and misuse of connectors were one of the most common reasons for coherence breaks in the texts (cf. also Wikborg 1985). Interestingly, the essays written in English were not significantly poorer in this respect than those written in Swedish. Even if the material was too limited for any far-reaching conclusions, this suggests that transfer from Swedish is not a major reason for Swedish learners' problems with English connectors.

2 Aim

In this study we shall examine the use of adverbial connectors – what Quirk et al. (1985: 631ff) call 'conjuncts' – in advanced Swedish learners' written English and compare it with the use in comparable types of native Swedish and native English writing. To broaden the picture we shall also briefly compare the Swedish learners' usage with that of advanced French learners of English.

Our interest in conjuncts (rather than other types of connectors) springs from the fact that advanced Swedish learners find them problematic and, in our experience, tend to underuse them. For this reason, our study will mainly be quantitative in character, i.e. we shall not be concerned with errors in connector usage but rather with such phenomena as under-/overuse by the Swedish learners in comparison with native writers. We want to emphasize that the terms 'overuse' and 'underuse' are used as purely descriptive labels – they do not necessarily imply incorrect usage. More specifically, we will examine the following questions:

- Do advanced Swedish learners use conjuncts to the same extent as native English university students?
- Do they use them to express the same semantic relations as native students?
- Do they choose stylistically appropriate conjuncts?
- Do they place their conjuncts in the same positions as native English writers?
- Does their use of conjuncts give evidence of transfer from their native Swedish?
- How do they compare with French learners and what can such a comparison tell us about mother-tongue influence vs. general learner problems?

3 Material

The main part of our material has been taken from the International Corpus of Learner English (ICLE) (see Granger, Chapter 1, this volume).

The Swedish component of the ICLE corpus contains essays written by Swedish students of English in their second year (third and fourth term) at Lund University. The essays have an average length of 500 words and deal with such topics as the roles of imagination and technology in modern society, environmental issues, Swedish immigration policy, and the integration of Europe. From this subcorpus we selected a sample of 86 untimed essays totalling about 50,000 words. We will refer to this sample as SWICLE.

From the native English control corpus we selected a sample of 70 essays, also totalling about 50,000 words, written by British students of French in their second and third years at the University of Surrey. The essays have an average length of 1,000 words and deal with such topics as Britain and the EU and various aspects of French culture and civilization. We will refer to this sample as LOCNESS.

To be able to compare the use of connectors in the Swedish learners' essays with native Swedish usage, we collected a sample of 35,000 words from 37 longer papers written in Swedish by native students of Swedish in their second term at the Department of Scandinavian Languages, Lund University. The papers deal with various linguistic topics such as male and female conversational styles, foreign students' proficiency in Swedish, Swedish dialectal features, and the role of prosody and body language in conversation. The excerpts, averaging 1,000 words, were taken from the discussion of the results and the conclusion of the papers. We will refer to this sample as 'L1 Swedish'.

Although the topics of the corpora are not identical, we regard the samples as sufficiently similar to be used for a comparative study. All the essays are argumentative or expository in character, i.e. besides presenting facts, they have the aim to explain, analyze and interpret these facts and, usually, to argue for a certain standpoint. The writers are all university students and most of them are in their early twenties. All can be regarded as 'advanced' in the sense that they are studying at university level, but their experience and training in argumentative writing may of course vary.

4 Comparing Swedish learners and native English students

4.1 Overall frequencies

Let us first look at the overall frequency of conjuncts in the material. Table 6.1 shows the number of conjunct types and tokens used in the three samples.

Since the samples differ in size the number of tokens per 10,000 words is also given. The table shows that the Swedish learners use fewer conjuncts in their essays than the native English students (72 vs. 95 examples per 10,000 words). This supports our impression that advanced Swedish learners of English tend to underuse conjuncts in their written English. Interestingly, the learners also use fewer conjuncts than Swedish students do when writing in their native language. This suggests that the problem facing the learners is not so much influence from Swedish as the fact that they have to express themselves in a foreign language.

The number of conjuncts per essay varies greatly in the material. In the Swedish learners' essays the number ranges from 0 to 16, in the English students' essays (which are generally longer) from 1 to 25, and in the native Swedish essays from 3 to 18. This shows that connector usage is not just a matter of EFL proficiency but closely connected with the individual writer's style and compositional technique.

Table 6.1: Overall frequency of conjuncts in L1 Swedish, SWICLE and LOCNESS

	L1 Swedish	SWICLE	LOCNESS
Tokens	329	366	481
Tokens/10,000 words	93	72	95
Types	48	50	48

4.2 Semantic relations

Another interesting question is to what extent Swedish learners use conjuncts to mark the same semantic relations as native students. To investigate this we analysed the functional roles of the conjuncts in the material, using Quirk et al.'s (1985: 634ff) classification, as shown in Figure 6.1. For the present purposes we disregarded the subdivision of the main categories and excluded the temporal subcategory, which we regarded as irrelevant. Instead we followed Granger and Tyson (1996) and added a category which they call 'corroborative' (cf. Ball 1986). This includes certain attitudinal disjuncts like *actually*, *in fact*, *of course* and *indeed* which are basically modal in character but which can also be said to have a cohesive function in that they tend to add a new point that strengthens or gives a new turn to an argument (see Granger and Tyson 1996: 20).

As shown in Table 6.2, the distribution of the different semantic categories is roughly the same in the three corpora: contrastive and resultive relations are most common, summative and transitional relations are rare, and clear cases of the inferential relation could not be found at all. The differences between the corpora are mainly confined to three categories. The Swedish learners tend to use more appositive conjuncts than the native students but fewer resultive and contrastive conjuncts. The learners' underuse of resultive and contrastive conjuncts is especially striking.

At first glance the learners' overuse of appositive conjuncts (such as *for example* and *for instance*) seems to be due to Swedish influence, since this category is also very common in the native Swedish essays. However, a scrutiny of the material reveals no clear evidence of L1 influence. Instead, what turns out to be the main reason for the Swedish learners' apparent overuse of appositive conjuncts is that the native English students generally prefer a connector that was not included in the study,

(a) Listing (i) enumerative (e.g. *for a start, finally*)
(ii) additive: equative (e.g. *in the same way, likewise*)
reinforcing (e.g. *moreover, further*)
(b) Summative (e.g. *in sum, altogether*)
(c) Appositive (e.g. *for example, namely*)
(d) Resultive (e.g. *as a result, consequently*)
(e) Inferential (e.g. *in that case, otherwise*)
(f) Contrastive (i) reformulatory (e.g. *more precisely, rather*)
(ii) replacive (e.g. *better, again*)
(iii) antithetic (e.g. *by contrast, instead*)
(iv) concessive (e.g. *in any case, however*)
(g) Transitional (i) discoursal (e.g. *by the way, incidentally*)
(ii) temporal (e.g. *in the meantime, meanwhile*)

Figure 6.1 Classification of conjunct roles (Quirk et al. 1985: 634)

Table 6.2: Distribution of semantic types of conjuncts

Category	**L1 Swedish**		**SWICLE**		**LOCNESS**	
	n	***n* per 10,000**	***n***	***n per* 10,000**	***n***	***n* per 10,000**
Listing	39	11.0	57	11.2	56	11.1
Summative	2	0.6	12	2.4	10	2.0
Appositive	69	19.5	70	13.8	53	10.5
Resultive	79	22.4	80	15.8	142	28.0
Contrastive	114	32.3	95	18.7	169	33.2
Transitional	0	0	2	0.4	0	0
Corroborative	26	7.4	50	9.9	52	10.3
Total	329	93.2	366	72.2	482	95.0

namely *such as*. This exemplifying connector, which is functionally equivalent to *for example* and *for instance* but not regarded as a conjunct in Quirk et al. (1985), is twice as common in the native English essays (42 tokens) as in the Swedish learners' essays (21 tokens). If we include this variant, the Swedish learners' overuse of appositive conjuncts disappears and is turned into a slight underuse. The fact that semantic relations can be expressed by connectors of different grammatical kinds emphasizes the danger of relying on strict grammatical criteria in a study of functional categories. We shall return to this problem in the following section.

The underuse of resultive and contrastive conjuncts in the learner essays does not seem to be L1-induced either, as there is no obvious underuse of these categories in the native Swedish essays. The explanation is more likely to be sought in problems the learners have when expressing these relations in English and we shall return to this question in the next section.

It is also interesting to look briefly at the type/token ratio of the conjuncts used to express the different relations. In most of the categories the difference between the corpora is negligible, but there are two exceptions: the Swedish students use a smaller set of listing conjuncts than the native English students (13 vs. 20) but a larger set of contrastive conjuncts (16 vs. 10).[1] Neither of these differences is statistically significant, but it is noteworthy that the difference in the number of listing and contrastive conjunct types used in the two corpora has a parallel in the native Swedish essays: the Swedish students also use fewer listing and more contrastive conjuncts than their English counterparts. However, whether the learners are influenced by their native language in this respect is impossible to say on the basis of the present material.

4.3 Individual conjuncts

We now turn our attention to the use of individual conjuncts in the material. The top ten conjuncts in SWICLE and LOCNESS are shown in Table 6.3. As we can see, seven of the listed conjuncts are identical in the two corpora, although their rank order differs somewhat. This means that both the Swedish learners and the native students rely heavily on roughly the same conjuncts. However, the tendency to exploit a limited set of items is especially strong among the native English students: the top ten conjuncts represent no less than 76 per cent of the total number of conjunct tokens in LOCNESS but only 60 per cent in SWICLE. The native students' strong reliance on *however* as a contrastive connector is especially striking: nearly every fourth conjunct in the native English essays is represented by *however*.

Yet, despite this general tendency to share a common set of high-frequency items, there are some notable differences between the corpora. If we concentrate on the most frequent items (those occurring at least ten times in either sample), we find that four conjuncts are significantly overused by the Swedish learners while six are underused (see Tables 6.4 and 6.5).[2]

Three of the overused conjuncts – *furthermore, still* and *for instance* – are remarkable in that they are rarely used by the native English students, who prefer other alternatives such as *also* (instead of *furthermore*), *for example* and *such as* (instead of *for instance*) and *however* and *yet* (instead of *still*). There are no obvious reasons for these differences except that the Swedish learners are evidently less familiar with the variants preferred by the native students (cf. the discussion of *such as*

Table 6.3: Top ten conjuncts in SWICLE and LOCNESS

SWICLE	*n*	%	LOCNESS	*n*	%
for example (*e.g.*)	39	10.7	*however*	122	25.4
however	32	8.7	*therefore*	55	11.4
of course	31	8.5	*thus*	42	8.7
so	26	7.1	*for example* (*e.g.*)	36	7.5
therefore	26	7.1	*so*	33	6.9
thus	18	4.9	*of course*	22	4.6
for instance	13	3.6	*in fact*	16	3.3
that is (*i.e.*)	13	3.6	*that is* (*i.e.*)	14	2.9
still	11	3.0	*yet*	13	2.7
furthermore	10	2.7	*indeed*	12	2.5
Total	219	59.8	Total	365	75.9

Table 6.4: Conjuncts overused by the Swedish learners

Conjuncts	SWICLE	LOCNESS
furthermore	10	4
for instance	13	2
still	11	0
of course	31	22

Table 6.5: Conjuncts underused by the Swedish learners

Conjuncts		SWICLE	LOCNESS
Resultive	*hence*	1	10
	therefore	26	55
	thus	18	42
Contrastive	*however*	32	122
	though	3	11
	yet	6	13

above). The fourth overused conjunct, corroborative *of course*, will be further discussed in section 5.

The conjuncts underused by the Swedish learners all belong to the resultive and contrastive categories (see Table 6.5). It is difficult to say for certain what the reason for these cases of underuse may be. We have already seen that both resultive and contrastive relations are frequently expressed in the native Swedish essays (see Table 6.2), so influence from Swedish is unlikely. Resultive relations are generally easier to infer from the context than contrastive relations and omission of resultive connectors is consequently less risky (cf. Wikborg 1985: 112). However, it is significant that with the exception of *though* all the underused conjuncts belong to the formal registers (*therefore, thus, however* and *yet*; see Altenberg 1984 and 1986). Since formal contrastive conjuncts (such as *emellertid, dock*) are not avoided in the native Swedish essays, the most likely explanation is that the Swedish learners are less familiar with formal English conjuncts and that they use a less formal style than the English students. This explanation receives additional support if we examine the distribution of the coordinator *but* in the material. *But*, which is especially common as a contrastive connector in informal registers in English (see Altenberg 1986), is significantly more frequent in the Swedish learners' essays than in the native English essays (276 vs. 207 occurrences). This is a clear indication that the Swedish learners tend to avoid formal contrastive conjuncts like *however* and *yet*, replacing them with more informal equivalents (This tendency for learners to adopt a more informal style has also been found in other studies. See e.g. Chapters 8 and 9, this volume.)

The fact that the learners also underuse an informal conjunct like *though* does not necessarily contradict this. Rather, it seems to suggest a general stylistic uncertainty about the use of connectors in argumentative writing.

4.4 The position of connectors

Many English conjuncts have a variable position in clauses or sentences, although some have favoured or restricted positions. According to Quirk et al. (1985: 643), clause-initial position is the norm for most conjuncts 'and many are virtually restricted to it' (e.g. *besides, so, what is more, yet*), but several are also common in medial position (e.g. *however, nevertheless*) or end position (e.g. *anyway, though*).

In this section we shall briefly compare the clause position of the connectors in the corpora to see if the learners deviate from the native English norm. Such a comparison is of special interest as Swedish is a V2-language which typically permits only one clause element before the finite verb. This affects the position of connectors, which tend to be postponed in cases where another clause element is judged to have greater claim to clause-initial (thematic) position. In a preliminary contrastive study of the English-Swedish Parallel Corpus (see Aijmer et al. 1996) it was found that while English conjuncts predominantly occur clause-initially, Swedish conjuncts favour medial position (cf. Jörgensen and Svensson 1986: 101). If the Swedish pattern is transferred to Swedish learners' EFL writing, we can consequently expect a lower proportion of clause-initial conjuncts in the Swedish learners' essays than in the native English essays.

The position of the conjuncts in the three corpora is shown in Table 6.6. In addition to initial, medial and final position, two other variants had to be distinguished in cases where none of the other positions was applicable. We have called these 'elliptic' and 'appositive'. Elliptic position was used for conjuncts occurring in coordinated and subordinated clauses where the subject or the subject and an auxiliary were omitted. In such cases the initial and medial positions are neutralized and impossible to distinguish (cf. Quirk et al. 1985: 496):

(1) People can not survive without any recreation or amusement and *consequently* find different ways to cope. (SWICLE SC93–11–001)

The label 'appositive' was used to describe the position of conjuncts introducing a parenthetically inserted element, typically in the form of an apposition:

Table 6.6: Position of conjuncts in SWICLE, LOCNESS and the Swedish essays

Position	**L1 Swedish**		**SWICLE**		**LOCNESS**	
	n	***n* per 10,000**	***n***	***n* per 10,000**	***n***	***n* per 10,000**
Initial	85	24	219	43	267	53
Medial	156	44	77	15	124	25
Final	0	0	9	2	9	2
Ellipsis	32	9	21	4	40	8
Appositive	56	16	40	8	42	8
Total	329	93	366	72	482	96

(2) Technology has given us a lot for which we are thankful, e.g. air-conditioning, and other things which we do not find that necessary, e.g. the egg boiler. (SWICLE SC93–11–001)

As Table 6.6 shows, the positional tendencies are radically different in the native Swedish and native English essays. While every other conjunct has clause-initial position in the native English essays (55 per cent), only every fourth conjunct has this position in the native Swedish essays (26 per cent). Instead, medial position predominates in Swedish (47 per cent). However, it is obvious that the Swedish pattern has not influenced the learners. If anything, they tend to overdo the English pattern, having an even stronger preference for initial position than the English students (60 per cent) and a corresponding weaker preference for medial position. In other words, there is no sign of transfer from Swedish.

5 Comparison with French learners

In their comparison of connector usage in essays written by advanced French learners of English and native English students, Granger and Tyson (1996) found no general overuse by the learners (as they had expected) but clear evidence of both overuse and underuse of individual connectors. They also found evidence of semantic, stylistic and syntactic misuse.

Since Granger and Tyson's study was based on comparable ICLE material, it is interesting to compare the French and Swedish students' use of connectors. As Granger and Tyson point out (1996: 18), such a comparison may give valuable information about L1-related and universal features of learner language and help us 'to draw a clearer picture

Table 6.7: Comparison of French and Swedish learners: overall frequencies

	Granger and Tyson		Present study	
	French NNS	**NS**	**Swedish NNS**	**NS**
Corpus size in words	89,918	77,713	50,697	50,648
Number of tokens	976	916	366	482
Tokens/100,000 words	1,085	1,178	722	950

both of advanced interlanguage and of the role of transfer for different mother-tongue backgrounds.'

A rough comparison of the two studies reveals both similarities and differences between the two learner groups. As shown in Table 6.7, the Swedish learners underuse conjuncts to a much larger extent than the French learners. What this may be due to is difficult to tell. As there is nothing in the Swedish system of connectors that may explain the Swedish learners' usage, we must assume that it is somehow connected with differences in the educational background of the two learner groups.

On the other hand, a comparison of over- and underused conjuncts in the two learner varieties (see Table 6.8) reveals a surprising similarity between the French and Swedish learners. With few exceptions the same items are over- and underused by the two groups. Since the Swedish sample is comparatively small, the status of some of the Swedish items is uncertain (e.g. *moreover, namely, on the contrary* and *hence*), but the general tendency is much the same in the two learner varieties. This seems to rule out L1-induced transfer as an explanation for the over-/underuse of most of these conjuncts.

Only a few comments on some striking features can be made here. Of the overused items, the corroborative adverbs *actually* and *indeed* are overused by the French learners only, while *of course* is overused by both groups. This difference is interesting since the three items overused by the French learners have also been shown to be overused by German learners (see Granger and Tyson 1996: 22). The Swedish learners thus deviate in some respects from the other learner groups. It is difficult to say how this difference should be interpreted. Granger and Tyson explain the French learners' overuse of *actually* as an L1-induced 'translation' of French *en fait*. This may well be so, but it is also possible that the tendency among some learners to overuse corroborative adverbs is due to their argumentative 'style'. As Biber and Finegan (1988) have demonstrated in a study of 'stance' adverbials in English, corroborative adverbs are typically associated with registers that reflect the speaker/writer's personal convictions, whereas a low frequency of

Table 6.8: Comparison of French and Swedish learners: over- and underuse of conjuncts

Categories		**Swedish learners**	**French learners**
Overuse:	Additive	*moreover*	*moreover*
	Appositive	*for instance*	*for instance*
		namely	*namely*
	Contrastive	*on the contrary*	*on the contrary*
		still	
	Corroborative	*of course*	*of course*
			actually
			indeed
Underuse:	Resultive	*hence*	*hence*
		therefore	*therefore*
		thus	*thus*
	Inferential		*then*
	Contrastive	*however*	*however*
		though	*though*
		yet	*yet*
			instead

such adverbs is characteristic of more 'faceless' and objective registers such as written expository prose. Moreover, there seems to be a difference between adverbs like *actually* and *in fact*, on the one hand, and adverbs like *of course* and *surely*, on the other. While the former tend to be especially common in interactive speech where they reflect 'the maintenance of a convincing or engaging dialogue in situations with little motivation and opportunity for careful argumentation' (ibid.: 18), the latter have a more persuasive function, serving to present information as obvious and 'beyond the realm of dispute' (ibid.: 21). The learners seem to be unaware of these functional and stylistic restrictions and the result is that they use a more 'personal' argumentative style than the native English writers are prepared to adopt in their essays.

Most of the underused conjuncts listed in Table 6.8 are also identical in the two learner varieties. Both groups tend to underuse resultive and contrastive conjuncts. To explain the French underuse of these categories Granger and Tyson (1996) suggest that the French learners use a different kind of argumentation than the native students and that they tend to avoid certain formal connectors. As we have seen (section 4.3), the latter is the most likely explanation for the Swedish learners' underuse of these types of conjuncts. The Swedes prefer less formal connectors (e.g. *but*) to the formal alternatives and it is significant that all but one (*though*) of the conjuncts listed as underused by the Swedish learners in Table 6.8, are formal in character.

Hence, what seems to be the problem, especially for the Swedish learners, is not so much that they underuse (or overuse) certain relations, but rather that they fail to use connectors that are stylistically appropriate to express these relations in a comparatively formal register like argumentative or expository writing. In other words, insensitivity to register distinctions in the target language emerges as a major learner problem for the Swedes.

6 Conclusion

The main conclusion of this study is that, in purely quantitative terms, the advanced Swedish learners' use of conjuncts compares fairly well with that of native English students. In contrast to many EFL learners of other language backgrounds, the Swedish learners tend to underuse conjuncts, which confirms our own impression of Swedish students' essay writing. However, this feature is mainly confined to resultive and, especially, contrastive relations, and it partly reflects a tendency among the learners to avoid formal connectors and replace them by less formal ones. In fact, what seems to be a major problem for the Swedish learners is their lack of register awareness, a feature that they share to some extent with advanced French learners. This is undoubtedly a reflection of their general language development but also of their EFL education. The main pedagogical conclusion to be drawn from this study is consequently that Swedish EFL students need to be exposed to a greater range of registers and to a more extensive training in expository writing.

Apart from these general tendencies, there is little evidence of mother-tongue influence on the learners' use of conjuncts. The English and Swedish use of connectors is evidently not different enough for transfer to play an important role, and even in areas where there are cross-linguistic differences, such as the position of conjuncts, the learners seem to have little difficulty in conforming to the target norm.

However, these conclusions are very tentative. Our study has been exploratory in character and its limitations are obvious. Our material has been restricted in size and our approach has been purely quantitative. Obviously, further research is needed which takes into account not only the quantitative aspects of connector usage but also its qualitative aspects – how connectors are actually used by the learners. To judge from the present study, such research would benefit from a wider definition of connectors and from more extensive comparisons with other interlanguage and native varieties. Coupled with contrastive studies of the native and target languages, corpus-based investigations of discourse produced by EFL learners from various mother-tongue backgrounds will greatly increase our knowledge of L1-related and universal features of connector usage. The ICLE corpus offers a very promising resource for such future research.

Notes

1 Listing conjuncts used by the native English students but not by the Swedish learners are *also, equally, fifthly, in particular, lastly, next, similarly* and *what is more*. Contrastive conjuncts used by the Swedish learners but not by the native English students are *after all, at the same time, in any case, of course, still* and *then again*.
2 Other less frequent conjuncts underused by the Swedish learners are *also, firstly* and *in fact*, and three less frequent overused items are *moreover, first of all* and *consequently*. However, these connectors are rare in both corpora and the differences are uncertain.

CHAPTER SEVEN

Direct questions in argumentative student writing

Tuija Virtanen

1 Introduction

The presence of questions in EFL proficiency essays seems to be something of a general characteristic of writing of the type and there are a number of reasons why this may be so. First, if students are faced with a topic lacking in personal interest, they often have problems inventing what to write about. The writing process is also affected by the unnatural setting, the ill-defined or fictional audience and the teaching/testing purpose of the task. These factors, not to mention the fact that they are writing in a foreign language, are bound to have an effect upon the confidence with which they address and perform the writing task and it is this lack of confidence and reluctance to assert themselves which may well result in a tendency to ask questions rather than make statements.

Interestingly, however, a study of the International Corpus of Learner English (ICLE), which consists of argumentative essays written by advanced EFL students from various L1 backgrounds, reveals that the frequency of direct questions varies across its subcorpora. This finding raises the issue of motivations behind the use of questions of various kinds in these data. This chapter is a first report of a study which explores discourse functions of direct questions in argumentative EFL and native speaker (NS) student writing, and my aim here is to answer the following two research questions, using ICLE and the comparable Louvain Corpus of Native English Essays (LOCNESS).

(1) What are the overall frequencies of direct questions in some ICLE and LOCNESS subcorpora, and are the differences statistically significant?

(2) Does the placement of direct questions in an essay show systematic differences across subcorpora?

In addressing these fairly straightforward issues, I will view all types of questions as a single group. Two ad hoc categories, however, emerge from close reading of the texts. In what follows, I will start with general considerations of the use of computerized corpora in the study of discourse phenomena, relating this discussion to the present investigation (section 2). I will then go on to deal with the two issues indicated above (section 3).[1]

2 Using computer learner corpora in the study of direct questions

The *raison d'être* of this report is the need to explore how we can profit from computer corpora in the study of discourse. This is a problematic area: the study of discourse involves investigation of processes which lie behind a given product, i.e. a spoken or written text. These processes can be studied indirectly by examining the product, which should therefore be considered in its entirety in relation to its situational context. Discourse processes can also be studied more directly, for instance, through on-line experiments. The use of a computer corpus, however, involves a shift of focus from the dynamic to the static: it is difficult to get at processes through a search procedure which initially demands rethinking of a given discourse phenomenon in terms of suitable formal units. At the same time, it is less straightforward to get sufficient 'recall' and 'precision' (cf. e.g. Brodda 1991: 276–8) for discourse phenomena than for problems concerning syntax or the lexicon. In other words, we are still very much at the mercy of the computer, working on what is possible in automatic analysis. To take an example of relevant previous findings concerning questions in NS data, Biber (1988) focuses on *wh*-questions because of the possibility of reaching sufficient recall and precision. Such decisions can be wise, as in the instance of Biber's study. Yet in the study of global discourse phenomena, choices dictated by this practice can, unfortunately, also be utterly misleading.

This chapter focuses on a formal category, direct questions, starting from the kinds of output that are retrievable from computer learner corpora (CLCs). As ICLE and LOCNESS consist of written materials, the scope of the study can be limited to questions indicated by a question mark, rather than *wh*-questions, and the output thus also includes *yes-/no*-questions. Other relevant material will, however, be lost, even after the application of a complementary search procedure based on lexical cues. Direct questions have been retrieved with the help of *WordCruncher*, which has the question mark as one of the items in the alphabetical list it creates of the texts indexed for it. Other uses of the question mark in these data have been deleted manually. Questions without a question mark thus lie outside the scope of the present study even if some of them can be retrieved using other search cues. More importantly,

Table 7.1: Data under scrutiny in this study: description of the NS and NNS subcorpora in terms of the number of essays, the number of running words, and the average number of words per essay

Subcorpus	Number of essays	Number of running words	Average number of words/essay
American	70	68,460	978
British	33	19,037	577
NS Total	103	87,497	849
Finnish	164	119,919	731
Finland-Swedish	84	55,332	659
Swedish	166	97,914	590
Belgium-French	329	198,709	604
Dutch	130	111,597	858
German	213	111,192	522
Spanish	94	57,216	609
NNS Total	1,180	751,879	637
NS and NNS Total	1,283	839,376	654

indirect questions, including a small number followed by a question mark in the NS and non-native speaker (NNS) data, are also excluded for the time being though they are potentially of interest. Stylistic preferences are a factor here: Swales and Feak (1994: 19, 72), for instance, recommend the use of indirect, rather than direct, questions in academic writing.

The frequencies to be presented below are based on the faulty assumption that direct questions, followed by a question mark, constitute a homogeneous category. Even though faulty, an assumption of this kind is to some extent justifiable at a first stage of a corpus study: existing programs force one to start from form, rather than function, and in view of the prospect of unexpected findings, search cues such as the present one may sometimes prove successful. The use of such formal cues can thus be motivated if the output is relevant enough to be used as a starting point for a qualitative analysis.

The present study is based on two comparable CLCs under compilation: ICLE and LOCNESS, consisting of argumentative student essays (see Granger 1993, also Chapter 1, this volume). Table 7.1 summarizes the data used for this study, which comprise 87,497 running words of NS writing and several NNS subcorpora totalling 751,879 words.

3 Findings

In section 3.1 I consider the overall frequencies of direct questions in the data presented in Table 7.1. Section 3.2 is devoted to the placement of direct questions in the essay, and here the focus is only on NNS essays written by Finnish-speaking and Swedish-speaking Finns. These two parts of the Finnish subcorpus, totalling 175,251 words, are compared with the NS data.

3.1 *Overall frequencies*

Table 7.2 displays the overall frequencies of direct questions in the NS and NNS data. An examination of the Finnish and Finland-Swedish essays indicates that the presence of a question in the title of the essay does not affect the number of questions in the text.

Table 7.2 covers 2,326 direct questions, appearing within a corpus of 839,376 words, which gives a relative frequency of 2.77 question marks per 1,000 words. Generally, these questions are somewhat randomly distributed across the essays constituting the subcorpora. Overall, the NS students seem to use fewer questions than the NNS students. If, as in *WordCruncher*, the question mark is regarded as a word, and as such

Table 7.2: Distribution of direct questions in NS and NNS argumentative student writing: absolute frequencies, and relative frequencies based on the number of question marks indicating a direct question per 1,000 words

Subcorpus	**Number of direct questions**	**?/1,000 words**
NS British	42	2.21
NS American	118	1.72
NS Total	160	1.83
NNS L1 Finland-Swedish	200	3.61
NNS L1 French	645	3.25
NNS L1 Finnish	367	3.06
NNS L1 Swedish	295	3.01
NNS L1 German	326	2.93
NNS L1 Dutch	234	2.10
NNS L1 Spanish	99	1.73
NNS Total	2,166	2.88
NS and NNS Total	2,326	2.77

related to the remainder of the words in a given subcorpus, we get a highly significant difference between the present NS and NNS data.[2] I will, however, comment on this way of counting below.

Both the NS and NNS data display internal differences. Hence, the British essays include more question marks indicating a direct question per 1,000 words than essays written by American students, though this difference is not statistically significant. Furthermore, the much larger category of NNS data manifests internal variation which suggests a major distinction between two groups of subcorpora: on the one hand, the large majority of NNS subcorpora (i.e. the Finnish and Finland-Swedish, French, Swedish and German subcorpora) show a highly significant difference in this respect in relation to the NS data; on the other hand, two subcorpora (i.e. the Dutch and Spanish subcorpora) do not show such a difference. The difference between the individual NNS subcorpora belonging to the one or the other of these two groups is highly significant. Table 7.2 also indicates that the highest relative frequency of occurrences is to be found in the Finland-Swedish data. In fact, the difference between these essays and the Swedish and German subcorpora is significant. In contrast, the French and Finnish essays do not show a significant difference in relation to the Finland-Swedish essays or the Swedish and German data.

The NS data thus seem to constitute a category together with the Dutch and the Spanish subcorpora. In particular, it is the American part of the NS corpus that in this respect shows a highly significant difference in relation to the remainder of the NNS subcorpora. The British part of the NS corpus shows a highly significant difference in relation to the Finland-Swedish subcorpus, and a less significant difference to the French and the Finnish subcorpora. One of the reasons why the number of questions in the British subcorpus is relatively higher than in the American one can be the nature of essay topic, which suggests that the influence of the topic should be investigated more thoroughly throughout the present data.

Relating the number of question marks indicating a direct question to the number of running words, as I have done above, seems odd. Despite variation in sentence length, a more natural solution would be one in which the number of sentences realized in the form of a direct question were related to the total of sentences in a subcorpus. In the instance of *WordCruncher*, this involves indexing of the data for sentence level searches, which has so far only been done for a small part of the subcorpora. Being able to select clauses would be even better but they are more difficult to get at automatically unless the data are parsed. At this stage of the study I have been able to relate the number of questions to the total of sentences in the NS data and the two parts of the Finnish subcorpus. These figures are shown in Table 7.3, which indicates that the NS students use fewer questions than the Finnish and

Table 7.3: Proportion of direct questions of the total number of sentences in NS and NNS (Finnish and Finland-Swedish) data

Subcorpus	Direct questions/sentences
NS Total	3.54%
NNS L1 Finland-Swedish	6.60%
NNS L1 Finnish	5.63%
NNS Total	5.94%

Finland-Swedish students, the difference being highly significant. In contrast, the two parts of the Finnish subcorpus do not show a significant difference in this respect. Overall, sentences are somewhat longer in the NS essays than in the Finnish and Finland-Swedish essays, the difference being one word on the average. Because of variation in sentence length, new counts based on the number of sentences rather than number of words will give a slightly different ordering of the remainder of the subcorpora in Table 7.2.

3.2 *Placement*

ICLE and LOCNESS permit discourse studies as they consist of entire texts which are similar enough for most purposes of comparison. Yet the lack of sophisticated software makes a combination of an automatic analysis of a CLC with an in-depth study of given texts obligatory for a deeper understanding of the discourse phenomenon at hand. In what follows, I am concerned with the placement of direct questions, since this is an issue of discourse relevance which can be investigated automatically. The focus is on the two parts of the Finnish subcorpus, i.e. essays written by Finnish-speaking and Swedish-speaking students in Finland (cf. Virtanen 1996). Accordingly, I will use the label 'NNS' to refer to these two groups and compare their essays with the NS data.

To start with, questions in these data turn out to be of two kinds: topical or rhetorical. Topical questions have a text-organizing function; they introduce or shift topics to be dealt with in the subsequent text. The discussion of these topics extends over a few sentences, one or more paragraphs, or the entire essay, as in (1) below, which is the beginning of an American essay on euthanasia. In contrast, rhetorical questions have an interpersonal function; they are used to persuade the reader and they therefore appear without an explicit answer in the subsequent text. The rhetorical question in (2) below appears at the very end of another American essay on the same topic. All questions of course encourage reader involvement. In view of previous studies of cultural

Table 7.4: Placement of direct questions in NS and NNS (Finnish and Finland-Swedish) essays

Subcorpus	First paragraph	Mid-paragraph	Last paragraph	Total
NS Total	39 (24%)	94 (59%)	27 (17%)	160 (100%)
NNS Finnish	64 (17%)	268 (73%)	35 (10%)	367 (100%)
NNS Finland-Swedish	35 (18%)	153 (76%)	12 (6%)	200 (100%)
NNS Total	99 (18%)	421 (74%)	47 (8%)	567 (100%)

differences between Finnish/Finland-Swedish and Anglo-American rhetoric, the placement of topical questions can be expected to vary systematically across the present data (see Isaksson-Wikberg 1992, 1996; Mauranen 1993).

(1) *Does a terminally ill person with only a few months to live have the right to choose between a seemingly peaceful death at the hand of their doctor, or must they continue living in pain? Also, if this situation is accepted, does this mean that other cases, not as severe, might also be considered for this option?* The issue of assisted suicide and euthanasia is now being addressed by society in response to the medical practices of Dr Kevorkian. . . . (NS)

(2) In closing, only one question need be asked. *Is it worth losing lives to violent protests just to allow a few others to lose their lives to euthanasia?* (NS)

Table 7.4 indicates the distribution of questions in the essays. I use the problematic notion of 'paragraph' here, well aware of the heterogeneity of paragraphing criteria (for a discussion, see e.g. Stark 1988). These figures also raise the issue of paragraph length, measured in number of words. Hence, the NS essays consist of longer paragraphs than the Finnish and Finland-Swedish essays, in that order. As pointed out above, existing software puts demands on the kinds of categories we can start from in corpus studies: we need formal units, such as sentences and paragraphs, or indeed, direct questions indicated by a question mark.[3] The student's decision to start a new sentence or paragraph can, however, be argued to reflect a need to provide the reader with helpful cues to discourse structure. Yet in a qualitative study, textual units are to be preferred to typographical paragraphs.

Not surprisingly, the majority of questions appear in the main body of the essay. The NS students also often place questions in the first and last paragraphs. In contrast, the NNS writers tend to favour mid-paragraphs. This suggests that it will be of interest to focus further

Table 7.5: Placement of direct questions within the first paragraph in NS and NNS (Finnish and Finland-Swedish) essays

Subcorpus	First sentence	Mid-sentence	Last sentence	Total
NS Total	8 (20%)	28 (72%)	3 (8%)	39 (100%)
NNS Finnish	9 (14%)	21 (33%)	34 (53%)	64 (100%)
NNS Finland-Swedish	5 (14%)	5 (14%)	25 (72%)	35 (100%)
NNS Total	14 (14%)	26 (26%)	59 (60%)	99 (100%)

on the first and last paragraphs and to differentiate mid-paragraphs more closely. The difference in the distribution of questions in the essay between the NS and NNS data in Table 7.4 is statistically highly significant.

Counting, instead, how many of all the essay-initial or essay-final paragraphs include questions reveals that the proportion of such paragraphs is fairly similar in these NS and NNS data. In contrast, the proportion of second paragraphs including questions of the total of second paragraphs in these two categories of data shows a highly significant difference. More specifically, 19 per cent of the second paragraphs in the Finnish and the Finland-Swedish essays include questions while the corresponding figure for the NS essays is only 6 per cent. The NS students thus seem to place their text-initial questions early, in the first paragraph, while the NNS students appear to use the second paragraph for a similar purpose.

Despite differences in paragraph length, it is relevant to investigate the distribution of questions across sentences in the first, second, and last paragraphs, to see whether students favour the outset of a paragraph or its very end; see Tables 7.5–7.7. In the instance of one-sentence paragraphs, the sentence has been classified as the opening one in the first paragraph and the concluding one in the final paragraph of the essay.

Questions appearing in the opening paragraph are generally topical and are often preceded by background information. Table 7.5 indicates that the NS students place their text-initial questions, firstly, in the middle of the first paragraph, and secondly, at the very beginning of the essay, cf. examples (3) and (1) respectively. The opening paragraph in (3) is from an American essay entitled 'Prayer in schools'. The NNS students, again, place these questions at the end of the opening paragraph, and secondly, in the middle. This latter position is favoured more by the Finnish-speaking than the Swedish-speaking students, and the remainder of the opening paragraph then typically refers to the many-sided or complicated character of the problem at hand. The paragraph in (4) is from the beginning of an essay on television, written by a Finnish-speaker, while (5) is the opening paragraph of a corresponding Finland-Swedish essay. All in all, the NNS students place their text-initial questions later than the NS students, of whom the British place them somewhat later than the Americans but not as late as the NNS writers. This tendency is in harmony with earlier studies on cultural differences in argumentative rhetoric, referred to above.

(3) Forty years ago, starting the day off in a public school often meant reciting the pledge of allegiance and a group prayer. Today, the American flag garners little attention and a public prayer contradicts constitutional law. *But why does praying in public schools receive such a negative reputation?* There is a strong movement in the United States to bring back prayer to the schoolhouse. The argument used to support the use of prayer in public schools, however, relies too heavily on shaky speculation, fallacies, and fanaticism for effectiveness. Those who oppose prayer in public schools focus on fairness and equality to everybody rendering their argument much more convincing and acceptable. (NS)

(4) The television generation seems to spend more and more time in front of a television set. Some people are almost addicted to some TV-series and organize their daily routines so that they can watch these programmes. On the other hand we get a lot of information through television. *Is television really 'opium for the masses' or is it an important and essential part of our lives?* Every story has two sides and this question is no different. (NNS-Fin)

(5) 'Telly came, was seen and conquered'. The story of the TV can be said to be one of success, ever since it first got invited to our living-rooms it has been treated like a member of the family. When it wants to show us something, we will surely watch, when it wants us to listen, we will pay attention. We always take its opinions into account, and it does get the last say very often. Television is indeed an important part of our world nowadays; an uncountable number of people watches TV daily and many people earn their living from working with television. *But can one really claim that television is like opium for the masses, like a drug to us? Are we addicted to television?* (NNS-FSwe)

Focusing on the second paragraph, we find few questions in the NS data whereas one-fifth of these paragraphs in the Finnish and Finland-Swedish essays include questions. Here as elsewhere in the main body of the text, both NS and NNS students often use questions to make the next move in the argument, thus highlighting a local topic. Moreover, in the second paragraph we start finding examples of rhetorical questions. Table 7.6 indicates that questions are mostly placed in the middle

Table 7.6: Placement of direct questions within the second paragraph in NS and NNS (Finnish and Finland-Swedish) essays

Subcorpus	First sentence	Mid-sentence	Last sentence	Total
NS Total	–	8 (100%)	–	8 (100%)
NNS Finnish	10 (19%)	39 (74%)	4 (7%)	53 (100%)
NNS Finland-Swedish	3 (13%)	13 (54%)	8 (33%)	24 (100%)
NNS Total	13 (17%)	52 (67%)	12 (16%)	77 (100%)

of the second paragraph. Particularly in the Finnish data, questions can also appear at the outset of this paragraph; in such instances, the first paragraph has usually dealt with background information leading to this very topic. In the Finland-Swedish data, again, the end of the second paragraph is a good candidate for questions.

Two topical questions appear in the second paragraph in (6), from a Finnish essay on punishment. Example (7) illustrates the use of questions, topical and rhetorical, in the first two paragraphs of a Finland-Swedish essay discussing the claim that the 20th century offers more choice for the individual than any other era.

(6) Punishment seems to be universal. In every culture there are ways of punishing people, only the means of carrying the punishments out vary. In Finland we fine or imprison people, in Singapore they cane them and in the United States the ultimate punishment is execution.

But why do people punish and get punished? A common answer to the latter question is that the person has committed a crime, or more generally, done something wrong. Therefore, he ought to be punished. One could argue that punishing does not do the crime undone and it can, in fact, make the situation worse. *If this is true, why do we inflict penalties on other people?* The answer is simple, we are afraid. We fear people who do not play by the rules we are used to, we fear that things will get out of our control. (NNS-Fin)

(7) This is said to be the century of choice, the century of freedom. Today you can do whatever you want to. You have the means and the technology to go wherever you want to. The individual is free. Equality for women and minorities has risen almost to its full extent. *Is this true? Are we happier today? Are we more independent? Are we free from the burdening pressure of society?*

Well, there are two sides to every story. Personally, I do not think that the majority of people, if they had the choice, would

Table 7.7: Placement of direct questions within the last paragraph in NS and NNS (Finnish and Finland-Swedish) essays

Subcorpus	First sentence	Mid-sentence	Last sentence	Total
NS Total	7 (26%)	14 (52%)	6 (22%)	27 (100%)
NNS Finnish	1 (3%)	26 (74%)	8 (23%)	35 (100%)
NNS Finland-Swedish	6 (50%)	5 (42%)	1 (8%)	12 (100%)
NNS Total	7 (15%)	31 (66%)	9 (19%)	47 (100%)

> choose to live in another era. *Why is this?* There has to be some reasons. First of all, there is convenience. *Who would want to give up their right to watch television if there were no such things? Or even the right to choose not to watch it, but record it on their VCR and watch it later? Or the right to reheat their food in the microwave instead of spending hours by the stove?* From a social point of view this is of course not what freedom of choice is all about. For the materialist, maybe, but otherwise it is just an example of one of the most basic problems of the 20th century child. We are spoiled. We make all kinds of demands just because we can. *Are these then good or bad?* That is the issue to be argued. (NNS-FSwe)

Table 7.4 pointed to a somewhat higher percentage of questions in the essay-final paragraph in the NS data, as compared with the NNS data. Both data include topical and rhetorical questions. Table 7.7 indicates that the NS questions are more evenly distributed across sentences than those appearing in the NNS essays. Compared with the second paragraph, the placement of the NNS questions shows a reversed tendency: the Finnish-speakers seem to include questions in the middle of their last paragraph, which can be relatively long, and secondly, at the very end of the essay. The Swedish-speakers, again, start the typically short last paragraph with a question or place it after its first sentence.

The beginning and the end of the essay are prominent positions and therefore of interest in view of discourse functions of questions in these data. Questions contribute to reader involvement. Further, topical questions included at the beginning of the essay facilitate processing of the subsequent text; at the end of the essay they have a summarizing or concluding function. Rhetorical questions, with their reversed polarity and implied statement, provide the writer with a powerful tool for effective argumentation. The placement of questions of these two types across the essay must clearly be studied separately, focusing on the local and global strategies at work in the text.

4 Conclusion

This study has provided preliminary answers to two research questions. First, the relative frequency of direct questions is considerably lower in the NS data as compared with the totality of the NNS data. At the same time, however, there are statistically highly significant differences in this respect between some of the NNS subcorpora. The highest relative frequency of occurrences is found in the Finland-Swedish essays. An overuse of questions can reduce their argumentative value and increase the often more informal style of their writing (see e.g. Chapters 8 and 9, this volume). Secondly, the placement of direct questions in the essay and within paragraphs varies between the NS data and the essays written by Finnish-speaking and Swedish-speaking Finns. This variation can, to some extent, be argued to support earlier studies of cultural differences in rhetoric as far as topical questions are concerned.

The present analysis has demonstrated the ease with which we can generate a multitude of counts on the basis of a computer corpus. It is therefore useful to remind oneself of the myth of objectivity created by such counts. Results of qualitative analyses, in contrast, make it easier for readers to keep in mind the role of the discourse linguist as a text receiver, bringing her/his own interpretation into the investigation. At the same time, only very little of the above information is of direct relevance to the important issue of why – or even how – questions are used in argumentative student writing. Hence, two subcorpora manifesting similar figures may, in close analysis, reveal very different uses of direct questions. The obvious next step is thus an in-depth discourse analysis, which can only be done manually and therefore lies beyond the scope of the present volume. For a discourse linguist, a computer corpus is, in the first place, an instrument for pilot studies, to test hunches which emerge from close reading and manual analysis of entire texts in context. We can also profit from representative computer corpora in the study of micro-level discourse phenomena. A number of practical problems referred to above will disappear once the corpora under attention are available in a tagged and parsed format. An important development of relevant software will, however, be necessary to switch the roles of the computer and the discourse linguist, from doing what is possible with the help of the computer to permitting the discourse linguist to address issues which need investigation.

Notes

1 I wish to thank Sylviane Granger, Stephanie Petch-Tyson, and Signe-Anita Lindgrén for valuable comments and suggestions which have considerably improved the present report, Signe-Anita Lindgrén also

for efficient help with text indexing, and Sarah Bannock for checking my English. Finally, discussions with Jan-Ola Östman have been helpful. I am, of course, alone responsible for the shortcomings of this chapter.

2 Due thanks go to Fredrik Ulfhielm for writing a computer program to count statistical significance using the chi-square test. I refer to a difference as statistically significant at the 0.05 level, and as highly significant at the 0.01 level.

3 KWIC (Key Word In Context) concordances of course allow us to avoid typographical units such as sentences or paragraphs but this does not solve the problem caused by the necessity of using formal units as search arguments in the study of global discourse phenomena.

CHAPTER EIGHT

Writer/reader visibility in EFL written discourse

Stephanie Petch-Tyson

1 Introduction

It is widely accepted that there are conventions governing the overt presence of participants in different types of discourse. In an Anglo-American context, it is difficult to imagine a conversation in which the interlocutors do not figure prominently in some way in the discourse and equally difficult to imagine a scientific treatise on genetics in which writer and reader are in strong evidence. In other words, the presence of the participants will be encoded more or less overtly, depending on the discourse type. Furthermore, studies have shown that there is cultural variability in levels of (acceptability of) interpersonal involvement in discourse and this variability may result in quite different realisations of particular discourse types. A study conducted by Tannen (1982) into storytelling by American and Greek women showed that the Greeks had a greater tendency to be involved in their stories. By constructing their stories around a particular theme and by making judgements about the characters, they told 'better' stories than their American counterparts who told their stories from a more objective, critical perspective, performing the retelling like a memory test and commenting on the filmmakers' technique rather than the content of the story. Thus in this instance, the overt presence and involvement of the narrator in the story led to a better story, or in fact it led to something which was more representative of a prototypical story than the output of the American participants. It is implicit in Tannen's study that the differences in retelling style are a direct result of different cultural backgrounds, with the Greek women coming from a more oral tradition and the Americans coming from a more literate tradition. According to Tannen however, it is not orality per se that is at issue but rather, 'to what degree interpersonal involvement or message content carry the signalling load.' (Tannen 1982: 3). From this Tannen develops the notion of a 'continuum of relative focus on interpersonal involvement vs. message content' (ibid.: 15).

In her study, Tannen equates higher focus on involvement with discourse types in the oral tradition (in this case, storytelling). It might therefore seem reasonable to put forward as a tentative preliminary hypothesis that there will be less focus on involvement in prototypical discourse types in the literate tradition.

This article is an exploratory corpus-based study of some features of involvement in a discourse type very much in the literate tradition: that of argumentative essay writing. As the study will have a narrower focus than is often the case in studies of *involvement*, the term *writer/reader (W/R) visibility* will be preferred here.

The study has been carried out within the framework of the International Corpus of Learner English (ICLE) project, the central aim of which is to identify the distinctive and shared features of a wide variety of interlanguages. The writing under investigation is that of EFL student writers from four different language and cultural backgrounds (French, Dutch, Swedish and Finnish). The EFL output is also compared to that of native English-speaking students. The primary objective of the study is to determine whether there are differences between the different language/cultural groups in the way the participation of writer and reader are explicitly coded in the discourse. In using a computer to support the analysis, a secondary aim is also to see to what extent this type of discourse phenomenon can be analysed with the help of the computer and thus to what extent it is a suitable candidate for large-scale study. It is understood that the mere presence or absence of features of W/R visibility says nothing about their effect on the success or otherwise of a piece of discourse, although some tentative comments based on a small-scale qualitative text analysis will be put forward. These comments will, however, be based solely on text-level phenomena, with no attempt being made at this stage to take into consideration socio-cultural aspects (for a criticism of this see Besnier 1994: 282). This initial piece of research is intended as a first step in a much larger-scale study[1] and aims to establish the potential interest of W/R visibility as an area of EFL research.

In the first section of the chapter, I review some of the literature on W/R visibility and draw up a list of features which indicate W/R presence in the discourse. In the following section, the results of a computer-aided corpus analysis are presented and discussed. In concluding, I discuss the potential of this area as a field of research and the merits and demerits of using computerised techniques for this type of analysis.

2 Signals of writer/reader visibility

As in many areas of linguistics, features of W/R visibility have been discussed under a variety of different headings. They are used to express personal feelings and attitudes and to interact with readers and as such, fall within the interpersonal function of language as discussed by Halliday (1985). They feature prominently in the study of metadiscourse (see Vande Kopple 1985 and Markkanen et al. 1993).[2] And as has already been shown in the previous section, they are important in the work of sociolinguists such as Tannen. They are also of importance in the work of discourse analysts such as Chafe (e.g. 1982) who aims to identify the linguistic features differentiating speech and writing.[3] According to Chafe (1982: 36) the difference between typical speech and typical writing is often attributed to the fact that 'speakers interact with their audiences directly, whereas writers do not'. This, he argues, has a crucial effect upon the type of discourse the speaker and writer produce. Whereas the obligation for the speaker will be 'to have less concern for consistency than for experiential involvement' (ibid.: 45), the writer must be 'more concerned with producing something that will be consistent and defensible when read by different people at different times in different places' (ibid.: 45).

The result is typical written discourse which he characterises by 'detachment' (in the spirit of Tannen's literate tradition) and which is marked by high use of such linguistic features as passive mood, nominalisations, and abstract subjects, and a spoken discourse which Chafe characterises by 'involvement' (in the spirit of Tannen's oral tradition), marked by high use of, amongst others, first person reference, pragmatic markers (such as *I mean, you know*), fuzzy reference and direct quotes. In his 1987 paper with Danielewicz he expands on this notion of involvement further, distinguishing between involvement with the audience, involvement with yourself and involvement with the concrete reality of what is being talked about (see also Korhonen and Kusch 1989 for an interesting discussion of the different ways in which the pronoun *we* is used in academic discourse).

Chafe is concerned with identifying differences in the linguistic realisation of typical speech and writing, but Smith (1986), in his article 'Achieving impact through the interpersonal component' takes a different approach. Starting from the fact that, contrary to what the textbooks say, professional writers use features of W/R visibility in their writing, he tries to identify the conditions for their being used successfully and conversely the reasons for their coming across as unsuccessful in unskilled writing.

He argues that these interpersonal features can be used successfully if the writer has paved the way for their use by setting a certain tone at the beginning of the discourse. He places the features on two continua, formal–informal and didactic–non-didactic (see Figure 8.1). Although these continua are presented as separate, the two will often be associated, with, for example, informal texts containing didactic grammatical features in the form of direct address.

Figure 8.1 shows that in Smith's ranking, second person is ranked above first person, since second person presumes the presence of a reader

INFORMAL
↑
Presence of the reader
particular second person pronouns
general second person pronouns
reference to situation of reading

Presence of the writer
first person singular pronouns
first person plural pronouns
reference to situation of writing
evaluative modifiers

Distance of the reader/writer
high proportion of passives
third person references to reader/writer
↓
FORMAL

DIDACTIC
↑
Clause mood and modality
full imperative
direct question
first person imperative
periphrastic imperative
rhetorical question
high proportion of indicative clauses
↓
NON-DIDACTIC

Figure 8.1 Ranking of linguistic features actualizing personal tenor and functional tenor (adapted from Smith (1986: 111)

and is therefore more interpersonal than *I* or *we*, for which a reader is not necessary. An important distinction is also made between specific and general second person reference. As regards situation of reading/writing, this relates to the writer's choice either to make absolute reference, e.g. 'in Belgium', or otherwise to refer to it as 'this country', 'our country', 'my country' etc. All of these choices have implications. The absolute reference contributes to the creation of a 'stand-alone' text, whereas the deictic reference anchors the text to its situation of occurrence, very much as in the speech situation.

After establishing these continua, Smith demonstrates that successful writers will set up a range early on in their piece of writing, and will not move outside that range throughout the discourse. The inexperienced writer on the other hand will often establish a particular range of tone throughout the discourse and then suddenly jump to a different tone which comes across negatively as a result.

Figure 8.2 gives a list of some of the main features of W/R visibility and is broadly based on Chafe's (1982) and Smith's (1986) listings. It is important to note that the list is by no means exhaustive and is merely intended to pave the way for a more comprehensive analysis.

3 Corpus analysis and discussion of results

For the present study, I selected from the list in Figure 8.2 those features which best lent themselves to automatic retrieval.

First person reference (singular, plural)
Second person reference (specific, general)
Speaker's mental processes (think, believe etc.)
Monitoring of information flow (you know, I mean etc.)
Emphatic particles (just, really)
Fuzziness (and so on, etc., '. . .')
References to situation of reading/writing (this X, here, now etc.)
Evaluative modifiers
Imperatives
Questions (direct/rhetorical)
Quotation marks
Italics

Figure 8.2 Features of writer/reader visibility

Table 8.1 gives the features which were used in the analysis and the frequency results. As mentioned above, four corpora of learner English and one corpus of comparable native English were analysed. *TACT* was used to obtain raw frequencies and the concordances, which are discussed later on.

The figures demonstrate beyond doubt that, with the exception of emphatic particles, all the non-native speaker (NNS) groups use more of all these features of W/R visibility than the native speaker (NS) group. Furthermore, they show that there is some sort of continuum of use, as illustrated in Figure 8.3, with the Swedish and Finnish writers using very many features at one end and the native American writers using very few at the other.

If one goes beyond simple frequencies and takes a look at concordanced data, a much richer analysis opens up.

To demonstrate the type of insights into the use of features of W/R visibility that concordances may provide, concordances of the first person singular pronoun *I* will be examined across the corpora.

The type of environment and function in which the *I* occurs can be revealing. For example, in the US corpus, almost half of all occurrences of *I* were with verbs in the past tense, and many of these represented chains which together recounted personal experiences (see Figure 8.4). The clustering or chain effect can be seen from the line numbers.

In the learner corpora, the only corpus in which this type of recounting of personal experience and talking about feelings and attitudes in real life is anywhere near as prevalent is the Finnish corpus (see Figure 8.5). There were also some instances in the Swedish corpus of recounting experiences, but almost none in the Dutch and French.

In the French, Dutch and Swedish NNS data, a main function of *I* seems to be to talk about the writer within the context of the piece of discourse, either saying something about the writer functioning within

Table 8:1: Analysis of features of writer/reader visibility

Feature	**Dutch 55,314**	**Finnish 56,910**	**French 58,068**	**Swedish 50,872**	**US 53,990**
Ist person singular pronouns	391	599	364	448	167
I, I'x, me, my, mine					
First person plural pronouns	484	763	775	1,358	242
we, we'x, us, our, ours					
Second person pronouns	447	381	257	227	76
you, you'x, your, yours					
Total first/second person pronouns	1,322	1,743	1,396	2,033	485
Total first/second person pronouns per 50,000 words	1,195	1,531	1,202	1,998	449
fuzziness words					
kind/sort of	53	69	54	34	11
and so on, etc.	43	32	27	31	2
emphatic particles					
just	85	140	48	54	66
really	61	59	28	31	31
reference to situation of writing/reading					
here	27	27	20	43	17
now	81	58	100	62	41
this essay	5	7	7	17	2
TOTAL features	1,677	2,135	1,680	2,305	655
TOTAL features per 50,000 words	1,516	1,876	1,447	2,265	607

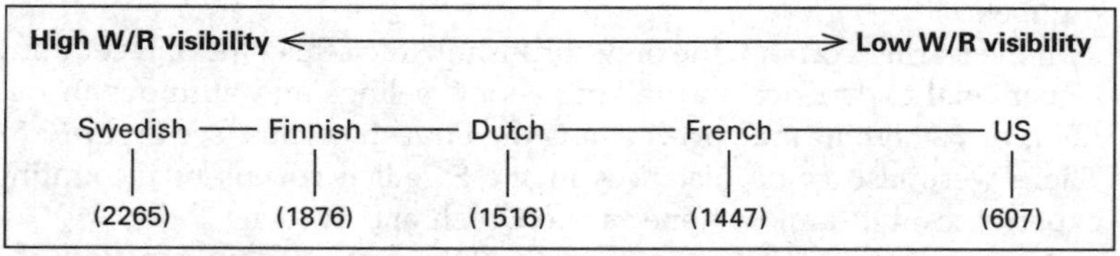

Figure 8.3 Continuum of relative focus on interpersonal involvement vs. message content

(585)	them in I the United States. <*>	> I honestly ran out of my room
(586)	honestly ran out of my room after I	> I read the above quote to ask
(593)	statement grabbed my I attention,	> I looked through the rest
(594)	it as a true argument. For all	> I know, I the author may have
(609)	magazine Christianity Today. As	> I was researching I my topic,
(610)	I my topic, using infotrac 2000,	> I found there were many I
(612)	Today. It was at this point that	> I realized I how popular of a
(881)	within the community.	> I attended school in the I
(884)	I program called Chapter 220.	> I was in seventh grade at
(885)	in seventh grade at the I time and	> I can verify that the battle
(3220)	<ICLE-US-MRQ-0028.1 I >	> I remember driving to northern
(3221)	Wisconsin with my Father I when	> I was twelve. On the way
(3223)	it off to embarrassment. Although	> I had I many questions for my
(3227)	I Finally at the age of eighteen	> I gave in to peer I
(3228)	to have sexual intercourse.	> I decided to have sex I with
(3235)	, my life would never be the way	> I expected I it. At eighteen I
(3236)	way I expected I it. At eighteen	> I needed to make life altering

Figure 8.4 Concordance of NS *I*: recounting personal experiences

(48)	I I I hate war.	> I fear it more than anything
(48)	it more than anything else. But	> I believe in I self-defence. I
(49)	But I believe in I self-defence.	> I am ready to defend my
(50)	my country by force of arms. I	> I think I owe it those almost
(50)	country by force of arms. I I think	> I owe it those almost 100.000
(51)	1939-45 I defending this country.	> I also think that it is every
(229)	way to get "rid" I of them. I I	> I think that the benefits of
(230)	it is used in a intelligent way.	> I couldn't I even think about
(232)	First thing in the I morning	> I turn on the television to
(233)	watch the news and every I night	> I watch at least a couple of
(234)	home though, because at home	> I have fourteen channels
(236)	rence but it's good because now	> I have the time to do my
(238)	rself in a oneroom appartment.	> I have learned most of my I
(1604)	quite the opposite. I I When	> I still lived at home with my
(1604)	lived at home with my parents	> I never had any bigger I
(1606)	were no bills for me to pay and	> I even got a little pocket I
(1608)	most essential parts of living.	> I never realized I that
(1609)	I never realized I that someday	> I am alone and counting every
(1610)	to I survive. For four years now	> I have been on my own. At the
(1611)	on my own. At the age of I 19	> I left home and moved in

Figure 8.5 Concordance of Finnish EFL *I*: thinking and recounting personal experiences

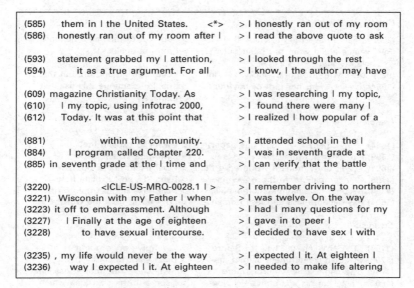

Dutch

(200) article, I have tried to show that > I am not of the same opinion
(394) I once again want to I point out clearly that > I am not against the
(928) ones who are not so lucky. I I And > I could go on and on, but that is
(1964) his/her girl- or boyfriend. > I could I continue this list endlessly.

French

(1684) man? I Through this paper, > I want to explain that
(1599) to bear out this I point of view, > I will first sketch the
(1601) in our I modern world an d then > I will try to find a possible
(3788) incompatible. In these few lines > I shall try to I explain how
(4764) become multinational companies. I > I can take the example of the
(1604) has become less and less human. > I'm I using here the word

Swedish

(1707) ICLE-SW-LND-0031.1> I I Before > I will give my arguments for
(1708) Swedish Government should have, > I just want to clarify the I
(1710) Swedish I society. Furthermore > I will show one more possible
(1801) play I in his sparetime. I I Now > I come to the next idea which
(1801) Now I come to the next idea which > I presented in the I
(1803) are very closely I connected. As > I said, I think that
(1803) closely I connected. As I said, > I think that imagination is a
(1804) is a condition I of technology. > I will explain why. I I I

Figure 8.6 Concordance of NNS *I*: writer operating within the text

the text or what the writer thinks. The uses in Figure 8.6 are typical of occurrences of *I* across these corpora.

This type of use is almost completely absent both from the native American texts and from the Finnish texts.

Another striking thing revealed by the concordances of *I* in the learner data is the chaining of sentence-initial features of W/R visibility (Figure 8.7, 1). In the NS concordances, there is usually one pre- 'topic' feature, whereas in the learner corpora, there is a much greater occurrence of chains of features, and a much greater occurrence of extra focus on these features, either by topicalisation structures or other means, such as emphatic particles. Also of interest are the frequent repetitions of phrases (Figure 8.7, 2 – rhetorical structure) which according to Tannen (1989) are a feature of conversational narrative. There are also quite frequent occurrences of end-placement of features such as *I think, I guess* which creates a more conversational style.

In summary, this analysis of the use of the first person pronoun *I* reveals both quantitative and qualitative differences in its use by the

1. Chains of interpersonal features

Dutch
(1715) by this > I mean that according to my opinion there
(3092) O.J. Simpson-case, f I instance, and you'll know what > I mean when I say that
(428) service. I I To conclude, I think > I have made it clear that we

Finnish
(3368) too old. I must admit though that > I am not sure if I would
(4974) a while it might seem like that if > I, I mean you . . . we imagine

French
(1124) to be. I As far as I am concerned, > I think that every man should
(3969) Community. I For this reason > I think we can easily say that
(5362) with. I As I am an optimist, > I do not think that things
(1533) A last thing I want to add is that > I do not agree with you when I

Swedish
(1193) the first vacuum-cleaner. I So > I guess you can say that we

2. Rhetorical structure

Dutch
(975) saying still counts: <*>. And > I thought all men were created
(979) men get the jobs thrown into I their laps. And > I thought all men were created
(988) a chance to solve their problem. And > I I thought all men were created equal.
(996) chance be regarded as democratic? > I thought democracy was I supposed to

Swedish
(1380) po·vers of human beings? > I think not. I I It is
(1383) entail a decrease in fairy-tales? > I think not. I I In this
(1424) in a society dominated by them? > I think not. I What I do think
(1425) by them? I think not. I What > I do think is that because of

3. End-focus

Finnish
(4608) fear until censorship disappears, > I think. It seems to be true

Dutch
(2506) most of them are about twenty three, > I guess. We were talking about

4. Emphasisers

French
(736) elaboration. On the contrary, > I am deeply convinced that in

Swedish
(290) imagination in modern I society. > I thoroughly believe that
(300) for dreaming and I imagination. I > I am quite sure that this was
(3554) I areas. I So in other words: Yes, > I definitely think that

Figure 8.7 Concordance of NNS *I*: (1) chains of features, (2) focus on writer/organising the text round the writer (3) end-focus, (4) emphasisers

different groups. Of the learner groups, only the Finns seemed to use the *I* to talk about first-hand experiences and feelings in a similar way to the NS writers. For the other learner groups, the *I* was the person organising and participating within the discourse.

The more general result of this study is that all the learner writers, to a greater or lesser extent, have been shown to use almost all of the features of W/R visibility under investigation much more often than the control NS writers, and can thus be said to be focusing more on interpersonal involvement. One result of this may be that their writing may be felt to conform less to the conventions of the particular genre.

As regards the effect that the presence of more interpersonal features of language will have on the reader, Lakoff (1982: 252) predicts that it may be negative, commenting that:

> In general then, the borrowing of a device from one medium into another is always overdetermined: it carries with it the communicative effect, or 'feel', of one medium into another (the metacommunicative effect) and at the same time attempts to utilise the language of one mode to communicate ideas in another (the communicative effect). It is no wonder that this sort of translation can create confusion in readers (or hearers) and can also create in them very strong feelings – typically negative.

Coming back to Smith's (1986) idea of a continuum of formality–informality however, I believe that there is a distinction to be made between texts which mix features from the two poles of the continuum and those which stick within a particular range. Of the two texts below, example 1 has the more informal tone and yet arguably creates a better communicative effect because the tone is consistent. In example 2, the jump at the end from the informal style to the more formal '*one*' disturbs the fluency of the writing.

(1) So, what has all that got to do with me? Well, I have to get along in this world – just like everybody else. As a student I have to cope with the high prices of food and other basic stuff I need to stay alive and well. My parents are not exactly rich and therefore I am forced to survive with practically no money at all (the lousy allowance from the state does not count). So, does it ever cross my mind to get the money 'somewhere else', in a less honest way? Well, yes it does. I never do it, though. Maybe I would if I knew just how. I am just a regular little citizen from a regular little town, who does not know shit about the littlest thing called cheating.

(2) We do talk quite a lot about equality, but what does the reality tell us? Are we people really that open-minded and just – tolerant? I know we like to think that we are all that – the most civilised generation that ever set its foot on Earth – but . . . If **one** opens **one's** eyes and faces the real world, that is out there, **one** can see that we still have a long way to go.

4 Conclusion

This preliminary study has shown that interesting quantitative and qualitative differences exist in the use of features of W/R visibility in NS and learner writing. Much research remains to be done and most of the questions remain unanswered. It seems reasonable to say however, that the learner writers are much more overtly present within the discourse than the NS writers and that this presence manifests itself in different ways. It could be culturally induced and due to differences in persuasive strategies and in this respect it will be useful to examine the relationship between the features of W/R visibility and Connor and Lauer's (1985) categories of persuasive appeal – rational, credibility and affective. Another potentially revealing line of enquiry would be to investigate whether the different groups are expressing different types of involvement (cf. the three types proposed by Chafe and Danielewicz 1987: 3), something which may be culturally or indeed teaching-induced. Finally, differences may be due to different perceptions of the writing task,[4] or indeed to the topics of the essays themselves.

This study has only looked at each learner population as a group and therefore individual differences have not been taken into consideration. It will be essential to do this in order to know whether most/all learners of one language background are using these features in similar ways, or if there are just a few using them all the time. Similarly, if the issue of range and consistency of tone is to be addressed in more depth, it will be necessary to look at individual whole texts.

For many of these aspects, as is often the case in the analysis of discourse features, analysis will be manual, but the computer can nevertheless play a useful supporting role. This study has shown how initial quantitative results can easily be obtained and the value of this should not be underestimated. With the aid of retrieval software, it is possible to ascertain the potential interest of an area of study without spending weeks identifying and counting features manually. It is possible not only to have frequency counts of an item in one corpus, but one can also have access to frequency comparisons between corpora, a facility which immediately highlights significant differences in the use of particular words. Concordancers and collocation facilities can often reveal patterns of use that may not be immediately apparent in a whole-text context, as was the case in the study of *I*. And finally, one can get information about the distribution of features within and across corpora. (For further information on automating lexical analysis see Meunier, Chapter 2, this volume.)

This type of automated analysis will help paint an initial picture of the use of features of W/R visibility by the different learner populations and has the significant advantage of being able to take into account data from a large number of learners. Combined with other types of analysis, it will help us understand where the differences lie in the use of these features between the different groups. As Markkanen et al. (1993: 41) point out in their study of metadiscourse: 'Metadiscourse is part of the pragmatics of language, but proficiency in this area is notoriously difficult to attain in a foreign language.' Once we are more aware of how (and why) features of W/R visibility are used by NS and NNS writers, we shall be better equipped to help learners use them to their advantage.

Acknowledgement

I would like to thank Sylviane Granger, Tuija Virtanen and Raija Markkanen for their helpful comments on my work. The many failings in this chapter are completely my own.

Notes

1 This study is the subject of my doctoral dissertation.
2 This is not meant to imply that what is understood by W/R visibility in this chapter is the same as what is included in Halliday's interpersonal component or in Markkanen et al.'s classification of metadiscourse. Both of these terms take in a much wider set of features but they also include the features dealt with in this article.
3 As Chafe and Danielewicz point out in their 1987 paper, neither spoken nor written language are a unified phenomenon and each allows a multiplicity of styles. For them typical writing would be formal academic papers and the like, and typical speech would be conversation.
4 The idea of the results being due to different interpretations of the task was put forward to me in a personal communication by Raija Markkanen.

CHAPTER NINE

Automatic profiling of learner texts

Sylviane Granger and Paul Rayson

1 Introduction

In this chapter Crystal's (1991) notion of 'profiling', i.e. the identification of the most salient features in a particular person (clinical linguistics) or register (stylistics), is applied to the field of interlanguage studies.[1] Starting from the assumption that every interlanguage is characterized by a 'unique matrix of frequencies of various linguistic forms' (Krzeszowski 1990: 212), we have submitted two similar-sized corpora of native and non-native writing to a lexical frequency software program to uncover some of the distinguishing features of learner writing. The non-native speaker corpus is taken from the International Corpus of Learner English (ICLE) database. It consists of argumentative essay writing by advanced French-speaking learners of English. The control corpus of similar writing is taken from the Louvain Corpus of Native English Essays (LOCNESS) database.[2] Though limited to one specific type of interlanguage, the approach presented here is applicable to any learner variety and demonstrates a potential of automatic profiling for revealing the stylistic characteristics of EFL texts. In the present study, the learner data is shown to display many of the stylistic features of spoken, rather than written, English.

2 Lexical frequency software

The lexical frequency software used for the analysis was developed at Lancaster University (see Rayson and Wilson 1996) as a front-end retrieval system to enable researchers to view semantically (word-sense) tagged corpora and perform statistical tests on frequency profiles produced from those corpora.

The software can provide frequency profiles and concordances (at all levels of annotation) from semantically and part-of-speech (POS)

Table 9.1: The word frequency profile

Word	NS frequency	NNS frequency	Overuse or underuse	χ^2 value	Log likelihood	Dispersion
the	14,912	17,728	X–	29.6	29.5	702
of	7,645	10,282	X+	17.4	17.4	702
to	7,597	9,585	X–	0.0	0.0	702
and	6,018	6,976	X–	23.7	23.7	702
a	4,726	7,034	X+	76.4	77.0	702
in	4,556	5,769	X+	0.0	0.0	702
is	4,465	6,518	X+	55.7	56.1	700
that	3,671	4,109	X–	28.3	28.2	701
for	2,177	2,324	X–	31.8	31.7	684
it	2,116	3,270	X+	52.5	53.0	693
be	2,066	2,792	X+	5.4	5.5	686
he	2,049	1,800	X–	127.6	126.6	377
as	1,978	2,368	X–	3.1	3.1	674
not	1,883	2,651	X+	13.0	13.1	678
this	1,872	2,469	X+	2.0	2.0	667
are	1,682	2,701	X+	60.1	60.8	668
they	1,479	2,340	X+	46.2	46.7	623
his	1,435	1,238	X–	97.7	96.8	416
with	1,396	1,614	X–	5.8	5.8	663
by	1,270	1,389	X–	13.8	13.7	619
have	1,252	1,891	X+	24.2	24.4	665
on	1,228	1,702	X+	6.2	6.2	658

tagged text and has been adapted to display the frequency of lemmas alongside word forms, POS disambiguated word forms and semantically disambiguated word forms. The user can load a file (or set of files) into the program which then displays a frequency profile with relative frequency and a dispersion value (which, in this case, shows how many essays mention each item) (see Table 9.1).

Using a classification scheme based on the SGML information encoded in the essay file headers, a user can select subcorpora and hide parts of the text not of interest in a particular study. A typical header is of the type '<p mt = 2 tt = 1 nr = A1001>', encoding *mother tongue* (mt), *text type* (tt) and an identification number for each essay. The classification scheme allows the user to display frequencies for different parts of the corpus alongside each other. The χ^2 statistic is used to show items whose frequency distribution across the subcorpora is statistically significant. Profiles can be resorted on any of the fields being displayed (including χ^2 value). The frequency profile can also be searched for, or limited by, a particular lexical item or tag, for example, to include only lexical verbs by matching on VV.

and sustained". Patients don't	feel	the up and down effect other" stre
, the architect mentioned before,	felt	less obsessed with his work and had
ncomfortable in the event that you	feel	you are constantly being viewed as
ing conditions should be like. He	feels	that, "*". How can this be if t
s? Pattullo, on the other hand,	feels	that homosexuals in the military wo
hat everyone is entitled to. Wall	feels	that, "*". Sexual discriminatio
ech is o.k. does not mean it would	feel	the same way about the amendment
s, especially Liberal Democrats,	feel	that the death penalty is an integr
us crime. Basically, some people	feel	that a strong death penalty through
penalty as immoral, and therefore	feel	that it is unneeded. Although, so
s a dark ring to it. Those who do	feel	that way see pictures of Oliver Twi
y such as Republican Newt Gingrich	feel	that support payments should be sto
this dehumanization factor, many	feel	that orphanages are no place for ch
create lasting relationships, and	feel	a sense of belonging. Speaking of
d to have sex with a class mate to	feel	socially accepted by my peers. My
mate on what our options were. We	felt	the right decision was to get marri
y that a person in a coma does not	feel	pain? Some people have little or n
in life to be breathing, eating,	feeling	, smiling, and most of all loving
would still be life. I would not	feel	the same about a terminal illness o
utlook on life. In conclusion, I	feel	that the restoration of the "Ameri
ne of the users of this system. I	feel	that this won't help, considering
ofits of the county's transit. I	feel	that the city might lose more money

Figure 9.1 The KIIC (Key Item In Context) display for the lemma 'feel'

Values of χ^2 are known to be unreliable for items with expected frequency lower than 5 (see Dunning 1993), and possibly result in overestimates for high-frequency words and when comparing a relatively small corpus to a much larger one. In this study the corpora are similar-sized, and results are usually checked using the dispersion value and concordances to take into account the distribution within the corpus. We also use the log-likelihood value (Dunning 1993) which does not suffer the same problems as χ^2 does with unbalanced sample sizes.

To produce a KIIC (Key Item In Context, see Figure 9.1) concordance for an item in the frequency profile, the user simply double clicks on the line in the list. Levels of annotation can be added to or taken away from the concordance lines so that the user can see patterns of tagging, for example, surrounding a key item. Essay headers can also be viewed for each concordance line.

3 Word category profiling

3.1 Word category set

One way of characterizing a language variety is by drawing up a word category profile. This method has been used in previous studies to bring out the distinctive features of learned and scientific English (Johansson

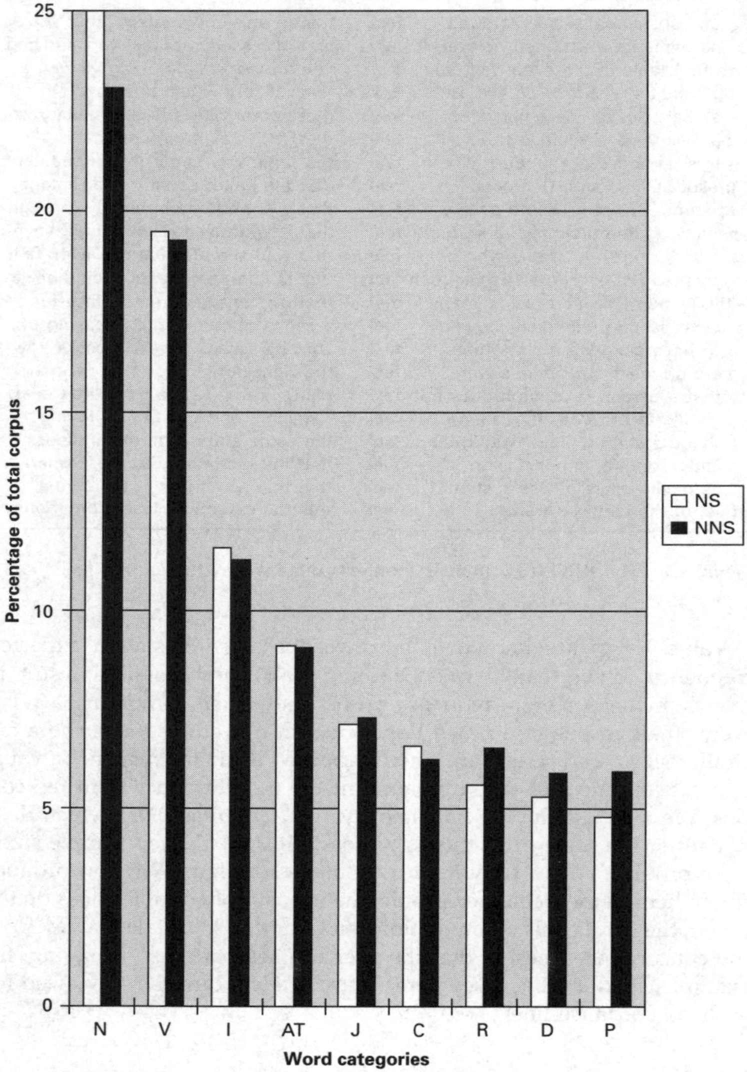

Figure 9.2 Major word category breakdown in NS and NNS corpora

1978, 1985), American vs. British English (Francis and Kučera 1982) and spoken English (Svartvik and Ekedahl 1995).

Claws4, the word category tagging system used for the analysis, employs 134 word category tags,[3] some of which were grouped together

Table 9.2: Reduced word category tag list

N	nouns (common and proper)	
J	adjectives	
I	prepositions	
AT	articles[4]	
D	determiners	
C	conjunctions	
	subcategorized into	coordinating conjunctions
		subordinating conjunctions
P	pronouns	
	subcategorized into	personal pronouns (including possessive and reflexive)
		indefinite pronouns
		wh-pronouns
R	adverbs	
	subcategorized into	prepositional adverbs; particles
		all the other categories of adverbs
V	verbs	
	subcategorized into	lexical verbs (finite forms, *-ing* participles, past participles, infinitives)
		modal auxiliaries *be/have/do*[5]

for this study, to allow significant patterns to emerge. The reduced tagset contained nine major word categories and 14 subcategories, presented in Table 9.2.

As appears from the list, five word categories are not subcategorized at all, while the other four have various degrees of secondary coding. Most of the new categories are merged categories. One category, for example, groups all categories of adverbs (general, locative, temporal, etc.) except for prepositional adverbs and particles.

3.2 *Frequency of major word categories*

Figure 9.2 displays the distribution of the nine major word categories in the native and non-native corpora. Three categories prove to have similar frequencies in the two corpora: articles (AT), adjectives (J) and verbs (V). But the non-native speaker (NNS) writers overused three categories significantly: determiners (D), pronouns (P) and adverbs (R), and also significantly underused three: conjunctions (C), prepositions (I) and nouns (N).[6]

Table 9.3: Top 20 lexical verbs in decreasing order of significance

Lemma	Overuse or underuse	χ^2 value	NS frequency	NS relative frequency	NNS frequency	NNS relative frequency	Dispersion
dream	X+	184.2	3	0.00	243	0.08	80
state	X–	112.2	145	0.06	27	0.01	93
think	X+	96.7	261	0.11	666	0.23	418
support	X–	96.0	105	0.05	13	0.00	57
continue	X–	74.3	115	0.05	29	0.01	92
forget	X+	73.9	20	0.01	152	0.05	131
live	X+	72.2	197	0.09	501	0.17	339
speak	X+	66.1	46	0.02	202	0.07	165
imagine	X+	60.8	8	0.00	102	0.04	81
create	X+	58.1	108	0.05	312	0.11	224
believe	X–	55.7	287	0.12	181	0.06	222
argue	X–	53.8	102	0.04	33	0.01	87
realise	X–	51.4	89	0.04	26	0.01	45
allow	X–	41.3	175	0.08	101	0.03	170
disappear	X+	41.3	5	0.00	68	0.02	66
let	X+	40.8	71	0.03	210	0.07	183
run	X–	40.3	66	0.03	18	0.01	54
reach	X+	38.8	39	0.02	144	0.05	124
lower	X–	34.4	32	0.01	2	0.00	10
attempt	X–	33.5	45	0.02	9	0.00	37

Not unexpectedly, this type of profile raises more questions than it answers. Aside from the question of whether overall similarity of frequency may conceal individual differences, there are questions relating to the over- and underused groups: is it coordination or subordination that accounts for the overall underuse of conjunctions? What types of pronouns are underused? To answer these questions, it is necessary to look both at the grammatical subcategories and the lexical items they contain. This more detailed analysis is the subject of the following section.

4 Significant patterns of over- and underuse

In order to determine significant patterns of over- and underuse, we produced profiles for lemmas in each major word category and subcategory and sorted them in decreasing order of significance. The software also indicates if the lemma is overused by learners (with *X*+) or underused (*X*–). Table 9.3 shows the top 20 lemmas in the category of lexical verbs in decreasing order of χ^2 value.

The most significant findings resulting from the comparison of word categories and lemmas in the two corpora are summarized in Table 9.4. The table only contains items which are either significantly over- or underused, not those with similar frequencies.

In the following sections these patterns of over- and underuse are interpreted in the light of the results of previous variability studies.

4.1 *Articles*

In the French learner corpus, the indefinite article *a* is overused and the definite article *the* underused. This proportionally higher use of indefinites by the NNS writers suggests that they are conforming less to the norms of formal writing. In his analysis of word frequencies in the LOB corpus, Johansson (1985: 30) notes that 'category J (learned texts), which has the highest frequency of the definite article, has the lowest frequency of the indefinite article'. These results also demonstrate that an analysis based on major word categories, such as that represented in Figure 9.2, can be very misleading since in the case of articles, it showed no difference between the native and non-native corpus.

4.2 *Indefinite determiners and indefinite pronouns*

Most indefinite determiners and pronouns are significantly overused by the French learners. A high frequency of such words has been found to be favoured in speech and disfavoured in formal writing. Devito (1966, 1967) notes that speech has more indefinite quantifying words and allness

Table 9.4: Patterns of over- and underuse in the NNS corpus

	Overuse	Underuse
AT	*a*	*the*
D	**most indefinite determiners**	
	all, some, each, a few, another	*many*
P	**most indefinite pronouns**	
	everybody, nobody, one, oneself, something, everything, a bit, a lot, lots	*no-one, no, anyone, everyone someone*
	first and second personal pronouns	
CC	*but, or*	*and*
CS	**some complex subordinators**	**most subordinators**
	as far as, as soon as, even if	*until, after, before, when, (al)though, while, whilst, whether (or not)*
I		**most prepositions**
	between, towards, without, above, during, of, on, about, before, among in spite of, in front of, thanks to, by means of, till	*for, over, throughout, upon, into, along, out, despite, regarding, per, including, by, off, after, to, amongst, until, up, than*
RP		**most adverbial particles**
RR	**short adverbs of native origin (especially place and time)**	***-ly* adverbs**
N		**overall underuse of nouns**
V	**auxiliaries**	***-ing* and *-ed* participles**
	infinitives	

terms, while Johansson (1978: 11, 27) points at the low frequency of indefinite pronouns ending in *-thing/-one/-body* in academic English. Table 9.4 clearly brings out the learners' tendency to opt for the more informal variants of these words: they overuse *a lot* and *lots* but underuse *many*. Similarly, they overuse the indefinite pronouns ending in *-body* but underuse those ending in *-one*, which are more common in writing than the former.[7]

4.3 *First and second personal pronouns*

There is also a very significant overuse in the learner corpus of the first and second personal pronouns. All variability studies associate this feature with the involved nature of speech and point to the low frequency of indices of personal reference in academic writing (see Poole and Field 1976; Chafe 1982; Chafe and Danielewicz 1987; Biber 1988; Petch-Tyson, Chapter 8, this volume and Rayson et al. forthcoming).

4.4 *Coordination vs. subordination*

The general underuse of conjunctions brought out by Figure 9.2 conceals a complex situation. While conjunctions of coordination display both overuse (*but* and *or*) and underuse (*and*), the majority of subordinators are underused. For reasons which are difficult to explain, the only subordinators that are overused are complex subordinators such as *even if* and *as soon as*. Interpreting these results would require a thorough analysis of each of these conjunctions in context, a task which is beyond the scope of this chapter. However, some results can be interpreted in the light of previous studies. A high frequency of *but* has been found to be a distinguishing feature of spoken language. Chafe (1982) finds over twice as many instances of *but* at the beginnings of idea units in speech as in writing.[8] As stated by Biber (1988: 107) subordination is not a 'functionally unified construct'. Some semantic categories of subordination are strongly associated with speech, and others with writing. It is striking to note that concessive subordinators, which, according to Altenberg (1986: 18) are more prevalent in writing, are significantly underused by learners. It is also noteworthy that the two subordinators which are usually associated with speech, namely *if* and *because*, are not underused by learners, unlike most of the other subordinators.

4.5 *Prepositions*

The category of prepositions is underused by the learner writers. According to Rayson et al. (forthcoming) use of prepositions differs more than for most other categories between speech and writing. A high proportion of prepositions is associated with the informative and nominal tendency of written language. As appears from Table 9.4, the overall learner underuse hides considerable differences between individual prepositions and again, an in-depth study will be necessary to investigate which prepositions are over- and underused and in what meanings and contexts. Where there are formal–informal doublets, learners again prove to opt for the informal variant: *in spite of* and *till* are overused, while *despite* and *until* are underused. In addition, complex prepositions, like the complex subordinators, have a tendency to be overused.[9]

4.6 *Adverbs*

As has now been shown to be the case for many categories, the general overuse of the category of adverbs in Figure 9.2 is the result of over- and underuse of individual adverbs or categories of adverbs. It is mainly short adverbs of native origin (*also, only, so, very, more, even, rather, quite*) which are significantly overused, especially those expressing place and time (*now, ago, always, often, sometimes, already, still, everywhere, here*). The underused adverbs are mainly *-ly* adverbs: amplifiers (*greatly, truly, widely, readily, highly*), disjuncts (*importantly, traditionally, effectively*), modal adverbs (*possibly, supposedly*), time adverbs in *-ly* (*newly, currently, previously, ultimately*).

This picture contrasts sharply with the type of adverbs frequently found in academic writing. According to Johansson (1978, 1985), academic writing shows a preference for *-ly* adverbs formed from adjectives of Romance origin which denote concepts other than place and time, and disfavours short adverbs of native origin (especially adverbs of place and time). Learners clearly favour speech-like adverbs. The list of overused adverbs contains eight of the 14 interactional adverbials listed by Stenström (1990: 175): *anyway, in fact, of course, indeed, absolutely, really, certainly, now*. It is noteworthy, however, that the underuse of adverbial particles, probably due to an underuse of phrasal verbs, seems to point in the opposite direction since phrasal verbs are typical of speech. A closer look at this category of adverbs is clearly necessary if we are to find out exactly what is happening.

4.7 Nouns

Johansson (1985: 30) contrasts the nominal style of informative prose with the verbal style of imaginative prose. Svartvik and Ekedahl's (1995: 27) study equally links up a lower density of nouns with the category of imaginative texts and conversations. The overall underuse of nouns that characterizes French learner argumentative writing is thus clearly a further sign of a tendency towards oral style. Further research is necessary in particular to assess the rate of nominalizations, which have been shown to figure prominently in academic writing (Chafe and Danielewicz 1987: 99).

A comparison of over- and underused lemmas proves enlightening. Among the underused nouns we find a whole set of items which are normally associated with argumentative writing, such as *argument, issue, belief, reasoning, claim, debate, controversy, dispute, support, advocate, supporter, proponent, denial*. By contrast, there is overuse of general and/or vague nouns such as *people, thing, phenomenon, problem, difficulty, reality, humanity* (see Petch-Tyson forthcoming for a discussion of the use of these nouns across several NNS corpora). Such lists clearly hold great potential for ELT materials design.

4.8 Verbs

Though the overall frequency of verbs is similar in learner and native texts, there are considerable differences in the verbal forms used. The first striking feature is the overuse of auxiliaries, a characteristic of

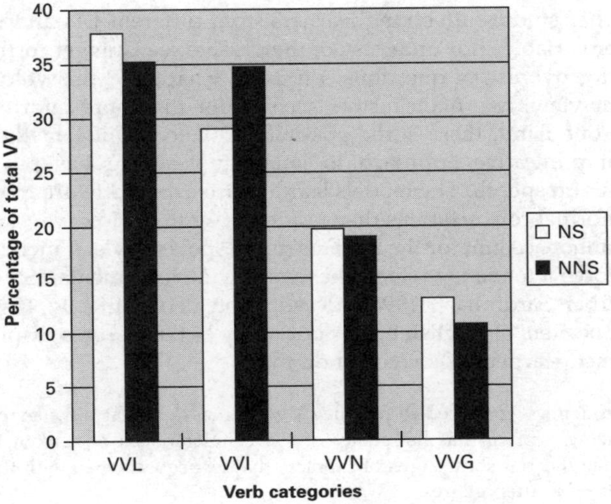

Figure 9.3 Verb forms in NS and NNS corpora

conversational English. The second difference concerns lexical verbs, both finite (VVL forms), which are underused and non-finite forms, which display a less uniform pattern, with learners using fewer participle forms, both past participles (VVN) and *-ing* participles (VVG), and more infinitives (VVI) (see Figure 9.3).

This is exactly the opposite of what one would expect in an academic text. Participles are the integrative device *par excellence* (Chafe 1982: 40) and studies such as Chafe and Danielewicz (1987: 101) show that 'language other than academic writing makes considerably less use of participles'.[10] On the other hand, a high frequency of infinitives, which goes together with a high frequency of auxiliaries, is indicative of speech (O'Donnell 1974: 108).

As for lexical variety, a look at Table 9.3 shows that learners underuse some of the typically argumentative verbs – *state, support, believe, argue* – a deficit which contrasts with an unusually high frequency of the 'cover-all' verb *think.*

5 Conclusion

The automatic profiling technique has highlighted the speech-like nature of learner writing. The essays produced by French learners display practically none of the features typical of academic writing and most of those typical of speech. This conclusion is reinforced by results from other studies, involving learners from different L1s and focusing on other variables (for underuse of the passive see Granger forthcoming a, and for overuse of questions, Virtanen, Chapter 7, this volume).

In our view, two main factors account for this more informal style. On the one hand, there is the possible influence of ELT methodology: the communicative approach to language teaching has put greater emphasis on speech. The models learners are exposed to are more likely to be informal conversations than academic writing. However, this factor alone cannot account for the learners' more spoken style. It merely serves to reinforce a tendency which is essentially developmental. Shimazumi and Berber Sardinha's (1996) investigation of writing by 15-year-old native speakers of English brings out many of the features displayed by the French learners. They conclude that

> The students were asked to produce a written assignment but they ended up producing a piece that has many of the characteristics of spoken language . . . . they did not show signs of literacy, that is, acquaintance with the formal aspects of written genres.

Orality and involvement are thus more to be viewed as features of novice writing, found in both native and non-native speakers. Whether primarily teaching-induced or developmental, however, the learners' stylistic immaturity has the same remedy, namely greater exposure to good quality expository or argumentative writing, as found, for example, in the editorials of quality newspapers.

Automated quantitative analysis is 'a very accurate quick "way in" for any researchers confronted with large quantities of data with which they are unfamiliar' (Thomas and Wilson 1996: 106). In this article, we have shown that automatic profiling can help researchers form a quick picture of the interlanguage of a given learner population and that it opens up interesting avenues for future research. Do all national interlanguages share the same profile or will each interlanguage have its own? Is the profile constant for a particular national interlanguage or does it evolve across time and if so, how? Automatic profiling applied to a wide range of learner corpora has the potential to help us answer these questions and thereby contribute to a better understanding of learner grammar and lexis.

Acknowledgements

This chapter was written within the framework of the Louvain-Lancaster Academic Collaboration Programme funded by the Fonds National de la Recherche Scientifique, the Commissariat Général aux Relations Internationales and the British Council.

Notes

1 Crystal (1991: 237) himself suggests extending the concept of profiling to other fields 'to see what might grow'.

2 The non-native speaker corpus consists of c. 280,000 words of formal writing (both argumentative essays on general topics and literature exam papers) by advanced EFL university students of French mother-tongue background. The native speaker corpus consists of c. 230,000 words of similar writing by British and American university students.

3 For a full description of the word tagging system, see Leech et al. (1994).

4 This category includes words which are usually not classified as articles, e.g. *no* and *every*.

5 In *CLAWS be/have/do* each constitute a class of their own, no distinction being made between their use as lexical verbs or auxiliaries.

6 Throughout this chapter the significance level has been set at 6.63 ($p < 0.01$).

7 A comparison of two subcorpora of the BNC – one representing informal speech, the other informative writing – found there to be a systematic preference for *-body* pronouns over *-one* pronouns in speech and the reverse in writing (except for *nobody* which was found to be more frequent than *no-one* in both speech and writing).

8 The NNS writers' underuse of *and*, also a speech-typical feature, seems to point in the opposite direction. Further analysis of the use of *and* in context will be necessary in order to identify how it is used by the different groups and in what functions it is underused by the NNS writers.

9 One of the reasons why complex subordinators and prepositions are overused may well be that, unlike single word prepositions, they tend to be semantically transparent and have one-to-one equivalents in the learners' mother tongue: *by means of* = *au moyen de; thanks to* = *grâce à*. Other reasons may play a part as well: the overuse of *as far as* is simply due to the massive overuse of the phrase *as far as X is concerned* by the French learners.

10 A recent study of non-finites in learner writing (see Granger forthcoming b) reveals an underuse of participle clauses in writing by EFL learners from different L1s.

CHAPTER TEN

Tag sequences in learner corpora: a key to interlanguage grammar and discourse

Jan Aarts and Sylviane Granger

1 Introduction

Although part-of-speech (POS) tagged corpora have been around for quite some time, relatively few linguists have been making use of them. Scanning through the comprehensive bibliography compiled by Altenberg (1991), Kennedy (1996: 219) notes that 'Even for many of the grammatical studies, the approach has been through lexical items, for example modals or complementizers.' He suggests that one of the areas which should figure prominently on the research agenda of corpus-based studies is the investigation of 'co-occurrence of tags as expressions of syntactic patterning and as the basis for quantitative studies of the use of syntactic structures and processes' (ibid.: 225).

Though frequency counts of individual grammatical categories are included in several register studies, most notably those of and following Biber (1988), quantification of tag sequences is a very recent development, mostly found in the area of stylometry. Authorship attribution studies, which aim to discover the 'stylistic fingerprints' (Holmes 1994: 87) of writers by quantifying a range of features in their writing, have begun to use tag sequences in addition to word frequency counts (see Felton 1996: 75; Glover and Hirst 1996: 165). Tag sequences are also making an entry into the field of literary text analysis (see Roventini 1996: 234).

If tag sequences can help us discover writers' fingerprints, one can assume that they can also help uncover EFL learners' fingerprints. Atwell and Elliott (1987) have been pioneers in this area. They had the idea of using tag pairs to detect errors, but had difficulty putting the idea into practice because of the lack of learner corpus data. Now that computer learner corpora are available, it is becoming possible to explore learner language automatically using grammatical annotation, notably POS tagging. This can be done by looking at the frequency of individual tags (see Granger and Rayson, Chapter 9, this volume) or tag sequences. In

Table 10.1: List of tags

ADJ	adjective	IT	cleft/ant/prop *it*
ADV	adverb	N	noun
ART	article	NUM	numeral
AUX	auxiliary	PREP	preposition
CONJUNC	conjunction	PROFM	proform
CONNECT	connective	PRON	pronoun
DISC	discourse item	PRTCL	particle
EXTHERE	existential *there*	PUNC	punctuation
GENM	genitive marker	V	verb

this chapter, which adopts the latter approach, we compare tag trigrams, i.e. sequences of three tags, in learner and native corpora with a view to discovering distinctive interlanguage patterns.

2 Data processing

The analysis is based on four similar-sized corpora of c. 150,000 words. Three of the corpora are from the International Corpus of Learner English (ICLE) database and contain argumentative essay writing by Dutch (DU), Finnish (FI) and French-speaking (FR) advanced learners of English. The fourth corpus is a native speaker corpus, extracted from the Louvain Corpus of Native English Essays (LOCNESS) database, and covers the same type of writing by American students (NS).[1]

The four corpora were tagged with the *TOSCA* tagger, using the TOSCA-ICE tagset. The *TOSCA* tagger is a stochastic tagger, supplemented with a rule-based component that tries to correct observed systematic errors of the statistical components. It operates with a wordform lexicon which currently contains about 160,000 wordform-tag pairs, covering about 90,000 wordforms. The TOSCA-ICE tagset contains 270 different tags. A tag normally consists of a label for a major word class, plus any number of 'features' indicating syntactico-semantic subclasses and/or morphological characteristics. For this study however, the information contained in the TOSCA-ICE tagset was drastically reduced by discarding the features and, in some cases, by conflating two or more TOSCA-ICE major word classes. This reduction resulted in the list of tags presented in Table 10.1.[2] Sentence breaks (marked as #) are also counted as one tag.

Standard UNIX tools were used to extract the tag trigrams from the tagged corpora. In the output files, each trigram is presented with the following information: absolute frequency, expected frequency, relative frequency (100,000 words) and χ^2 value. The threshold for statistical significance was set at 6.63 ($p < 0.01$). The native speaker (NS) corpus served as normative for the non-native speaker (NNS) corpora and was taken as standard for expected frequencies and χ^2 values.

3 Top-ranking trigrams

One way of finding possible distinguishing features of learner writing is by looking at the top-ranking trigrams. The Appendix to this chapter lists the top 20 trigram types in each of the four corpora, calculated on the basis of the first 100,000 word tokens. When we compared the four lists, we found that the trigram types in the top 20 were in general roughly the same. Taking the NS corpus as our standard, we found that the Dutch corpus shared 18 of the 20 trigrams with the NS corpus, while for the Finnish and French corpora this number was 17 and 19 respectively. There were, however, differences in the ranking of the trigram types and even bigger differences in their frequency.

When, for each of the trigrams, we inspected the difference in ranking between a NNS corpus and the NS standard rank and counted the total number of different rank positions between the NNS corpus and the NS corpus, we got a rank deviation index for the NNS corpus with respect to the NS corpus. For the three NNS corpora the deviation indices were roughly in the same range, with French slightly higher: DU 40, FI 42, FR 47. To see what this rather abstract observation means in practice, one needs to examine the trigram frequencies.

A comparison of the frequencies of the top trigrams showed that only a minority were similar in the native and non-native corpora. Table 10.2 gives the over- and underuse values of the NS top ten trigrams (excluding punctuation but including sentence beginnings) in the three learner corpora: a plus sign indicates significant overuse, a minus sign significant underuse, a bracketed minus sign nearly significant underuse, while the '≅' symbol marks cases where there is no significant difference in frequency.

The most striking feature is the amazing similarity between the three categories of learners: except for two trigrams, the patterns of use are exactly the same. Particularly noteworthy is the consistent underuse of the four most common trigrams in NS writing, all of which contain prepositions. Also very striking is the difference in sentence beginnings: nouns are underused and pronouns overused in sentence-initial sequences in all three learner corpora. In the following sections, we will take a closer look at some of the distinctive trigrams, i.e. trigrams which have a significantly higher or lower frequency in NNS writing than in

Table 10.2: Over- and underuse values of top ten trigrams in NNS corpora

NS top ten		Dutch	Finnish	French
1	PREP ART N	–	–	–
2	ART N PREP	–	–	–
3	N PREP N	–	–	–
4	N PREP ART	–	–	–
5	ART ADJ N	≅	≅	+
6	V ART N	–	–	–
7	ADJ N PREP	–	≅	–
8	## PRON	+	+	+
9	PREP PRON N	(–)	–	–
10	## N	–	–	–

NS writing. We will first focus on cross-linguistic invariants (section 4). In a second stage, we will look into trigrams which are specific to only one learner variety (section 5).

4 Distinctive trigrams: cross-linguistic invariants

4.1 Overall frequency

In total, 133 trigrams displayed a significant frequency difference between all three NNS corpora and the NS corpus, i.e. around 7 per cent of the overall number of trigram types in each corpus (6.6 per cent in FI, 6.7 per cent in DU and 6.8 per cent in FR). In the overwhelming majority of cases (129/133, i.e. 97 per cent) the three NNS corpora display the same pattern of use equally divided between overuse (66 trigrams) and underuse (63 trigrams). In only four instances do the NNS corpora display divergent behaviour (i.e. overuse in one learner variety and underuse in another). This shows that the common base of deviation in advanced interlanguage is relatively narrow (c. 7 per cent) but that the patterns of use within it are highly convergent.

This technique provides a wealth of data, which can only be fully interpreted by breaking down the major categories into subcategories (distinguishing for example between coordinating and subordinating conjunctions) and looking at the lexical sequences underlying the patterns. Within the limited confines of this article, we will restrict ourselves to a brief presentation of two sets of overuse/underuse patterns

Table 10.3: Prepositional patterns

	Dutch		Finnish		French		Total	
	exp.	abs.	exp.	abs.	exp.	abs.	exp.	abs.
PREP ART N	3,682	3,220	3,713	2,977	3,876	3,196	11,271	9,393
ART N PREP	3,308	2,567	3,336	2,539	3,483	3,058	10,127	8,164
N PREP N	3,023	2,526	3,049	2,515	3,183	2,615	9,255	7,656
N PREP ART	2,567	2,117	2,588	2,021	2,702	2,409	7,857	6,547
PREP PRON N	1,421	1,247	1,433	1,249	1,496	1,361	4,350	3,857
PREP N PREP	953	725	961	652	1,003	738	2,917	2,115
PRON N PREP	848	655	855	713	893	740	2,596	2,108
N PREP ADJ	656	458	661	580	690	517	2,007	1,555
N V PREP	580	488	585	472	611	484	1,776	1,444
V N PREP	570	429	575	483	600	455	1,745	1,367
PREP PRON PUNC	284	339	287	443	299	404	870	1,186
ADV ADJ PREP	240	298	242	302	252	300	734	900
PREP N V	430	323	434	290	453	261	1,317	874
Total	18,562	15,392	18,719	15,236	19,541	16,538	56,822	47,166

which are common to all three categories of learners: sentence-initial patterns and patterns with prepositions.

4.2 *Sentence-initial trigrams*

There are very striking differences in the way learners and native speakers begin their sentences. The three learner varieties display an overuse of sentence-initial (SI) connectives, adverbs, auxiliaries and pronouns, and an underuse of nouns, conjunctions followed by nouns and prepositions followed by *-ing* verbs.

All three categories of learners prove to overuse SI connectives. A look at the text files shows that two of the overused patterns, namely # CONNEC ADV and # CONNEC CONJUNC mainly involve the connectives *but* and *and* with sequences such as *But today, But anyhow, But now, But then, But actually, But if, But whereas, And so, And still, And yet, And maybe, And when, And if.*[3] Learners' tendency to start the sentence with something other than the subject is confirmed by an overuse of SI adverbs. Auxiliary-initiated sentences mark an overuse of questions by learners. Though the overused patterns are shared by all three groups of learners, the much higher χ^2 values displayed by FR show that some of the patterns – notably connective-initial and interrogative ones – are especially prominent in French learners.

Sentences starting with nouns are clearly underused by learners, in particular subject-initiated # N V sequences. The underuse of the # CONJUNC N sequence shows that the same structure is underused in subordinate clauses (*Although creationists, If ideas, When information, Once people*). Learners' underuse of SI nouns has to be put in parallel with their overuse of SI pronouns and is undoubtedly at least partly related to the higher degree of involvement that characterizes learner writing (see Petch-Tyson, Chapter 8, this volume). Another structure underused by all learners is the SI preposition-headed *-ing* clause, such as: *By arguing that . . ., By using this example,* which plays an important frame-setting or linking role in academic writing.

Some of these findings are corroborated by research into learner language based on other retrieval methods, either manual retrieval or word-based automatic retrieval (see Granger and Tyson 1996 for connectives; Virtanen, Chapter 7, this volume for questions and Granger forthcoming b for preposition-headed *-ing* clauses).

4.3 *Prepositional patterns*

Another constant among learners is the underuse of patterns involving prepositions. Table 10.3 lists these patterns together with their absolute and expected frequencies. Patterns with a total absolute frequency under 500 are not given. For practically all patterns and for all three languages, there is a consistent, significant underuse of PREP. The overused patterns PREP PRON PUNC and ADV ADJ PREP show the opposite tendency, but this too is consistent for all three corpora.[4]

One major cause of learner underuse of prepositional patterns is explained by a study of postnominal modifiers by Biber et al. (1994). They compared the treatment given to postnominal modifiers in EFL/ESL grammar textbooks and their frequency in three registers (editorials, fiction and letters) and found that prepositional postnominal modifiers received the least attention in grammars although they proved to be much more common than relative or participial clauses in all three registers. This shortcoming cannot fail to have negative repercussions for EFL/ESL learners:

> it is not accurate to argue that prepositional phrases as noun modifiers are an easy construction that requires little attention. In fact, from a cross-linguistic perspective, this is a marked construction. While it is typical for languages to employ a range of phrases to mark various case relations to verbs, it is unusual to find these same kinds of phrases functioning as nominal modifiers. Thus, in addition to being extremely common in English, prepositional phrases as noun modifiers are likely to be troublesome for L2 students' (ibid.: 173).

5 Distinctive trigrams: L1-specific patterns

Table 10.4 lists the trigrams which have a significantly higher or lower frequency in only one learner variety. The first striking result is that – just like the proportion of cross-linguistic trigrams – the proportion of L1-specific trigrams is approximately the same in each learner corpus, accounting for c. 20 per cent of the trigram types (20.5 per cent in DU, 22.5 per cent in FI and 26 per cent in FR). These figures suggest that the L1-specific part in advanced interlanguage is much bigger than the cross-linguistic one (c. 20 per cent vs. 7 per cent).

Table 10.4: L1-specific trigrams in each learner corpus

	Dutch	Finnish	French
number of trigram types	1,975	2,016	1,962
number of L1-specific trigram types	404 (20.5%)	455 (22.5%)	510 (26%)
overuse	256 (63.4%)	315 (69.2%)	312 (61.2%)
underuse	148 (36.6%)	140 (30.8%)	198 (38.8%)

Table 10.5: Patterns with particles

	French rel. freq.	χ^2	Dutch rel. freq.	χ^2	Finnish rel. freq.	χ^2	NS rel. freq.
CONJUNC PRTCL V	82.4	114	35.2	0.1	32.3	0.0	33.4
PUNC PRTCL V	88.6	97	31.3	2.6	40.7	0.0	39.5
N CONJUNC PRTCL	39	73	16.9	1.1	9.7	1.7	13.6
# PRTCL V	60.7	65	28.7	0.1	29.7	0.3	27.3
V CONJUNC PRTCL	16.7	62	4.5	0.2	6.4	2.5	3.7
# # PRCTL	61.3	49	29.3	0.0	31.0	0.0	30.6

The type of divergence *vis-à-vis* the NS corpus is surprisingly similar in the three corpora: it is mostly one of overuse (c. two-thirds of the cases) with underused trigram types accounting for only one-third of the divergent types.

To illustrate the kind of insights that can be gained from a careful analysis of L1-specific patterns, we will focus on one set of distinctive patterns which occurs in the French learner data but not in the Dutch or Finnish. A look at the top 15 distinctive patterns in FR reveals one striking feature: six of these patterns include a particle (PRTCL). Table 10.5 lists these patterns in decreasing order of χ^2 value in the French corpus. The relative frequencies clearly show that the French learners stand out from all the other categories of writers: they use these patterns twice as often as the natives and the other learners.

An investigation of the lexical sequences underlying these patterns shows that the following three types of structures are overused: (1) sentence-initial marked infinitive used as adverbial of purpose, as in <u>To answer</u> *the question, it seems necessary to . . .* ; (2) sentence-initial marked infinitive instead of gerund used as subject, as in <u>*To live*</u> *in the same nation also means . . .* or <u>*To unite*</u> *of course includes . . .* ; (3) coordinated marked infinitives, as in *a real opportunity to develop* <u>*and to find*</u> *new outlets.*

6 Conclusion

The material in this chapter has been used merely to illustrate our methodology and we are well aware of its limitations. We might have presented more or different material, such as trigrams that are exclusive to native speakers or learners, for example; we could have used a more refined tagset or investigated other n-grams. Our main aim here, however, was to present the technique of automatic tag extraction and assess its potential for SLA research.

The results are encouraging. Our analysis has shown that the technique can highlight distinctive interlanguage patterns, marking off those that are common to all learners from those that are specific to one learner variety. Our analysis suggests that there are more L1-specific features of advanced interlanguage than 'universal' ones. This does not mean, however, that the different learner corpora have nothing in common. They do share a number of features and the striking thing about these is that they deviate from NS writing in the same way, in that the same patterns are either underused or overused by the three groups.

Automatic tag sequence extraction can also serve to rank interlanguages according to their degree of divergence from the native speaker norm. In this exploratory study French learner writing came out as more 'marked' than Dutch or Finnish writing on several variables.

Generally speaking, our study highlights the benefits of tagged corpora over raw corpora for the analysis of grammar and discourse features. Tagged corpora have their limitations, however, and there is no doubt that parsed corpora would be more useful for the analysis of learner grammar and discourse. If, as demonstrated by Baayen et al. (1996), syntactic annotation can contribute to more accurate authorship attribution, one can expect the same benefit in the field of learner language. However, fully automatic parsers that serve our purpose are not yet available, while automatic taggers are. In the meantime, researchers have every interest in working with tagged material. By adding the technique of tag sequence extraction to their supply of heuristic devices, they can hope to gain totally new insights into learner grammar and discourse.

Acknowledgements

We owe special thanks to Hans van Halteren, who extracted our data from the four corpora and showed unfailing patience whenever we changed our mind about what data were needed. Jan Aarts would like to acknowledge the support of the Centre for Advance Study of the Norwegian Academy of Science and Letters.

Notes

1 The breakdown of the corpus is as follows: NS: 204,195 words; Dutch: 146,780 words; Finnish: 144,765 words; French: 152,765 words.
2 Because of their use in analysing sentence beginnings and endings, sentence breaks (#) were also counted as one tag.
3 In the *TOSCA* tagging system *and* and *but* are tagged as connectives when they are sentence-initial.
4 The overuse of the second pattern is probably due to the general overuse of intensifiers noted by Lorenz (Chapter 4, this volume).

Appendix: Top 20 trigrams

Rank	Dutch	Finnish	French	NS
1	PUNC # #	PUNC # #	PUNC # #	PUNC # #
2	N PUNC #	N PUNC #	N PUNC #	PREP ART N
3	PREP ART N	PREP ART N	PREP ART N	N PUNC #
4	ART N PREP	N PREP N	ART N PREP	ART N PREP
5	N PREP N	ART N PREP	ART ADJ N	N PREP N
6	ART ADJ N	ART ADJ N	ADJ N PUNC	N PREP ART
7	N PREP ART	# # PRON	N PREP ART	ART ADJ N
8	ADJ N PUNC	N PREP ART	N PREP N	V ART N
9	V ART N	ADJ N PUNC	# # PRON	ADJ N PUNC
10	ART N PUNC	V ART N	PREP N PUNC	PREP N PUNC
11	# # PRON	PRON AUX V	V ART N	ADJ N PREP
12	PRON AUX V	ADJ N PREP	PRON AUX V	# # PRON
13	PREP N PUNC	PREP N PUNC	N AUX V	ART N PUNC
14	ADJ N PREP	ART N PUNC	ADJ N PREP	PREP PRON N
15	N AUX V	N AUX V	ART N PUNC	# # N
16	PREP PRON N	PREP PRON N	PREP ART ADJ	N PREP PRON
17	AUX V PREP	N PREP PRON	PREP PRON N	N AUX V
18	V PREP ART	N CONJUNC N	N PREP PRON	PREP ART ADJ
19	N CONJUNC N	V PRON N	PRON N PUNC	V PREP ART
20	N PREP PRON	AUX V PREP	V PREP ART	PRON AUX V

Part III

Pedagogical Applications of Learner Corpora

CHAPTER ELEVEN

Comparing native and learner perspectives on English grammar: a study of complement clauses

Doug Biber and Randi Reppen

1 Introduction

Most teachers and students in the ESL/EFL classroom rely on three major resources to answer their questions about English grammar: reference grammars (such as Quirk et al. 1985; Dirven 1989) and ESL/EFL textbooks (such as Davis 1989, or the four-book series directed by Larsen-Freeman 1993), and their own intuitions. All three sources provide a wealth of information concerning the structural characteristics of grammatical features, and in some cases they also provide guidance in the use of a feature.

More recently, these traditional descriptions have been complemented by empirical investigations of text corpora. While corpus-based analyses do not necessarily provide better structural descriptions, they do provide more accurate and insightful analyses of language use. That is, when traditional descriptions have included guidance on language use, it is usually based on the author's perceptions of appropriateness. In contrast, corpus-based analysis allows us to discover what typical speakers and writers actually do with the grammatical resources of English. Surprisingly, the actual patterns of use in natural discourse are often quite different from linguists' perceptions, and many patterns simply go unnoticed until they are uncovered by empirical analysis.

In designing empirical studies of language use, we have found it useful to investigate 'association patterns': the systematic ways in which linguistic features are used in association with other linguistic and non-linguistic features (see Biber 1996; Biber et al. 1996, forthcoming). This approach requires a register perspective, studying the extent to which a target feature is used in different registers. In fact, corpus-based analyses show that linguistic association patterns are generally *not* valid for the language as a whole; rather, there are usually striking differences in the use of grammatical features across registers.

In addition to register differences, we consider here two systematic kinds of linguistic association patterns: lexical and grammatical. Lexical associations are the tendencies for a target grammatical construction to co-occur with particular words, while grammatical associations identify contextual factors associated with structural variants.

In this chapter, we focus on complement clauses to compare the kinds of grammatical information presented in traditional grammars/textbooks with the actual patterns of use discovered from corpus analysis of native and L2 student texts.

In section 2, we summarize traditional descriptions of complement clauses from both reference grammars and ESL/EFL textbooks. Then in section 3 we present empirical results about the language use patterns for each type of complement clause, comparing native English registers to L2 student essays. The empirical analysis is divided into three parts. First, we compare the overall patterns of use for all four complement clause types. Next, we focus on native/learner similarities and differences in the lexical associations of *that*-clauses and *to*-clauses. Finally, we take a detailed look at two structural variants for *that*-clauses, considering the extent to which *that* is omitted in native vs. learner texts and the grammatical factors favouring omission in both cases. In conclusion, we summarize the corpus findings and discuss implications for language teaching.

2 Traditional descriptions of complement clauses

English has four major types of complement clause (also known as 'noun clauses'): *that*-clauses, *to*-clauses, *ing*-clauses, and WH-clauses. The following sentences from conversation illustrate the four structural types, with the complement clause in italics. In all four examples, a verb in the matrix clause (shown in square brackets) is the controlling element.

(1) *that*-clause:
I always [thought] *that I reminded him too much of his mom.*

(2) *to*-clause:
I don't [want] *to talk it over.*

(3) *ing*-clause:
So I [enjoy] *working for him.*

(4) WH-clause:
I don't [know] *what I'll do with it.*

There are many structural variants for these four major types. For example, infinitive clauses can occur as *to*-clauses, *for . . . to*-clauses, or bare infinitives. Further, the controlling element can be a verb (as in the above examples), or an adjective or noun, as in:

(5) *that*-clause controlled by an adjective:
I'm just [glad] *that someone's doing their job.*
(6) *for . . . to*-clause controlled by an adjective:
I'm [happy] *for somebody else to do it.*
(7) *that*-clause controlled by a noun:
Plus the [fact] *that one of my friends thought it was a really funny idea.*

In the present study, we focus only on complement clauses controlled by a verb and filling an object slot in the matrix clause, as in examples 1–4 above. However, we do consider one major structural variant: *that*-clauses occurring with the complementizer *that* omitted, as in:

(8) I [thought] *you liked it.*
(compare: I [thought] *that you liked it*.)

Comprehensive reference grammars (such as Quirk et al. 1985; Dirven 1989) describe the structural characteristics of the full range of complement clauses. Many of these treatments also describe differences in meaning between the types of complement clause (e.g. the difference between *I like to make pasta for dinner* and *I like making pasta for dinner*). Lexical associations are usually given a great deal of attention, since many verbs and adjectives control only one or two types of complement clause; for example, *want* occurs only with a *to*-clause, and *show* occurs with *that*-clauses, while *forget* can occur with all four major types of complement clause. (The chapter by Horiguchi in the Dirven grammar includes an extensive appendix listing verbs, adjectives, and nouns controlling each type of complement clause.)

ESL/EFL grammars are obviously much more selective in their treatment of complement clauses, focusing on only the most important distinctions. Further, most ESL/EFL grammars have a sequenced presentation, with 'advanced' topics – including complement clauses – coming in later chapters. In most cases, the different types of complement clause are treated separately, with little or no discussion of how to choose among them. Finally, examples of controlling verbs and adjectives are given for some of the complement clause types.

Several aspects of use are disregarded by both reference and ESL/EFL grammars. Such treatments do not address questions such as: Which structural types of complement clause are common and which are rare? Are these structures found primarily in speech or writing? Are any particular verbs especially common controlling complement clauses? If two structural variants mean essentially the same thing, what factors influence the choice between them? Considerations such as these are obviously important for ESL/EFL instructors and students. Such information is also centrally important for the authors of ESL/EFL textbooks, given their selective treatment: to insure that textbooks present the structures most likely to be encountered and used by learners.

The following sections present findings from corpus-based analyses addressing many of these issues. Then, in the conclusion, we return to the implications of such research for ESL/EFL textbooks and instruction.

3 Corpus-based analysis of complement clauses

3.1 Corpora and methods of analysis

The present study is based on separate analyses of a large native language corpus and a much smaller learner corpus. However, the same computer tools and analytical techniques were used for both analyses: texts in both corpora were analysed using an automated grammatical tagger in combination with hand editing of KWIC (Key Word in Context) concordance files.

The analysis of complement clauses in native English texts was carried out as part of the *Longman Grammar of Spoken and Written English* (Biber et al. forthcoming, Chapter 10). The findings reported here are based on analysis of the four core registers in the Longman Grammar Corpus: conversation, fiction, news reportage, and academic prose, with c. 5 million words of text for each register.[1] All native texts used for the present study were from British English.

The analysis of L2 texts is based on an early version of the Longman Learners' Corpus. We analysed the language use patterns in four language groups, as shown in Table 11.1.

The sub-corpus for each language group consisted of student essays, written in either class or exam settings. Most essays in the corpus were written by intermediate or advanced students. There was a large amount of overlap in the tasks and topics included in the four sub-corpora. All four included personal opinion essays (e.g. comparing the merits of movies based on a book and the original book), descriptive essays (e.g. descriptions of self, a close acquaintance, a national hero, the capital city, cultural traditions), and personal/business letters (e.g. to a

Table 11.1: Breakdown of texts analysed from the Longman Learners' Corpus

Native language	Number of texts	Number of words
French	177	44,776
Spanish	438	152,389
Chinese	139	31,946
Japanese	237	55,793
Total	991	284,904

friend while on vacation, responding to a wedding invitation, to a hotel attempting to recover a lost purse/wallet, for a job application).

Both corpora were automatically tagged, using the grammatical tagger developed by Biber for multi-dimensional analyses of register variation (see e.g. Biber 1995); this tagger has been modified and extended for analyses relating to the *Longman Grammar of Spoken and Written English*. The tagger automatically identifies complement clauses, relying on both grammatical and lexical information.[2] To check the accuracy of these automatic analyses, we wrote a program to produce concordance listings for each type of complement clause. These listings were then edited by hand to include only the clause types under consideration here.

Although grammatical errors were relatively common in the essays written by all four language groups, there were relatively few errors in the choice of complement clause type. When errors did occur, they would often involve the incorrect use of a *to*-clause instead of a *that*-clause or an *ing*-clause, as in:

(9) I would suggest him to play tennis.
(10) You would never enjoy to encounter any 'alien' or monster in your daily life.
(11) My grandmother and grandfather make an speech they are going to say when we finish to eat.

For the most part, though, students tended to rely on the most common verbs controlling each type (e.g. *think*, *say*, and *know* controlling *that*-clauses, and *want* and *like* controlling *to*-clauses – see section 3.3 below). As a result, there were generally few errors relating to the correct choice of complement clause type.

The major threat to validity in this study comes from the differences in representativeness between the native and learner corpus. Whereas the native corpus is very large and designed around well-represented register categories, the learner corpus is relatively small and is not coded for register differences. As a result, the findings here must be interpreted cautiously. In particular, we expect that different varieties of Learner English (e.g. conversation vs. narratives vs. formal expository prose) will show quite different patterns of language use. We return to this issue in the conclusion, suggesting the need for further research investigating the patterns of register variation within Learner English.

3.2 *Overall patterns of use*

Figure 11.1 presents frequencies (per million words of text) for each of the four major types of complement clause.[3] As this figure shows, the four types of complement clause are not equally common, with *that*-clauses and *to*-clauses being generally more common than *ing*-clauses and WH-clauses. Further, there are striking differences across registers.

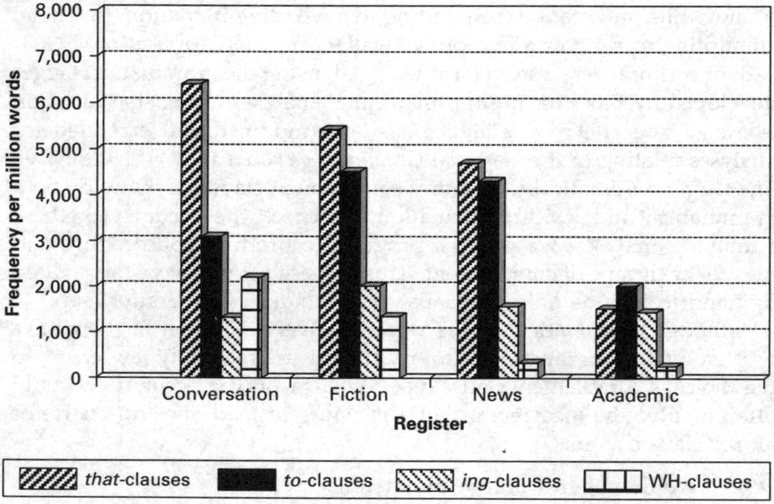

Figure 11.1 Frequencies of verb + complement clause across registers

For example, *that*-clauses are overwhelmingly the most common type of complement clause in conversation, while all four structural types are relatively rare in academic prose (when controlled by a verb). WH-clauses are only moderately common in conversation and fiction, but they are quite rare in news and academic prose.

Figure 11.2 presents the same information for the four learner groups included in our study. The extent of similarity across the four L1 groups is striking, with two general patterns being immediately obvious from a comparison with the native language registers (Figure 11.1). First, *that*-clauses and *to*-clauses are extremely common in all four student groups, and second, *ing*-clauses and WH-clauses are generally rare in all four groups.

That-clauses in the student essays occur with roughly the same frequencies as in native conversation (actually being considerably more common in the L1-Spanish essays). *To*-clauses are even more noteworthy, being much more common in all four learner groups than they are in any of the native registers. In contrast, *ing*-clauses and WH-clauses are consistently rare across all four groups. This pattern is particularly marked for *ing*-clauses, which are considerably less common in all four learner groups than they are in any of the native registers.

These differences between the native and learner patterns appear to reflect a kind of transfer effect. As far as we can tell,[4] none of these other languages allows participial clauses or WH-clauses[5] functioning as complement clauses. In contrast, at least French and Spanish

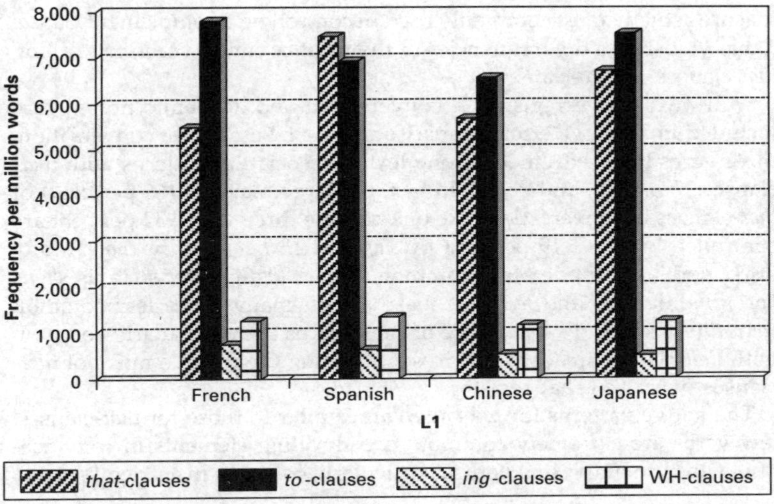

Figure 11.2 Frequencies of verb + complement clause across L1

clearly distinguish between finite complement clauses (similar to English *that*-clauses) and non-finite complement clauses (similar to English *to*-clauses). Thus, by relying on their L1 strategies, students from these languages might be expected to produce patterns similar to those shown in Figure 11.2.

More detailed cross-linguistic research is needed to account for some of the other patterns. For example, why are infinitive complement clauses, but not *that*-complement clauses, so much more common in all four student groups in comparison to the native registers? Why is this difference especially marked in the case of the L1-French students? Why do the L1-Spanish students differ in using *that*-clauses to a greater extent than *to*-clauses? We predict that some of these patterns relate to the influence of 'use transfer' (see Wu 1995), that is, preferred patterns of use in a first language being transferred to a second language. However, detailed corpus investigations of the languages in question are required to test this possibility.

3.3 *Lexical associations*

The overall differences in the use of complement clauses – across registers and across native/student groups – can be further understood by considering the lexical associations of each structural type. Instead of itemizing the verbs that are grammatical with each type of complement clause, we use the notion of 'lexical association' to identify the verbs that are actually most commonly used in controlling a complement clause. Table 11.2 shows the frequencies of the most common verbs controlling *that*-clauses and *to*-clauses.

Only two native registers – conversation and academic prose – are included in Table 11.2, for comparison to the L2 essays. In conversation, three verbs have extremely strong lexical association patterns with *that*-clauses: *think*, *say*, and *know*.[6] In fact, the large majority (66 per cent) of *that*-clauses in conversation take one of these three verbs: 32 per cent are controlled by *think*, 19 per cent by *say*, and 15 per cent by *know*. Many other verbs are moderately common with a *that*-clause, such as *show*, *hope*, *find*, *believe*, and *feel*, but these are all many times less common than *think*, *say*, and *know*. None of these verbs are particularly common with *that*-clauses in academic prose, reflecting the relative rarity of *that*-clauses overall in that register.

The native patterns for *to*-clauses are similar to those for *that*-clauses: few verbs are extremely common as controlling elements in conversation, while no individual verb is particularly common in academic prose.

Table 11.2: Most common verbs controlling *that*-clauses and *to*-clauses

***That*-clauses:**

Native English	Conversation	Academic prose
think	********************	*
say	************	**
know	*********	*
show	*	***
hope	*	–

L2 essays:

	French	Spanish
think	***************	*********************
say	*****	*********
know	*******	***********
show	–	–
hope	************	********

	Chinese	Japanese
think	*************	*********************
say	***	******
know	******	****
show	–	–
hope	********	********

Table 11.2: (cont'd)

To-clauses:		
Native English	Conversation	Academic prose
want	**********	–
try	***	*
like	**	**
seem	*	*
L2 essays:		
	French	Spanish
want	***********	*************
try	******	*******
like	********************	****************
seem	***	*
	Chinese	Japanese
want	*************	*************
try	****	****
like	****************	*********************
seem	***	***

Notes: Each * represents 100 occurrences per million words
– represents less than 50 occurrences per million words

In conversation, there is actually only one verb that is especially common controlling *to*-clauses: *want*. However, clauses controlled by *want* account for as much as 38 per cent of all *to* complement clauses in conversation.

The lexical association patterns for the L2 essays are equally revealing. First of all, the extent to which these patterns are the same across all four language groups is noteworthy. In part, these similarities might be due to the central influence of register, reflecting the special kinds of communicative tasks required in student essays. However, these cross-linguistic similarities need further study.

Beyond that, there are several interesting points of similarity, as well as difference, between the patterns for native and L2 texts. For *that*-clauses, all four languages are similar to native conversation in using *think* as the controlling verb much more commonly than any other verb (accounting for c. 30 per cent of all *that*-clauses). The verb *know* is also relatively common, while *say* is less common as the controlling verb (probably due to the nature of the essay tasks). The most interesting difference from native conversation relates to the notably high frequency of *hope*: whereas *hope* is not even among the ten most common verbs controlling *that*-clauses in the native corpus, it is the second most common verb in all student groups except for L1-Spanish.[7]

All four languages are additionally similar to conversation in that they use the verb *want* very frequently controlling *to*-clauses. There is also a major difference, though, in that the student essays make even more frequent use of the verb *like* controlling *to*-clauses – occurring about twice as often as *want* in French and Japanese. Thus, in the student essays, clauses controlled by *like* account for 25–40 per cent of all *to*-clauses; in comparison, only c. 8 per cent of the *to*-clauses in conversation are controlled by *like*. Further investigation shows that 60–80 per cent of the occurrences of *like* + *to*-clause in the student essays are part of polite requests taking the form *I would like to*. . . . It thus seems likely that both the extremely frequent use of *hope* with *that*-clauses and *like* with *to*-clauses are due to the tasks required in the student essays, especially in the personal and business letters, rather than reflecting a genuine native/learner difference.

3.4 Discourse factors associated with that *omission*

Corpus-based analyses are particularly useful in trying to understand the discourse factors that influence the choice among structural variants. One of the most important variants with *that*-clauses is the choice to omit or retain the complementizer *that*. As Figure 11.3 shows, this

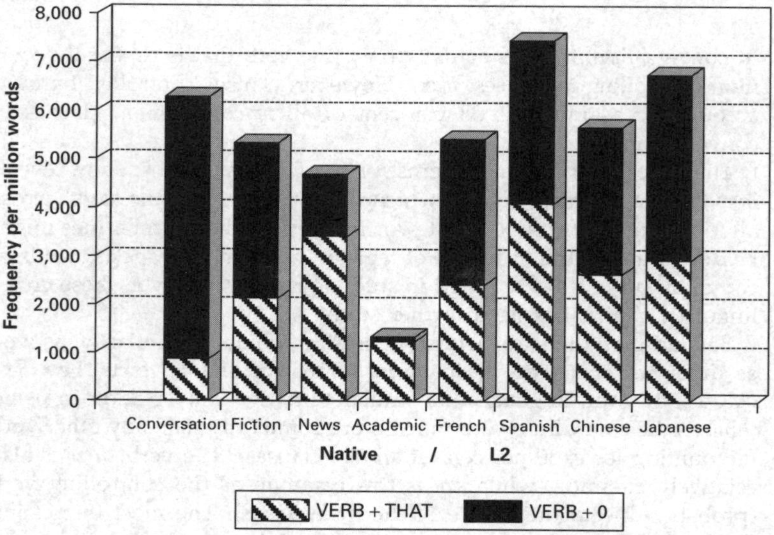

Figure 11.3 Frequencies of *that* retention vs. omission

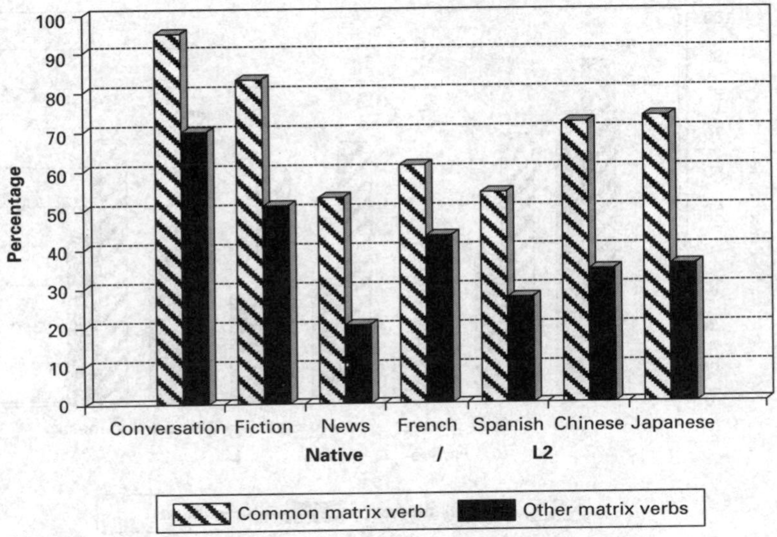

Figure 11.4 Percentage of *that* omission: influence of matrix verb

choice is strongly influenced by register factors: in conversation, the complementizer *that* is usually omitted (almost 90 per cent of the time), while in academic prose, *that* is almost never omitted. Interestingly, *that* is omitted a high proportion of the time in all four student groups, with the L1-Japanese group showing the highest proportion of omission (c. 55 per cent). These overall frequencies do not tell the whole story, however, since there is also considerable variation among the different student writing tasks. In particular, a very large percentage of the *that*-omissions occur in the personal/business letters written by students, while *that* is retained much more often in the opinion and descriptive essays.

Beyond register, there are two contextual factors that are particularly influential for this structural choice: the co-occurrence of a common matrix verb (*think* and *say*, and also *hope* for the student essays), and the use of a subject pronoun in the *that*-clause. As Figures 11.4 and 11.5 show, both of these factors are very influential for both native registers and L2-student essays. That is, the complementizer *that* is omitted a much higher proportion of the time with a very common matrix verb than it is with other matrix verbs; and *that* is omitted a much higher proportion of the time with a pronoun as subject of the *that*-clause than with other subjects. Both of these factors conform to stereotypical characteristics of *that*-clauses, making the presence of an overt complementizer

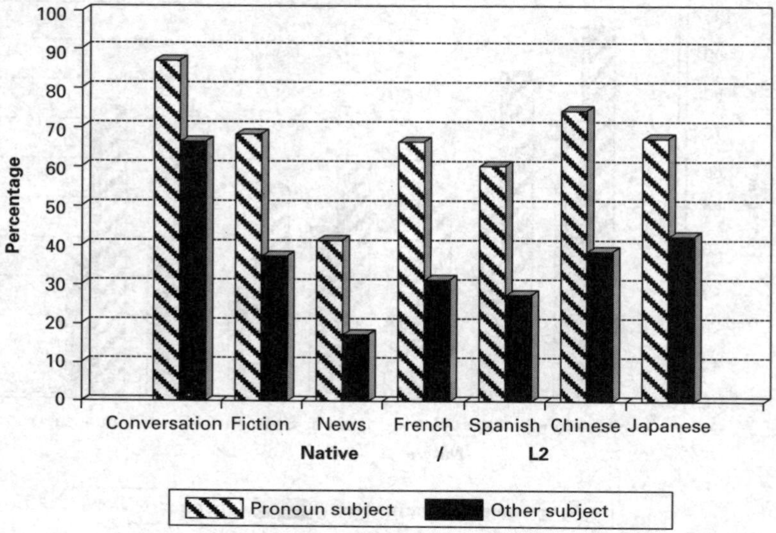

Figure 11.5 Percentage of *that* omission: influence of complement-clause subject

less essential. That is, the use of *think*, *say*, or *hope* (in the essays), raises the expectation that a *that*-clause will follow. Similarly, the occurrence of a subject pronoun marks the start of a new clause. In both cases, the complementizer *that* becomes less essential in marking the start of a *that*-clause.

The three factors discussed here – register/task, common matrix verb, and pronominal subjects – work together in the student essays. That is, in the personal/business letters, students were most likely to use constructions with *think* and *hope* as matrix verb, and with a pronominal subject in the *that*-clause, resulting in structures like *I think I . . .* or *I hope you. . . .*

4 Discussion and conclusion

Two of the most surprising findings from this investigation are the extent to which these four student groups have similar patterns of use for complement clauses; and the observation that many of those patterns are consistent with the patterns found in native registers. There were some major differences found in the distribution of structural types: most notably, *that*-clauses and *to*-clauses were much more common in all four student groups than in any native register. Further cross-linguistic research is required to fully understand those differences. However, the patterns of lexical association and the influence of discourse factors on *that* omission were much more similar across native registers and L2 essays. In particular, native and L2 texts showed similar lexical associations for *that*-clauses and *to*-clauses, with the major differences (with respect to *hope* and *like*) probably being due to the special tasks required in student writing (especially for the letters).[8] Further, both native and L2 texts showed similar patterns for the factors influencing *that* omission.

At the same time, there were major differences found in the distribution of structural types. For example, *that*-clauses and *to*-clauses were much more common in all four student groups than in any native register. Further cross-linguistic research is required to fully understand those differences.

Even more importantly, any overall assessment of similarity (or difference) turns out to be inadequate when we consider the patterns across registers; and these latter patterns raise important issues about learner writing and the construction of learner corpora. In particular, the patterns of use in the learner essays are very similar to those found in native conversation and fiction, but strikingly different from those found in native academic prose. It seems likely that there is also considerable variation among the different tasks required for student writing, although it is also possible that no sub-register of learner essays actually conforms to the patterns of use found in native academic prose. In order to investigate issues like these, we need learner corpora designed to represent the full range of student writing (and speaking) tasks.

In this brief comparison of native and L2 grammar, we have illustrated the highly systematic nature of language use, and shown how corpus-based investigations can be used to describe patterns that are usually disregarded in traditional treatments. These findings have in turn raised a whole new set of research questions, many of which require additional study. However, it is only by investigating actual language use in natural discourse that we can begin to understand how best to help students develop competence in the kinds of language they will encounter on a regular basis.

Notes

1 The Longman Grammar Corpus was designed to provide the empirical basis for the *Longman Grammar of Spoken and Written English*. The corpus is designed around four 'core' registers, in an attempt to balance breadth of coverage with economy of analysis and presentation: these four registers cover much of the range of variation in English, while being restricted to a manageable number of distinctions. In addition, the full corpus includes text samples from 'context-governed' speech, general prose, as well as American English conversation and news reportage.

2 For example, the tagger checks whether the word preceding a *that* or a *to* is a verb, adjective, or noun. Further, in the cases of *that*-clauses, the tagger checks a dictionary of possible words that can control a *that*-clause (e.g. *think, know, certain* – but not *begin, like,* or *try*). By using this dictionary, it is also possible to identify occurrences of *that*-clauses with the complementizer *that* omitted.

3 Figures 11.1 and 11.2 present frequencies only for complement clauses controlled by verbs. Complement clauses controlled by adjectives and nouns are somewhat more common in academic prose.

4 Linguistic generalizations concerning the languages other than English are based on a survey of grammars, confirmed by discussions with native speakers.

5 In at least some of these languages, a near equivalent to English WH complement clauses can be formed as a kind of relative clause with a generalized noun or demonstrative pronoun as head, something like *I know the thing that you want* or *I know that which you want*.

6 All inflected forms are included in the counts for these verbs.

7 Other specific differences are also noteworthy here, such as the particularly low frequencies for *say* in the L1-Chinese essays and *know* in the L1-Japanese essays. Given the availability of native corpora for these languages, it would be interesting to investigate whether these patterns reflect general cultural/linguistic dispreferences.

8 Additional sub-corpora are needed to investigate these patterns more adequately. In particular, the patterns of use should be studied in native English student essays and native English personal and business letters. In addition, a learner corpus organized by task would provide a much more principled basis for comparison, so that patterns in letters could be distinguished from those in expository or descriptive essays.

CHAPTER TWELVE

Using a learners' corpus in compiling ELT dictionaries

Patrick Gillard and Adam Gadsby

1 Introduction

The importance of corpora in ELT dictionaries has grown steadily. At first the emphasis was on corpora of written native-speaker English, but more recently spoken English and then learners' English have become the subject of corpus analysis.

The very first ELT dictionary, Michael West's (1935) *The New Method English Dictionary* drew heavily on the author's pioneering work in 1934 in which he analysed the frequency and meanings of words in a million words of text to produce his *General Service List of English Words* (1936). The *Longman Dictionary of Contemporary English* (1979) used citations from the 1-million-word Survey of English Usage, developed by University College, London. By the time the second edition was published in 1987, Longman had developed the 30-million-word Longman Lancaster Corpus (of native-speaker written English), in collaboration with Lancaster University. This corpus establishes the principles which Longman has followed for later corpus developments: the importance of balance and representativeness in corpus development.

ELT dictionaries have always tended to be at the forefront of lexicographical development. They have made early use of corpus analysis; they are often the first dictionaries to record new usages; and they take notice of developments in grammatical analysis and grammatical presentation. One reason for their innovation, apart from the need to remain competitive in the marketplace, is that the target user, the ELT student, has certain specific and recognizable needs. Publishers have to address those needs as effectively as they can.

The ELT student needs things such as: full information about grammar; reliable sociolinguistic information about register; and information about spoken English which may be ignored by many dictionaries for native speakers. All ELT dictionaries now use corpora of native-speaker English to garner information about current usage. The surprising thing is that some of them have been slow to apply the same analysis to the

English produced by learners of English. There have been quite a few books about common learners' errors and interlanguage errors. *Les Faux Amis des Vocabulaires Anglais et Américain* by Maxime Koessler and J. Derocquigny was published in France in 1975, and there have been collections of common errors such as *Common Mistakes in English* by T.J. Fitikides which was first published in 1936. It took a long time for this error information to appear as explicit information in ELT dictionaries (although the extensive grammatical information in these dictionaries is certainly intended to remedy some of the common learners' errors by showing full models of correct usage). Explicit error information was first seen in the form of usage notes, where there was a particular well-known student error (such as the learners' use of the word *actually* to mean *now*).

In the mid-1980s various researchers pointed out that it was important for ELT dictionary publishers to analyse learners' errors (e.g. Maingay and Rundell 1985). In 1987 Longman started collecting samples of learners' writing to build a corpus of learners' English. This corpus (the Longman Learners' Corpus – LLC) was intended to help in compiling ELT dictionaries and other ELT resources. The earliest information from the LLC was used in writing the *Longman Language Activator*, published in 1993. The LLC was used to a greater extent in the 3rd edition of the *Longman Dictionary of Contemporary English* in 1995 and now the full 10-million-word version has been used to help compile the *Longman Essential Activator* (*LEA*) (1997).

In the LLC each script is coded for the student's nationality, level, text type (essay, letter, exam script, etc.), target variety (British or American English), and country of residence. As with the native speaker corpora in the Longman Corpus Network, the corpus is designed to give balanced, representative coverage across each of these categories. The corpus contains over 27,000 individual scripts from students of 117 nationalities.

In compiling dictionaries for learners of English, the lexicographer's task is to predict what the student will want to know, and then to explain it in a way that the student can understand. A dictionary is only of use to the student if it includes the word or phrase the student wants, if the student can find it, and if he can understand the information when he does find it. The Learners' Corpus can help with each of these stages.

2 Inclusion

The first decision in compiling a dictionary is to decide which words and phrases to include. In seeking to maximise the usefulness of the dictionary to the student, it helps if we first get a good picture of the vocabulary level and range of the target user. By generating frequency listings from the LLC we can see which words students are using at a particular level.

One of the first things that you notice about learners' vocabulary is the way that they use the most common words in the language, particularly the common adjectives. These words are much more common in learners' English than in native speakers' English, and they are more common in lower-level learners' English than in higher-level learners' English.

As an example of this, Table 12.1 shows the frequency and distribution of the words *nice* and *happy* by student level in the LLC, and gives the native-speaker frequencies from the British National Corpus (BNC[1]):

Table 12.1: Frequency of the words *nice* and *happy* in the LLC, shown by student level (all figures show the occurrences per million words at each level)

Student level	***nice***	***happy***
Beginner	1,628	826
Elementary	1,508	1,061
Pre-intermediate	1,260	935
Intermediate	923	997
Upper intermediate	624	725
Advanced	425	349
Proficiency	261	330
Academic students	151	178
Average in LLC	752	689
Native speaker average (BNC)	77	109

Another feature of learners' English is that they do not usually have access to a range of synonyms for particular meanings. They are much more likely to use the same word each time they express a particular idea. Table 12.2 (overleaf) shows the relative frequencies of the words *big*, *enormous*, *massive* and *huge* in learners' and native speakers' English. The graphs in Table 12.2 show that the learners are far more likely to use the word *big* to express the idea, where a native speaker is almost as likely to use one of the other available words.

Not all the differences between learners' English and native-speakers' English are as predictable as this. For example, learners' writing often has an unexpectedly high use of vocabulary from specialised topic areas, such as the environment or literature, which they are frequently asked to write about. Table 12.3 (overleaf) shows the frequencies per million words for the words *pollution*, *environment*, and *traffic*, which often occur in student writing tasks on environmental issues, and for the word *characters*, which often occurs in students' reviews of books. For comparison, it also includes the frequencies for the words *mental* and *fully*, which are unlikely to feature strongly in students' writing topics.

Table 12.2: Frequency of the words *big, enormous, massive,* and *huge* in the LLC (learners' corpus) and the BNC (native speakers) (all figures show occurrences per million words of text)

Word	BNC	LLC
big	220	990
enormous	42	33
massive	44	10
huge	82	63

Table 12.3: Frequency of the words *pollution, environment, traffic* and *characters* in the LLC and in the BNC (all figures show occurrences per million words of text)

Word	LLC	BNC
pollution	180	45
environment	201	137
traffic	146	57
characters	69	42
non-topic vocabulary:		
fully	30	94
mental	35	62

3 Access

In the *Longman Language Activator,* we explain the meanings of words by grouping them together with their near-synonyms under about 1,000 'Concepts' such as WALK, HAPPY, INTELLIGENT, and FORGIVE. In the 'Concept' WALK, the student will find words like *stroll, stride, amble* and *jog,* with detailed definitions and several examples to show clearly the differences in meaning, and exactly how and when each word or phrase is used. In order to make sure that students would understand the words (such as WALK) that we used as Concept names, we looked at each word in the Learners' Corpus to see how frequently it was used, whether it was used in the meaning needed for the concept name, and whether there were any problems with false friends or other sources of confusion. As a result, the list of Concept names was revised to eliminate the more difficult names.

4 Definitions

All definitions in Longman dictionaries are written using a controlled vocabulary of around 2,000 words (the Longman Defining Vocabulary). The list has been revised a number of times, to include words like *computer* which had become universally known by the 1970s. The most recent revision involved a two-stage process, looking first at the Learners' Corpus and then testing students' knowledge of words in context. As the first stage, we compared the words in the Longman Defining Vocabulary against the 3,000 most frequent words in the BNC, the Longman Lancaster Corpus and the LLC. The first 1,500 words present fewer problems, and are more or less the same across the three corpora. Beyond this point, however, differences begin to emerge. Patrick Snellings[2] looked at the band of 400 words in the Defining Vocabulary with the lowest frequency counts on the LLC, and then examined each one through concordances to see what percentage were correct. He was also able to identify differences in distribution of words by language group, to identify whether words in the defining vocabulary were known and used correctly only by speakers of certain languages, because of cognates in their own language, or used incorrectly because of false friends. Having identified the words which were most likely to cause problems for learners, he then chose definitions from the *Longman Dictionary of Contemporary English* which used these words, and provided three possible translations plus a 'don't know' option, in each of four languages (German, Italian, Japanese and Korean). By testing the learner's understanding of the words within a dictionary definition, we were able to see whether they understood the words within the context we needed, rather than in isolation.

The skill of lexicography for ELT dictionaries lies in being able to write definitions which are clear and which accurately pinpoint the key aspects of the word or phrase being defined. By having constant access to a very large body of students' writing, lexicographers are sensitised to and reminded of the needs of their audience far more thoroughly than they could achieve through their previous teaching experience.

5 The use of the Learners' Corpus in compiling the *Longman Essential Activator (LEA)*

5.1 *Help boxes*

The *LEA* is a new 'production dictionary', semantically organized like the *Longman Language Activator*, but aimed at intermediate-level students. The aim of the *LEA* is to help students move from reliance on a small number of simple words which they learn in the early stages of their studies, to being able to express themselves naturally and accurately using a much wider range of words and phrases.

We used the Longman Learners' Corpus to find out how learners were using the words that we were covering in the *LEA*. Primarily, we wanted to find out which of their errors were common enough and correctable enough for us to put a specific 'help box' note into the dictionary text. The idea of the 'help box' is to clearly show a typical learner error, to make clear that it *is* an error rather that an example of correct usage, and to give the learner the correct way of expressing the idea that prompts the error.

There has always been resistance to the idea of showing 'wrong' usage, particularly in grammars and dictionaries, because of the danger of reinforcing the error by showing the incorrect form. We decided that it was appropriate to use examples of errors within the *LEA* text for several reasons:

- The *LEA* is a production dictionary, so the users are trying to make sentences with the words which we are defining (rather than trying to understand a word that they come across). This means they need more specific information than they would need for 'decoding' purposes.
- The *LEA* deals with single senses of particular words or phrases. For example the word *soft* appears in one part of the book (the concept SOFT) when it describes objects or materials and it appears in another part of the book (the concept QUIET) when it describes sounds. This means that the entry for each sense can be self-contained and can concentrate on describing the behaviour of the word *in that particular sense*, rather than describing its total behaviour in English.
- The *LEA* is designed for intermediate-level learners, students who particularly benefit from information about common errors.
- Above all, we have good evidence from the LLC to help us to decide which errors students are most likely to make and how to prevent the students from making those errors.

Figure 12.1 shows an example of an entry (the verb *mention*, from the concept SAY, together with its accompanying 'help box'). Learners are given the 'help box' at the end of the entry, so that the first thing they see is the definition, grammar and example set for the word they are

> **mention** /'menʃən/ [*v* T] to talk about someone or something, but without giving details or saying very much about them:
> *He mentioned something about a party, but he didn't say when it was.*
> + *(that)*: *I forgot to mention that I won't be in tomorrow.*
> *mention where/who/what etc*: *Did they mention where they were going?*
> Don't say 'mention about something'. Say **mention something**.

Figure 12.1

looking up. The 'help box' is separated from the entry but comes straight after it, so that the learner can make use of it without mistaking it for an example of correct usage.

5.2 *Error types*

It is easiest to give specific error information (and it is easiest for the learner to respond to the information) when the error is connected to one particular sense of one particular word. It is less easy to correct errors such as misuse of articles and misuse of tenses which apply equally across the whole of a learner's language production. For this reason, we have focused on words with errors in the following areas: collocational errors; grammatical/syntactical errors; spelling errors and word division errors; word order problems.

5.2.1 COLLOCATIONAL ERRORS

The most obvious of these are:

(a) complementation of verb headwords: e.g.
he **told that he was going*
she **mentioned about it to me*
we must **obey to the teacher*
It **reminds me my home town*

(b) prepositions after adjective headwords: e.g.
They were all very **kind with me.*
Who was **responsible of this crime?*

(c) operating verbs for noun headwords: e.g.
I **make my **homework** and then I go to bed.*
She **said a **joke** and I laughed.*
He **did a **crime***

(d) intensifying adjectives for noun headwords: e.g.
The husband died of a **heavy illness.*

(e) selection restrictions on which objects a verb can take: e.g.
We **looked the **TV** until about 10 o'clock.*
She **drove her **bike** into the town.*

5.2.2 GRAMMATICAL/SYNTACTICAL ERRORS

The most frequent of these are:

(a) errors over countability: e.g.
There are 500 **peoples live in our village.*
Here is another **information he gave me.*
I had to sit and do my **homeworks for two hours.*
You didn't follow my **instruction.*

<CL>an, in her early thirty, and that woman	<NW>reminded</NW> me an old friend, who I haven't</CL>
<CL>t like rice to be sticky. Debora's meat	<NW>reminded</NW> me Czech food "cauliflower brai</CL>
<CL>way through a long white corridor which	<NW>reminded</NW> me of a hospital. Our first sto</CL>
<CL> about the mistakes we had made, and it	<NW>reminded</NW> me one point of effective langu</CL>
<CL>ally stayed with me for a long time and	<NW>reminded</NW> me something important for a fa</CL>
<CL>n street and tried to catch a mark that	<NW>reminded</NW> me the "old" Barcombe. Too tire<CL>
<CL>wonderful and romantic. The whole event	<NW>reminded</NW> me the story of Apollo in the m</CL>
<CL>relation between us and this church. It	<NW>reminded</NW> us our history, our ancenstors </CL>
<CL>lso, everything he sees and does always	<NW>reminds</NW> him the shadow of Laura, like "t</CL>

Figure 12.2

(b) errors over use of progressive tenses: e.g.
I wasn't **needing it anymore.*
I am **liking it a lot.*

(c) gradable/non-gradable adjectives: e.g.
They live in a **very lovely house near the sea.*
The cake was **very delicious.*

5.2.3 SPELLING ERRORS AND WORD DIVISION ERRORS

For example:

Pour a pint of milk **in to the pan.*
We **allways go to the beach at the weekend.*
We hear it **everyday in the news.*

5.2.4 WORD ORDER PROBLEMS

For example:

I am **tall 180 centimetres.*
The apartment is not **enough big.*

Some of these errors are very frequent in the corpus. For example, there are 432 examples of the wordform *peoples* in the LLC and almost all of them are errors. At the other end of the scale there are errors such as *mention about something*, which has only 27 examples in the LLC but which still represents a significant percentage of all the 1,111 examples of the verb *mention*.

5.3 *Examples of how the 'help boxes' are used*

Here are two examples of how we used the 'help boxes' to warn against typical learners' errors.

EXAMPLE 1: VERB COMPLEMENTATION ERROR WITH THE WORD REMIND

The first one is a warning against omitting the word *of* between the direct and indirect object of the verb *remind*. The learner writes:
**it reminds me her*

instead of:

it reminds me of her

There are 42 examples of this error out of the 314 examples of the use of the verb *remind* in the LLC. Figure 12.2 shows a few of them.

Because of the way the *LEA* is organized, the word *remind* occurs in the concept called REMEMBER. This concept covers the whole semantic

> **remind** /rɪˈmaɪnd/ [*v* T] to make someone remember a person, thing, or time from the past
> remind sb of sb/sth: *That perfume always reminded him of his mother.* | *This song reminds me of that time we all went to Brighton.*
> Don't say 'it reminds me her'. Say **it reminds me of her.**
> Don't use **remind** (=make you remember) when you mean **remember.**

Figure 12.3

area connected with remembering. For example, it contains the words *remember, memory, nostalgia,* and *memorable*. The words are defined in a way that makes clear the differences between them, so that the user can choose which word is the most appropriate for expressing a particular idea. The headword *remind* occurs in two of its senses in the concept. The sense that we are concerned with occurs in the section headed: 'when something makes you remember something from the past'. Figure 12.3 shows the entry for the word *remind*.

The entry has a definition and two examples. The examples come after a 'propositional form' (*remind sb of sth/sb*). The 'propositional form' shows the grammatical behaviour of the word by giving a basic template of 'verb + object + preposition + object' that can be mapped onto the examples that follow it.

At the end of the entry the 'help box' warns the learner against making the typical learners' error in which the preposition *of* is omitted. We give an example sentence within the help box (*it reminds me of her*) rather than a propositional form (*remind sb of sb/sth*) because the example sentence is likely to be closer to the real sentence which the learner is trying to write.

We think it is helpful for learners to be able to compare directly a correct structure and an incorrect one. It helps them to see what the error looks like and it lets them compare their own sentence with the two examples to check if their own sentence is right or wrong.

EXAMPLE 2: COUNTABILITY ERROR WITH THE WORD *PEOPLE*

This is a common error with learners' use of the word *people*. Learners often add an 's' by applying the normal rule about pluralizing. There are over 300 examples of this error on the LLC. Figure 12.4 shows a sample of them.

The word *people* occurs at the concept PERSON/PEOPLE in the *LEA*, with the entry shown in Figure 12.5.

The 'help box' is phrased in a similar way to the one at *remind*. It starts off with the words: 'Don't say . . .', followed by an example of the error. Although it is true that the word *'peoples'* can be used in some

EE	EL	h in a future They will must find some other planet.	Peoples will live on the Moon But there isn't anythin
EE	EL	ples will go on the Saturn on weekend. I think, that	peoples will instruct and they will live normal. </TX
GRK	EL	t of them must know more languages than theirs. More	peoples will travel in other countries, more products
	AD	portant fields. Nations expense many money for their	peoples and all peoples has pribilige about education
OTH	PI	n ??? to others places, in the places of the florest	peoples will make factories, ofices, or many other th
JAP	EL	ared the introduce paper. My family consists of five	peoples. I have brother and sister. They are collegia
CHN	UI	d also to new house respectaly. Now there are three	peoples in my small family my wife and son and I. My
EE	IN	creation. I can broden my mind and learn about other	peoples, and cultures by visiting famous places, lear
OTH	PR	e media are nowadays one of the fastest ways to call	peoples attention to the worlds problems, difficultie

Figure 12.4

people /'pi:pəl/ [*n* plural] people in general: *I don't want people to feel sorry for me.* | *People are getting tired of all these politicians.*
most people: *Most people hate exams, but my brother loves them.*
Don't say 'peoples'. **People** is a plural noun.

Figure 12.5

well-formed English sentences – e.g. *the indigenous peoples of the Americas* – it is very unlikely that the learner looking at PERSON/PEOPLE in the *LEA* is trying to express this idea. The *LEA* concentrates on the typical tasks facing learners. We predict that most will be concerned with a use of the word in its central meaning, not with a specialised and comparatively infrequent use.

6 Conclusion

All of the 'help boxes' in the *LEA* (there are over 1,200 in the whole book) are presented in the same style as the examples above. We have concentrated on making them as clear and useful as possible by being careful about their style, placement, and selection. We believe that they improve the dictionary and make it more useful for the particular intermediate students that the book is aimed at.

Our work so far with Learner English has provided concrete evidence and useful statistics to back up and expand our existing knowledge of learner errors. It has become clear to us, while working with the LLC, that there are other very productive and interesting ways of exploiting its potential. For example, we have started using it for the following purposes:

- to analyse vocabulary size at the different learner ability levels
- to compare learners' patterns of collocation with native speakers' patterns (taken from the BNC) so that we can give learners a whole 'palette' of common native-speaker collocations for a particular word that they are interested in (and at the same time tell them which learners' collocations are untypical even when they are grammatically correct)
- to analyse the level at which a particular word enters a learner's vocabulary and to find the context in which the word is first used.

The LLC has already been very useful to us in compiling the *LEA*, and it is opening up very rich possibilities for future ELT dictionary projects. It already seems a very odd idea to try to compile an ELT dictionary without access to this information.

Notes

1 The British National Corpus is a collaborative initiative carried out by Oxford University Press, Longman, Chambers Harrap, Oxford University Computing Services, Lancaster University's Unit for Computer Research in the English Language, and the British Library. The project received funding from the UK Department of Trade and Industry and the Science and Engineering Research Council, and was supported by grants from the British Academy and the British Library.

2 Patrick Snellings, University of Utrecht research project.

CHAPTER THIRTEEN

Enhancing a writing textbook: a national perspective

Przemysław Kaszubski

1 Introduction

Contrastive studies of computerised learner corpora (CLCs) reveal the presence of persistent errors, some of them L1-specific,[1] in advanced-level EFL composition. It has been claimed by Granger (1996a, forthcoming c) that such findings should be increasingly used in designing new, L1-sensitive, teaching materials. In full accordance with this line of reasoning, I seek to demonstrate in this chapter how existing ESL/EFL writing textbooks[2] fail to cater for the lexical needs of learners in mono-national classrooms. I also argue in favour of redressing the balance between the process and product approaches towards greater product awareness and postulate ways of enhancing EFL writing textbooks on the basis of CLC-derived evidence.

The corpus used to illustrate the CLC-based[3] textbook enhancements, the International Corpus of Learner English (ICLE),[4] contains advanced-level argumentative/expository essay writing written in a (semi-)formal, semi-academic style. Such a corpus should clearly only be used to improve textbook teaching of this type of written English. Some of the findings in this study may indeed be relevant to other learner text-types, but one should not make assumptions. Improved textbook teaching of particular text-types needs to be based on solid analysis of corresponding learner data. This kind of product-awareness is in line with current developments in ELT and in L2 writing theory, both of which give prominence to aspects of conventionality in language and language use.

2 ESL/EFL writing – an overview of theories

According to Silva (1990: 11–17), the four most influential approaches to ESL writing theory in the post-war period have been: controlled composition, current-traditional rhetoric, the process approach, and – most recently, though to a limited extent – the English-for-academic-purposes approach. The first two approaches were both heavily product-oriented and relied on formal drilling of previously introduced linguistic models; their primary goals were to lead learners to achieving, respectively, syntactic and rhetorical correctness. Although now very much dominated by the process orientation, both approaches – particularly current-traditional rhetoric – still find application in language teaching.

The early 1980s saw a major philosophical change as many people began to feel:

> that neither approach adequately fostered thought or its expression – that controlled composition was largely irrelevant to this goal and the linearity and prescriptivism of current-traditional rhetoric [i.e. working to a fixed plan-outline-write sequence, P.K.] discouraged creative thinking and writing (Silva 1990: 15).

It was to overcome these perceived limitations that the process approach emerged. In this approach, writing – 'even the most mundane and routine' (White and Arndt 1991: 5) – started to be viewed as an independent thinking, and learning, process. This process consists of a number of complex stages – the four basic ones identified as 'getting started', 'drafting', 'revising' and 'editing' – which overlap and influence one another. Thus,

> in the process approach, the students do not write on a given topic in a restricted time and hand in the composition for the teacher to 'correct' – which usually means to find errors. Rather, they explore a topic through writing, showing the teacher and each other their drafts, and using what they write to read over, think about, and move them on to new ideas (Raimes 1983: 10).

As in communicative language teaching, content is believed to determine form.

The process approach, which dominates the current ELT scene, is not without its faults. Advocates of what Silva (1990: 16) calls 'an English for academic purposes orientation' have criticised it, among other things, for disregarding variations within writing processes caused by differences in individuals, writing tasks and writing contexts. The communicative tenets, inherent in the process approach, have also been discredited widely by many ELT authors. Hammerly (1991: 21), for example, demystifies the slogan 'Practice makes perfect' and replaces it with a more accurate 'Practice makes permanent', arguing that 'Communicating in a second language with many errors makes the faulty rules underlying the errors permanent.' Much in the same vein, a number of other authors have recently spoken in favour of keeping the balance between process and product, fluency and accuracy, and content and form.[5]

Although not so widely influential, the academic approach, with its pragmatic emphasis on conventionality, has a lot to offer to advanced EFL learners, who, themselves, are often university students expected to comply with academic standards, among them standards in essay writing. In parallel with that, the general awareness of the pervasiveness of conventions in language has been growing recently and a new interest in product and form has emerged – greatly inspired, it seems, by the advancement of the lexical approach and popularity of computerised corpus linguistics research.

3 The lexical profile of the ESL/EFL textbooks

The evolution of L2 writing theory seems to indicate that the greatest amount of lexical coverage should probably be contained in the older, product-oriented textbooks, and in (recent) academic-related materials, rather than in process-focused sources. In addition to this, the distinction between British and American sources is worth noting. The former, traditionally concerned with 'ideas' and 'self-expression', seem to rely to a great extent on students' creativity and on teachers' resourcefulness, which leads them to the inclusion of a substantial number of open-ended exercises and minimum theory. By contrast, American sources are generally analytical, advice-oriented, and equipped with extensive theoretical background; they rarely fail to mention the importance of the final 'packaging' (syntax, grammar, mechanics etc. are always covered, even if only at basic, remedial levels) and contain a fair amount of controlled practice. For these reasons, American textbooks might be regarded as generally more helpful with respect to product-related suggestions than British publications are.

Despite all these considerations, it must be admitted that most ESL/EFL textbooks, even those product-oriented ones, offer limited lexical and stylistic help to students. Concrete and exemplified coverage is usually given only to words and expressions related to organisation, coherence, grammar and relationships between ideas. In particular, the following sets are emphasised:

(a) connectives (also called connectors, linkers, conjunctives, transitions, conjunctive/linking/transitional devices etc.);
(b) certain categories of sentence-level adverbs and adverbial phrases, e.g. frequency, place, time;
(c) closed grammatical categories, such as prepositions, conjunctions, articles, pronouns;
(d) matrix structures with keywords for expressing relationship types, e.g. 'There is absolutely no chance that+SENTENCE' (Arnold and Harmer 1978: 93) which expresses lack of probability.

Other forms of aid, such as lists of common or typical errors, are very scarce; the amount of lexical reference in them is limited to terse lists of confusables, such as Jordan's (1990: 99–100) *practice–practise*, *logic–logical*,

Table 13.1: A typical example of vocabulary tabulation

Beginning	**Middle steps**	**End**
First	*Second(ly)*	*Lastly*
Firstly	*Third(ly)* (etc.)	*Finally*
To begin with	*Next*	
Initially	*Then*	
	Subsequently	
	After this	
	At the same time	
	(etc.)	

(Hamp-Lyons and Heasley 1987: 71)

and *do–make*. Collocation and phraseology are hardly touched on at all and are quite deliberately relegated to dictionaries.

The manner in which the lexical items that *can* be found in the textbooks are presented also leaves much to be desired. Table 13.1, summarising 'common sequencers used when describing a process', illustrates the typical listing/classifying technique.

Several weaknesses undermine this type of presentation. One is obscurity of subjective frequency criteria (cf. 'common' in the quote above); this inadequacy, however, can be resolved easily thanks to the current access to corpus-derived frequency lists. A second, and more serious drawback of listing/categorising items – and this especially concerns situations when new or unknown vocabulary is presented – is that learners may be led falsely to assume interchangeability of words or expressions grouped together – even though these may differ on stylistic and statistical grounds (compare, for example, the common and slightly informal *then* with the rather rare, formal *subsequently* in the middle column of Table 13.1). Still another disadvantage, particularly characteristic of process-based textbooks, is that lists are often not exhaustive and miss less obvious, though useful, examples. For instance, the column containing sentence-initial sequencers in Table 13.1 could well include expressions such as *in the first place* or *at the outset*.

Having looked at some general trends, let us now see how each of the identified L2 writing approaches relates to the matters of lexicon and style. Controlled-writing textbooks examined words mostly from the point of view of sentence-level grammar and offered rather little inherently lexical advice. To help his readers to achieve the heights of a 'simple and direct' English style, Alexander (1965) proposes only two grammatical and two lexical solutions: avoidance of contracted forms (p. 15), avoidance of the first person pronoun (pp. 84, 105); the use of linking expressions (p. 15), and avoidance of longer words where a

Table 13.2: A vocabulary table with graded stylistic information

Style	**By explaining or clarifying**	**By giving examples**	**By making more precise/exact**
<Normal> in both spoken+written	in other words that is (to say)	for example for instance	in other words to be precise
Rather <formal> spoken+written			namely
<Formal> written (mostly technical texts)	i.e.	e.g.	viz.
	By making more accurate	**By emphasising part**	**By strengthening**
<Normal> in both spoken+written	(or) at least	particularly in particular especially	what is more (and) in fact and actually
Rather <formal> in both spoken+written	(or) rather (or) better		furthermore

(Arnold and Harmer 1978: 57)

short one might work (p. 84); no examples illustrating the practical implementation of the last two rules are provided.

The current-traditional approach brought an interest in words, phrases and structures expressing relationships between ideas. In addition, rhetoric-oriented textbooks may sometimes highlight differing levels of formality: e.g. Smalley and Ruetten (1990: 108) compare the use of relative pronouns, the less formal *that* and the more formal *which*, in restrictive clauses. A unique well of fine-grained register distinctions drawn between numerous rhetorically and functionally grouped items is to be found in Arnold and Harmer (1978). Table 13.2 shows how qualifying or re-expressing statements are summarised there. On the whole, although confined to rhetoric-related lexis and rather dogmatic in tone, the current-traditional sources stand out for their comparatively rich and detailed coverage of lexical material.

Process-oriented sources concentrate on 'global' rather than 'local' aspects, and consequently offer only scattered and non-direct lexical and stylistic suggestions. White (1987: 14), for example, only notes that writing is characterised by a wider range of linking expressions than speech and that 'the repeated use of *and* or *so* or *then* is regarded as bad style'. Nolasco (1987: 25) gives one general piece of advice: 'Use common words such as "end" rather than "terminate" or "try" rather than "endeavour", where possible'; his discussion of expository and argumentative writing carries no further suggestions. Commenting on their selective table of sequencers (Table 13.1), Hamp-Lyons and Heasley (1987: 71) tell the reader that, when describing a process,

> you might decide to use a sequencer to make each step of the process clear. On the other hand, ... you might decide that sequencers are not needed because the process is described in natural time order and the reader's knowledge of the world will make the sequence clear to her or him.

In this, albeit illuminating, remark the authors do not manage to say directly whether, for the type of product discussed (i.e. academic and professional writing), the use of sequencers is conventional in English or not; they merely seem to be hinting at a possible overuse problem.

ESL/EFL textbooks of a (semi-)academic profile are, as mentioned before, more explicit and product-conscious, and so we find in them more specific suggestions about the kind of language required. Still, they also may deal with stylistic matters only in a brief or simplistic way. Jordan (1990: 99–100), for example, clarifies a number of features of formal academic style (e.g. no contractions, no hesitation fillers, no personal pronouns, careful use of phrasal verbs, tentative expression), and even supplements them with relevant examples and exercises; unfortunately, his presentation covers only three pages. In his turn, Smalzer (1996) – an American author – attends regularly and at length to 'Language conventions' but is sometimes not challenging enough. For example, in a section 'Shifts in Tone' he rightly advises that 'Colloquial language and slang should ... be avoided in academic writing', but then gives too many examples of an oversimple kind – e.g. *hang out with sb, buck, scream one's head off, pretty cool, yucky*' (ibid.: 183). This, as CLC evidence (and also teaching experience) shows, is unrepresentative of advanced EFL student writing, where tone/register problems are usually of a subtler nature.

Although one of the most widely recognised types of 'foreign-soundingness' in student writing is over- and under-representation of items, current ESL/EFL textbooks hardly address overuse/underuse problems at all. The only case in point is probably that of connectives,[6] which, however, is often treated too sweepingly, as in Smalley and Ruetten's (1990: 142) statement: 'Do not overdo the use of transitions; it could be repetitious. Generally, two or three transitional expressions in a paragraph are sufficient.' In reality, as Granger and Tyson (1996) have recently demonstrated, EFL learners' usage of connectives can be much more complex – with some subsets being overused and others underused.[7]

At this point, we come to the question of language-specific patterns, in the acquisition of which, as Granger (forthcoming c) argues, 'L1 plays an important role'. If this role is indeed so crucial, then the creation of a source which would comprehensively cover foreign learners' lexical and stylistic needs can only be possible if the type of learner at which this source is aimed is limited to a single mother tongue. Publications designed for *all* EFL learners, even if based on international learner corpora, are inevitably bound to suffer from superficiality and redundancy.

On the whole, as this short overview demonstrates, the degree of *explicit* lexical advice that students receive in ESL/EFL textbooks is very limited in terms of both content and manner. This forces many teachers and students to seek advice elsewhere – in dictionaries and thesauruses, as well as in native speaker (NS) textbooks and guidebooks. However, as the subsequent section will show, even these sources often fail to satisfy as they, too, are not in tune with the L1-specific needs of EFL learners.

4 Other sources of lexical aid

As regards the study of words, the most comprehensive source of information comes from dictionaries, books of collocations, thesauruses and other such works of reference, which are increasingly being based on modern corpus research data. Although they are rich in content, provide frequency and register information, group entries thematically and have a number of other advantages – they also suffer from limitations. The greatest one is probably the fact that they concern themselves with NS rather than non-native speaker (NNS) language, and aspire to describe the whole of L2 rather than only aspects of *written* L2 . Helpful as they are, their lack of definite focus may cause this help to appear rather diluted and abridged.

For more direct advice on lexical and stylistic usage, one needs to turn to style guidebooks, which, unfortunately, are mostly aimed at NS readerships. Such publications contain a lot of generalised advice, e.g. 'Suit the word to the occasion' (Warner 1961: 31), 'Write as you speak' (Legat 1989: 52), or 'Write with nouns and verbs' (Strunk and White 1972: 64), but they also, unlike any other source discussed so far, abound in authentic phraseological material: stock phrases, clichés, circumlocutions, jargonistic expressions and the like. Unfortunately, a large majority of these expressions are more typical of journalistic prose[8] than of student writing, let alone of writing by foreign students. Of more relevance are guidebooks written for NS student writers, such as Barrass (1982) or Collinson (1990), but even here, as a preliminary study of noun-headed circumlocutions has shown,[9] many of the flagged expressions are not representative of EFL written interlanguage. And catering as they do for NS writers, it goes without saying that these guidebooks do not include comments on the sometimes idiosyncratic language used by EFL writers.

NS writing textbooks, another possible source of lexical help, often give rather generalised guidelines similar to those in style guidebooks, e.g. that there is *no* 'proper' style in English or that a well-written paper is one that reads well aloud. The NS student may also be advised to have a good dictionary, pay attention to mechanical accuracy and turn to the teacher if in need (cf. Lewis 1979: 48). American sources can be more heuristic and analytical: for instance, discussing editing for style, Flower (1981: 172–80) suggests a few definite steps, such as eliminating or replacing abstract words, key-word editing (a procedure for eliminating 'nonfunctional padding' from text), lowering the noun/verb ratio, restructuring sentences to transform long nouns into verbs, avoiding linking *be*, changing negative expressions to positive ones, and transforming passive constructions into active ones. The most explicit, exhaustive, and instructive coverage of lexical issues is to be found in American college handbooks, which – due to the heterogeneous, often multinational, character of American educational institutions – are usually aimed at *both* NS audiences and ESL students. Marius and Wiener (1988), for instance, assign over 50 pages of their book to a section called 'Using Words Effectively' which features specific chapters on 'Appropriate Diction', 'Imagery and Figurative Language', 'Including Needed Words', 'Avoiding Wordiness' and 'Sexist Language'. Like guidebooks, these chapters contain general guidelines (e.g. 'Use foreign words only when they are necessary' ibid.: 242, or 'Avoid using worn-out expressions and clichés' ibid.: 255) as well as extensive practical sections, where we can find examples of incorrect usage and revision, lists of inappropriate expressions, and controlled practice exercises. Although sometimes the advice received may sound dogmatic and controversial – since grammaticality and economy rank high among the authors' priorities – their directness and commitment to detail make American college publications especially valuable and appealing to an EFL learner. Nowhere else – except, perhaps, in NS student guidebooks and sources published in one's native country – can one hope to find as specific suggestions for, say, avoiding 'empty expressions' as in US college materials. Table 13.3 is an extract from one of the books.

Finally, there are learning aids published in the students' mother country. Macpherson (1994: 5) is an example of a particularly valuable L1-sensitive reference and practice book that has been 'addressed to Poles who wish to express themselves in academic English'. It meets many of the requirements discussed in this chapter: the focus is on a specific type of product; there is comprehensive coverage of vocabulary and expressions; and register/style specifications are frequently given. The book also contains a selection of important collocations and synonyms, and lists of recurrent errors made by Polish writers. In addition, there is a list of 'words liable to confuse' (Polish–English false friends). Although formally not based on CLC data, and free from contrastive frequency

Table 13.3: A substitution table for polyword 'filler phrases'

For	Substitute
at all times	*always*
at the present time	*now*
at this point in time	*now*
by virtue of the fact that	*because*
in the final analysis	*finally*

(Based on Fowler 1986: 416)

information, the book – authored by an experienced British teacher working in Poland – is very relevant to Polish advanced students' needs, and is in many respects superior to what ESL/EFL and NS sources can offer. This shows the clear advantage of taking a contrastive, learner-centred perspective.

Regardless of the praise that some of the publications discussed above deserve, there is a substantial amount of information which they still lack and which only CLC-based, L1-sensitive sources would be able to provide. The next section gives examples of what can be done to enhance the existing teaching materials and to make them better target the needs of EFL learners and how this can be achieved.

5 'Enhancement' – what CLCs can provide

Studies of CLCs can add to EFL textbooks in at least two simple ways: by supplementing existing material with L1-L2 comparative frequency information on overuse/underuse/misuse; and by supplying new, hitherto lacking, content (e.g. collocations and phraseology) – also in a helpful contrastive format. Discussed below are a few examples of possible procedures of enhancement, illustrated with results of some analyses comparing data from Polish EFL and student and professional NS writers.

Comparing frequency lists drawn from native and non-native corpora, even without resorting to statistical measures of significance, can shed light on possible overuse and underuse patterns. While access to grammatically annotated texts and lemmatised frequency counts allows a much higher degree of complexity in the comparisons made (e.g. all nouns or past participles can be studied), even word-form-based frequency lists enable analyses of unambiguous, single-form words, such as modal verbs or frequency adverbs. For example, a study of adverbs of certainty for Polish and NS data revealed that Polish learners greatly overuse some words expressing higher degrees of certainty (*probably, simply, definitely*) and avoid hedging their statements with *perhaps*.[10] The underlying assumption – that Polish student writers generalise too much – found further substantiation in their less significant overuse of other certainty adverbs: *actually, certainly, indeed, probably, truly* and *undoubtedly*. It seems that both types of conclusions reached – the specific and the general – might be of direct interest to the Polish learner: the former introduces concrete usage problems, and the latter affords an interesting contrastive insight into the philosophy underpinning L2 written expression.

Whereas comparing frequency lists can reveal cases of over- or under-representation, concordancing can be applied to uncover instances of misuse. A study of the word *case* as found in the Polish ICLE sub-corpus led to the discovery of an overused formula *in (the) case of* (apparently a transfer from the common Polish '*w przypadku* + genitive') and of its frequently incorrect use without the definite article (possibly due to overapplication of idiomatic *In case of fire/emergency etc.* used in English warning notices). Here are four examples of this misuse:

. . . as it happened ***in case of** 'Jurassic Park', for example.
***In case of** many, it awakes creativness . . .
. . . they know that ***in case of** problems they do not just . . .
. . . difficult ***in case of** single parents.

Concordancing can also be applied in frequency studies of lexical items which appear in varying forms and with diverse meanings, such as nouns or verbs. While studies of individual nouns or verbs might not lead far, since content words are topic-sensitive and difficult to compare even across standardised corpora, certain classes of words, such as hypernyms (nouns of general reference), can be investigated successfully. The process is laborious since it requires disambiguation of forms, then conditional lemmatisation (e.g. the words *experience* and *experiences* cannot be lemmatised because of the difference in meaning) and finally manual counting of the selected occurrences. A comparison conducted between the Polish and NS corpora indicated that Poles overuse hypernyms as a whole set, and also in a number of individual cases – five lemmas: *case, factor, kind, situation, thing*; and two word-forms *conditions* and *time*. The findings corroborate the above-mentioned hypothesis about the Polish tendency towards generalisation.

Finally, as Granger's studies (1994, forthcoming c) convincingly demonstrate, CLCs prove useful not only for the study of words and word-classes but also for the study of phraseology and collocations. Of great help here are powerful software facilities, such as the collocation generator in *TACT* or the cluster detector in the *WordSmith*

Table 13.4: Attributive collocates for *attitude* as attested in the Polish and NS data

NNS (PICLE)		NS (LOCNESS/LOB)	
Collocate	**Frequency**	**Collocate**	**Frequency**
	Judgemental – positive		
accepted	1	*welcoming*	1
'healthy'	1	*professional*	1
positive	2		
right	1		
stressless	1		
Total	6	Total	2
	Judgemental – negative		
chauvinist	1	*care-free*	1
hostile	2		
intolerant	1		
negative	6		
permissive	1		
Total	11	Total	1
Grand total	17		3
	Non-definite/referential adjectives and pronouns		
such	3	*different*	2
certain	1	*these*	1
different	2	*this*	2
first	1		
general	1		
kind of	2		
this	1		
Total	11	Total	5
Grand total	28		8
	Neutral – descriptive		
changing	1	*basic*	1
personal	1	*bosses'*	1
present	1	*Britain's*	1
		British	2

Table 13.4: (cont'd)

NNS (PICLE)		NS (LOCNESS/LOB)	
Collocate	**Frequency**	**Collocate**	**Frequency**
		'wind of change'	1
		changing	1
		'laissez-faire'	1
		fatalistic	1
		Malthusian	2
		national	1
		new	1
		people's	1
		social	1
		Anglo-Soviet	1
		weary	1
Total	3	Total	17

Tools Concordancer, which can measure statistical proximity and show recurrent word combinations. But even if we do not have these tools, we can, by concordancing alone (as I have done), observe whether, for example, instances of cliché, jargon or slang found in NS style guide-books surface in learner data. It is also possible to test whether the same language 'chunks' attested for NS are represented in NNS learners' English. To take a collocational example, a study of the word *attitude* (see Table 13.4) has shown that Polish users place before it adjectival collocates of a rather restricted nature – mainly hyponyms of *good/bad* and non-descriptive, referential expressions – while native users tend to apply a wider selection of purely descriptive, non-judgmental collocates.

The above examples show that CLC studies can support writing text-books with a lot of new and detailed information. Specific suggestions for ICLE-based Polish-learner-oriented enhancement might include the following:

- longer lists of synonymous items, accompanied with frequency band information, register/style description, and (gradable) overuse/underuse/misuse warnings (if applicable). In cases of misuse, Polish and NS contrasting samples could be given;
- (following Macpherson 1994) lists of common collocations, with additional information on contrasts between Polish and NS use;
- listings of commonly misused words and phrases as well as examples of serious over- and underuse.

Whilst this list is obviously not exhaustive, what is essential here is the understanding that the only way that any textbook can incorporate this amount of detailed information is through assuming a national perspective, since only co-ordinated efforts of CLC research teams and ELT publishing houses can develop a type of learning aid whose content is made maximally relevant to the needs of its users.

6 Conclusion

'There is a decidedly "English" way of handling a topic, of putting the sentences together, and of connecting the sentences' (Raimes 1983: 115). This 'Englishness' manifests itself in organisational, syntactic, grammatical and other preferences. Unfortunately for a language learner, similar cultural constraints operate in his or her own mother tongue, which may be a cause of persistent problems with L2 acquisition.

The lexical problems affecting advanced-level EFL writers concern not only grammar and semantics, but also – and this is often overlooked or covered superficially in ESL/EFL writing materials – style, which requires, among other things, the application of acceptable *proportions* of usage – in accordance with the conventions characterising the desired type of linguistic product, such as a (semi-)academic essay. It is heartening that computer learner corpora, which enable massive statistical analyses of national varieties of EFL interlanguage, can now be applied successfully to pinpoint and diagnose the troublesome areas of overuse/underuse and misuse which have long been escaping attention. At present, the remaining, daunting task, 'if we are serious about giving learners the most efficient learning aids' (Granger forthcoming c), is to begin designing L1-sensitive materials which will make the most of CLC-based research and which will have their content and form 'customised' to the discrete 'national' needs of EFL learners.

Acknowledgement

I would like to express my thanks and gratitude to Professor Sylviane Granger for her encouragement and her precious comments on earlier versions of this chapter. They have played an important role in crystallising my ideas.

Notes

1 Transfer-related errors are reported, for example, in Granger and Tyson's (1996) investigation of the use of connectives by French

EFL learners. For an introduction to contrastive studies of CLCs, and to Contrastive Interlanguage Analysis (CIA), see Granger (1996a) and Chapter 1 of this volume. For more examples of the practical application of CLCs, see Part 3 of this volume.

2 I focus mainly on upper-intermediate- and advanced-level ESL/EFL textbooks published from 1980 onwards; a few earlier titles appear as well.

3 The CLC analyses of Polish learners' interlanguage referred to later in this chapter were based on the following corpora:

LOCNESS (NS: English ICLE sub-corpus) – 95890 tokens;
LOB B+F (NS: sub-corpus of LOB, *not* ICLE) – 83082;
PICLE (NNS: Polish learner ICLE sub-corpus) – 95588.

The version of LOCNESS used was British only and included also literature essays. Since these might have been incompatible with the argumentative/expository format and content of PICLE, the LOB B+F sub-corpus of LOB was added, which consisted of continuous expository texts (dialogues and narrative excluded) from Categories B (press: editorial) and F (popular lore).

4 For information on ICLE, and the ICLE Project, consult Chapter 1 of this volume, and also Granger (1993, 1994, 1996a).

5 E.g. Ur (1996: 163), Hammerly (1991: vii–viii), Harris (1993: 14).

6 See e.g. Hayward and Wilcoxon (1994); also Granger and Tyson (1996) for an investigation of the connectives overuse hypothesis.

7 Granger and Tyson (1996: 5) state that '[French] learners use most frequently those connectors which add to, exemplify, or emphasise a point, rather than those which change the direction of the argument or take the argument logically forward.' The authors admit that 'The cases of underuse were unexpected.'

8 Expressions such as *bring back to reality, work against time, blinkered view, dark horse, moving experience*, and many others, are not found in CLCs; consequently, their avoidance by EFL learners need not be specifically required.

9 Here are five circumlocutions of the kind tested (the nouns assigned as 'nuclei' are underlined): *have an <u>ability</u> to; at that <u>point</u> in time; in this day and <u>age</u>; in the final <u>analysis</u>; make an <u>attempt</u> to*. Many of them failed to appear in *both* NS and NNS corpora, which might be a tentative indication that their use in student writing is marginal.

10 It was found that although many Polish students do use the less appropriate informal word *maybe* (which is hardly present in the NS data), it does not compensate for the underuse of *perhaps*.

CHAPTER FOURTEEN

Exploiting L1 and interlanguage corpora in the design of an electronic language learning and production environment

John Milton

1 Introduction

This chapter first briefly describes manual and semi-automatic analyses of an electronic interlanguage corpus. It then outlines electronic exercises, tutorials and tools designed to address some of the infelicities in the writing of the English learners exposed by these analyses. The integration of such empirically based programs into a conventional EFL curriculum is discussed.

2 Background

As attested by other authors of this volume, the collection and study of corpora of interlanguage are powerful and necessary prerequisites to the understanding of the production, and therefore the communicative needs, of EFL learners. From such research follows the obligation to find ways of providing language learners with timely and comprehensible access to the increasing amount of information we are discovering about language. Conventional classroom methods are often inadequate for conveying to learners our growing understanding of language features, and inappropriate for providing learners full access to, or significant experience with, the features of target language behaviours and how particular features of their own production deviate from these targets.

The need for better (or at least better augmented) pedagogies is especially sharp in environments such as Hong Kong, where most EFL learners, after spending their entire primary and secondary education in 'English Medium' schools, complain of having received inadequate or unhelpful advice and feedback in the English classroom, as well as inadequate exposure to the L2 outside the classroom.[1] One would not expect either learning or acquisition, to use Krashen's (1981) dichotomy, to be very successful under such circumstances. The system described later in this chapter is an attempt to supplement instruction in and exposure to the L2 by an *Electronic Language Learning and Production Environment*, which is meant to enhance the ability of learners to attend to lexical, grammatical and discoursal aspects of their reading and writing.[2]

Computer-Assisted Language Learning (CALL) is often associated with dreaded behaviourist principles, and the case is sometimes made that machine-based practice discourages fluency. However, there is no reason to believe that the attention to linguistic detail made possible by autonomous programs is necessarily incompatible with fluency (although the excessive stress-intensive examination drill that is a feature of many Asian classrooms may). Declarative and procedural knowledge of *how* to write can surely be useful for effective communication if there is also attention to *what* is written.[3]

3 Analyses

The corpus study on which this development is based has proceeded in two stages:

(1) the analysis of the EFL learners' written English text for lexico-grammatical errors; and
(2) the comparison of this interlanguage corpus with an L1 corpus of the writing of native speakers of English so as to determine quantitative lexico-grammatical differences between the native speaker (NS) and non-native speaker (NNS) texts.[4]

The first analysis resulted in a typology of the most common grammatical errors in the interlanguage text; the second analysis has produced comparative databases of word sequences commonly used in the academic expository writing of these adolescents, indexed according to how frequently they are used by the English NSs and by this group of English NNS writers (for a similar analysis of prefabs in speech, see De Cock et al., Chapter 5, this volume).

3.1 Stage 1: Lexico-grammatical analysis

First, the corpus of NNS writing was part-of-speech tagged,[5] after which about 100,000 words were manually coded for occurrence or non-occurrence of error at the most restricted level possible to account for the error (mainly at word, and to some degree at phrase and clause level: this process is more fully described in Milton and Chowdhury 1994). This resulted in a free-text database of words, word classes, and sentence-level grammatical categories (such as concord), and information on how frequently and in what circumstances they were used correctly[6] and incorrectly. The primary purpose of the error coding procedure was to allow retrieval and facilitate further study of the errors, rather than to attempt complete explication by means of the codes. It should be noted that the determination of error is not possible when the semantic or pragmatic intention of the writer is not clear or the syntax or lexis is so entangled that the most heroic measures cannot disambiguate meaning – especially common among the weakest writers (e.g. **Moreover, the extra-curriculum activities should be immature*). The codes primarily act as lookups to tables where context, possible node words and the most obvious and localized error types can be listed for more detailed analysis. This at least allows a ranking of general structural and lexical error categories according to their absolute and relative rates of frequency, as well as according to rate of dispersion (i.e. how frequently they occurred in separate scripts). Within this pragmatically designed typology (organized under morphological, lexical, grammatical and stylistic headings), ambiguous structures and lexis are cross-indexed so that they can be assigned alternate explanations. This cross-referencing is exploited in a hypertext grammar, as explained later in this chapter.

I make no claim to having adequately dealt with the methodological and theoretical issues associated with error analysis techniques, such as problems in the precise identification and description of error (Ellis 1994: 47–71). Although these problems have been partly to blame for the decline in the academic interest in this area, they should not prevent us from exploring various linguistic learnability issues so that we have some basis for addressing discrepancies between the learners' interlanguage and the target language. Because my interest is in providing whatever feedback is most useful to the learners, in most cases only the surface features of error in this corpus were coded (as suggested by Dulay et al. 1982). Clearly, however, many errors have difficult-to-resolve theoretical or instructional issues that ultimately need to be addressed. Because the coding is intended as far as possible to be theory-neutral, the features can be retrieved and explored when time permits, and references to apparently transferred Chinese structures can be made where possible and useful (as Corder 1981 suggests).

It would be premature to attempt to apply the findings of this typology to an automatic analysis or correction of error. The indeterminate nature of many of the errors makes it difficult to work out parsing rules and therefore to reliably flag or automatically correct the errors. This is perhaps not surprising given the difficulty of parsing even well-formed text (see Black et al. 1993). It should nevertheless be noted that this 'ill-formed' text has systematic properties (at least partly due to the restricted nature of the grammatical structures and lexical expressions used by these writers) and does appear to conform to patterns, if not always readily defined rules.

3.2 *Stage 2: word-sequence analysis*

This error typology, based as it is on a manual examination of the interlanguage corpus, falls well short of quantifying the differences between the L1 and interlanguage texts. One relatively economic method of more systematically discovering differences between the two corpora, not based on error identification, is to extract and compare all words and word sequences of up to six-word sequences[7] from the L1 and interlanguage texts. This was done and the frequencies of the resulting words and word strings were compared using a log likelihood measure (an alternative to chi-square: i.e. the 'G-score' described by Dunning 1994). From the resulting several million strings, those that occurred once only were filtered out. The resulting tables (about 200,000 strings) were sorted by the degree (i.e. the 'G-score') to which NNSs underuse and overuse the expressions. Next, the topic-independent expressions were identified by deleting those strings which contain content words present in the examination questions and prompts (the 'rejected' strings were checked for polysemous expressions). This procedure was easier for the longer strings: relevance of one- and two-word strings was mainly based on degree of de-lexicalization: function words, delexicalized verbs and common modifiers were counted as non-topic-dependent. Table 14.1 lists eight randomly chosen four-word sequences underused by NNSs and eight four-word sequences overused by NNSs: these are sorted by the difference in occurrence (as measured by the

Table 14.1: Some four-word strings underused and overused by NNSs, sorted by G-score

		Word 1	Word 2	Word 3	Word 4	G-score	NNS	NS
Underused by NNSs	1	*In*	*this*	*case*	*the*	12.33	0	9
	2	*It*	*has*	*also*	*been*	10.96	0	8
	3	*It*	*can*	*be*	*seen*	10.96	0	8
	4	*An*	*example*	*of*	*this*	10.96	0	8
	5	*good*	*example*	*of*	*this*	9.59	0	7
	6	*This*	*is*	*not*	*to*	9.59	0	7
	7	*In*	*an*	*ideal*	*world*	9.59	0	7
	8	*A*	*century*	*ago*	*,*	8.22	0	6
Overused by NNSs	9	*First*	*of*	*all*	*,*	198.39	149	1
	10	*On*	*the*	*other*	*hand*	178.34	233	31
	11	*In*	*my*	*opinion*	*,*	86.02	102	11
	12	*All*	*in*	*all*	*,*	67.90	59	2
	13	*In*	*fact*	*,*	*the*	48.08	40	1
	14	*In*	*addition*	*,*	*the*	38.44	43	4
	15	*In*	*a*	*nutshell*	*,*	37.88	27	0
	16	*As*	*we*	*all*	*know*	30.62	27	1

'G-score') in each corpus. Words are listed uniquely by case and punctuation counts as 'words' (preserving full stops and other punctuation marks tells us much about the positioning of 'word chunks' in sentences).

Even the small sample of word strings in Table 14.1 is illustrative of both the constraints and value of this technique. A procedural limitation is that the automatic extraction of strings and the subsequent manual delimitation according to topic independence have not produced ideally usable databases. For example, this technique has indiscriminately attached commonly collocated words to fixed phrases (e.g. the table suggests that *In this case*, a fixed phrase, is often followed by *the*). Some expressions allow optional embedded modifiers (e.g. *An example of this / A good example of this*) and therefore need to be grouped (without losing their unique numerical values). Also, the technique has thrown up what might be argued are incomplete lexical phrases (e.g. *This is not to . . .*). The topic-independence of certain expressions (e.g. *A century ago*) is admittedly questionable: my intention is simply to retain those expressions which might be of use in a conceivable variety of topics. The expressions are currently being sorted into coherent lexical and syntactic units, and organized into pragmatic and semantic categories, with polysemous expressions cross-indexed.

We should note that this interlanguage data clearly warns of the pedagogical danger of exaggerating the significance of lexical classification. The functional and notional classification of language features that resulted from the work of Wilkins (1974) and others has become a staple of many teaching materials. This categorization lends an order and priority to the language syllabus, but like any order, it can become overgeneralized, restrictive and dogmatic. One unfortunate result of the application of this language model, at least on the syllabuses of Hong Kong schools, is that a narrow range of words and phrases have been elevated to the level of an academic catechism. Students are drilled in the categorical use of a short list of expressions – often those functioning as connectives or alternatively those which are colourful and complicated (and therefore impressive) – regardless of whether they are used primarily in spoken or written language (if indeed at all), or to which text types they are appropriate. There is a strong correlation between the expressions overused by NNSs and notionally classified lists of expressions distributed by Hong Kong 'Tutorial Schools'.[8] The relative frequencies with which expressions occur in the two corpora indicate the effect that misinformed instruction has on the learners' writing. The contrived and unlikely contexts in which the expressions are taught add to the impression made on learners that they are more frequent, and the meanings less subtle, than they in fact are in either published English or in the academic writing of English NSs (cf. Milton and Tsang 1993).

The NNSs make use of a much smaller repertoire of word sequences than do the NSs, but the high frequencies with which they use expressions which they 'know' and believe they can manage (e.g. *First of all* and *On the other hand*) is startling.[9] Contrasted with this is the infrequent use that the NSs make of the most common expressions at their disposal. NSs use a much wider range of lexis and syntax and are thus less likely to use any one string very often.

Most of the multi-word expressions commonly used by the NNSs are fixed lexical phrases, and many of these are made to function as logical connectors (so much the better if a connector is metaphorical, such as *In a nutshell*). Little of this appears to be the result of L1 transfer; rather it seems clear that the NNSs are using those expressions which they have been instructed to use (either because their instructors believe the lexis is characteristic of written English of this type or for other reasons).[10]

The NSs use grammatical structures avoided by the NNSs, such as passives (e.g. *It can be seen*). There are also marked differences in the discoursal roles of the expressions used by the NSs and the NNSs. A major difference is that the NSs tend to indirectness by hedging, qualifying or 'impersonalizing' their statements (often expressed by passive structures such as *It can be seen* and *This is not to say*), whereas the NNSs appear to often overstate their case by using intensifying and categorical expressions such as *As we all know* (this is discussed in more detail in Milton and Hyland 1997, see also Lorenz's discussion of 'overzealous' use of intensifiers by German learners of English, in Chapter 4, this volume). Of course it may be that the writing of NS adolescents (even at the level of repeated phrases) is not an ideal model for NNSs. Undoubtedly adjustments to the databases will be needed as we better understand the differences between the features of various styles of writing and text types.

Despite the high incidence of 'local' grammatical and lexical errors exposed by the Stage 1 analysis described in this chapter, very few of the word strings repeatedly used by the NNSs are identifiably wrong in these restricted contexts. This is further evidence that automatic grammatical/lexical checking routines based on simple string matches are unlikely in themselves to be reliable for automatically flagging error. It also raises questions of how learners can be best taught to modify their style. Learners might be helped to focus when they read and write if they had access to a wider and more empirically determined range of lexical and grammatical expressions. One technique which may ameliorate learners' tendencies to exaggerate usage of a small subset of expressions is described in the next section.

4 Empirically based CALL

The two types of research data just described are being exploited in the development of a number of tutorial exercises and tools to assist EFL learners in the acquisition and production of written language. Here I can only give the briefest outline of some of the components of the system, such as:

- an error recognition (i.e. 'proofreading' or 'editing') exercise intended to sensitize learners to the most common or most 'serious' errors exposed by the first analysis;
- a hypertext online grammar designed to give context-sensitive feedback and based on these errors;
- databases of the 'underused' lexical and grammatical phrases exposed by the second analysis, and made interactively available to learners from their wordprocessor; and
- a list-driven concordancer which interacts with text in these programs and databases.[11]

4.1 *Providing practice and declarative knowledge*

For CALL programs to be accepted as a part of the language syllabus at either level by instructors and students in Hong Kong, they must provide practice in language skills in examination mode as well as autonomous mode. This is because at their worst, Hong Kong curricula, at least at the secondary level, are often unashamedly examination focused, frequently emphasizing, as we have seen, the memorization of hothouse lexis that examination markers are presumed to admire. At tertiary level those tens of thousands of students who are considered to require remedial English may have no more than one semester of formal instruction, which is usually given to task-based communicative work, although assessed work (usually in the form of essays or reports in the English classroom) remains the students' main concern.

Editing/proofreading tasks are an important part of the territory-wide secondary examination, and at least intuitively seem a sensible way for students to practise a necessary writing skill. The CALL system under development features an electronic version of this task (Figure 14.1). The program displays authentic error types (randomly: a different error each time, but maximum one per line) that users must locate and correct.[12] The exercise provides learners with contextualized practice in those lexico-grammatical aspects of their English which demonstrably present them with the greatest difficulty. An online hypertext grammar is linked to each error so that the learners can call for context-sensitive explanations, and feedback is structured so that they are encouraged to work out the problem for themselves (see Milton 1996 for a fuller description).

Taking an initially instructional approach rather than attempting to implement a wide coverage grammar checker seems justified if for no other reason than that we are still at the stage where it is easier to manually replicate error than it is to automatically identify it. The proofreading program is 'authorable' and error replication is made easy by a file editor that lists and exemplifies the most frequent errors made by these learners and exposed by the earlier analysis, thus guiding the author (ideally, the EFL instructor) in replicating and coding errors in selected text. The hypertext grammar, which is coded with the same tags used in the error analysis, provides explanations of the lexical patterns and grammatical rules governing each language feature. The interaction of the grammar with 'real' error types embedded in an authentic context offers more than mindless drill to the learners. Students are encouraged to consult the online grammar as they work within the program and (in the case of those syllabuses in which this program has already been implemented) through the printed materials in the course. Much of the indeterminate nature of error encountered in error classification (Stage 1 of the analysis) can actually be exploited by the cross-referencing possible within a hypertext system, so that the learners have multiple access points to examples, rules and correct patterns. Figures 14.1, 14.2 and 14.3 show the screens at various possible stages in a learner's progress through a proofreading exercise. Figure 14.1 displays the passage and program as it first appears. In Figure 14.2 the user has clicked for help to understand the error, and has requested a 'full explanation' of the error, which is presented in the pop-up hypertext grammar. Within this hypertext system the user can jump to related problems and practise recognition of correct and incorrect patterns.

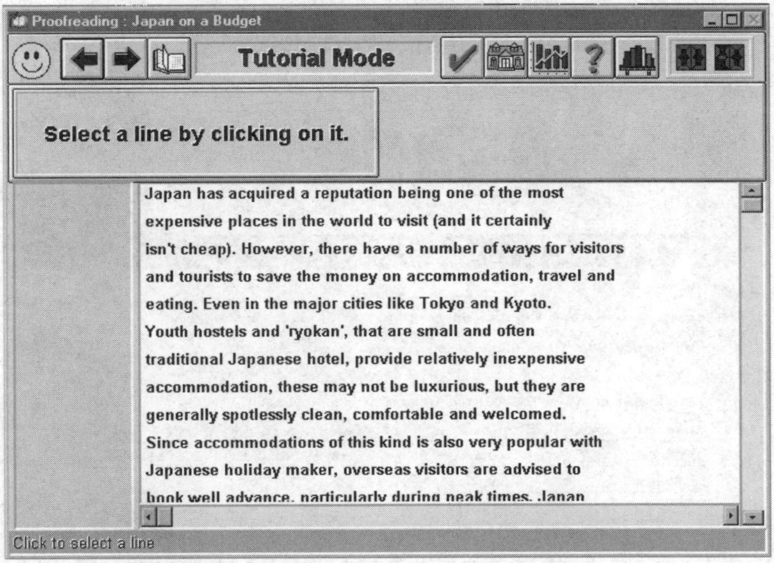

Figure 14.1 A proofreading exercise

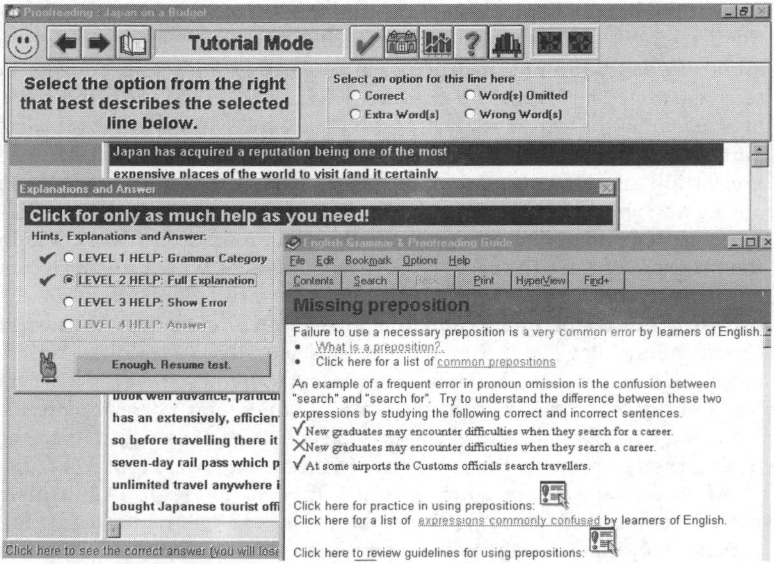

Figure 14.2 The proofreading exercise with the interactive grammar displayed

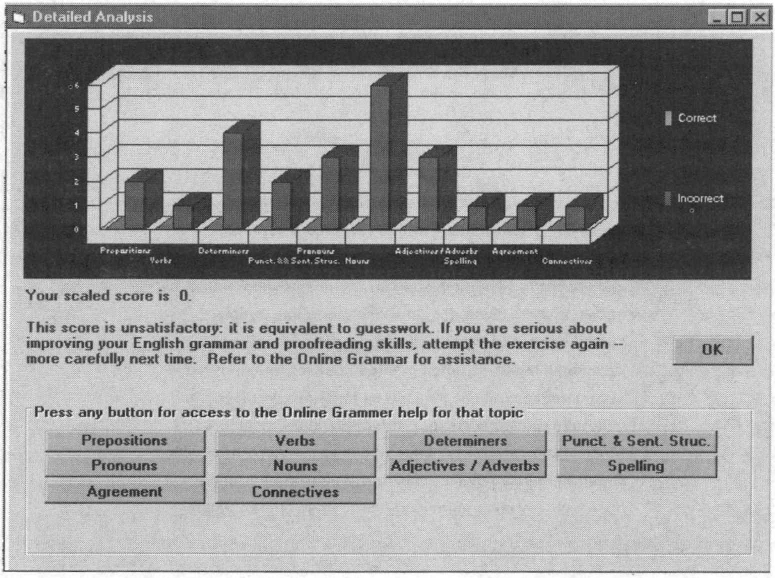

Figure 14.3 A grammar profile of the proofreading exercise

At any time in his progress the user can also access a profile such as that in Figure 14.3, from which the hypertext grammar can be further explored.

4.2 *Encouraging inductive and procedural learning*

The introduction of concordancing techniques for 'data-driven learning' (Johns 1991) has greatly expanded the potential for language exploration by EFL learners. However, the occasional user often has difficulty in using a concordancer as an autonomous pattern detector. For such a tool to be fully practicable by most EFL learners, it needs to be integrated with other programs, such as the user's wordprocessor, and it should provide some guidance to EFL learners in identifying those word patterns that are most problematic for them. The concordancer developed for this system 'communicates' with other programs and is linked to databases such as those of the underused and avoided lexical and grammatical phrases isolated in Stage 2 of the analysis, described earlier. Learners are thus guided in the contextualized use of specific words and phrases: they can view concordanced lines, see expanded context, test themselves on similar expressions etc. This concordancer can be called from a wordprocessor and other programs to access words and 'word chunks', which can be sorted by grammatical and semantic categories. This tool and associated databases is aimed at assisting writers in the selection of collocationally and discoursally appropriate language.[13]

This 'list driven' concordancer is demonstrated in Figure 14.4, which displays a partial list of 'hedging' phrases, of which Cantonese-speaking learners of English in Hong Kong seem unaware (a similar phenomenon has been noted in speech, see De Cock et al., Chapter 4, this volume). A number of techniques will have to be explored in order to avoid having the learners substitute one set of overused and misused expressions for another. Items in the list will be linked to notes in the hypertext grammar and can be annotated by the learner from within the concordancer. The user will be informed of the frequency with which the selected expressions occur in the text type and in the particular text being explored. Various sorting options will also encourage learners to use the entire range of available expressions.

5 Conclusion

The implementation of wide coverage, reliable grammar checkers for NNSs may be some way off yet, but there are a number of ways in which the data from the separate and comparative analyses of NS and NNS texts can be used now to create electronic learning experiences and writing assistants for English NNS writers. For such programs to be

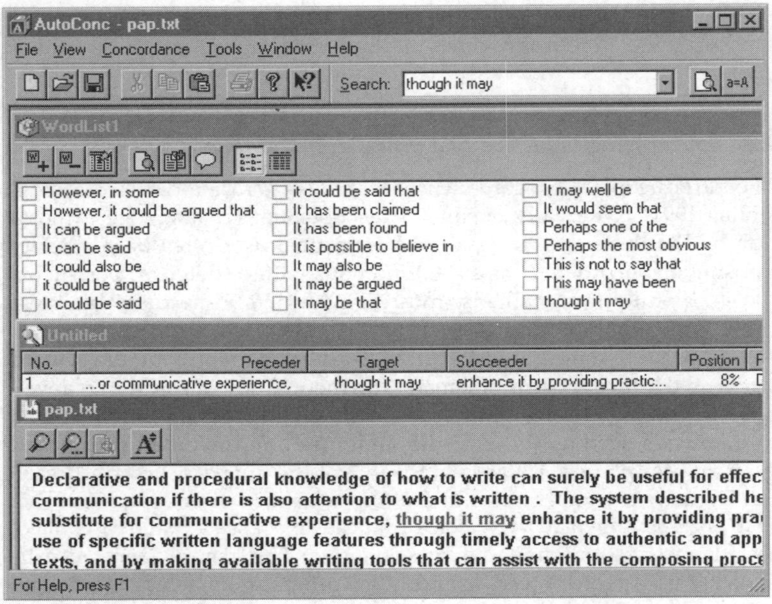

Figure 14.4 A list-driven concordancer

effective they should provide users with optional ways of accessing information: for example, through declarative resources such as the online grammar described here and through techniques which can lead to inductive and procedural learning, such as the list-driven concordancer.

Finally, we recognize the reality that, to be accepted by educational establishments, the relevance of such electronic tools and exercises to institutional procedures may be as important as the pedagogic principles which they model and the empirical foundations on which they are built. The exercises and tools described here meet some of the practical requirements of an EFL syllabus: they can be accessed autonomously and can supplement classroom instruction; they satisfy the institutional need for assessment (but also make both declarative and inductive language knowledge and skills available during practice); and they provide students with focused activities which have clear and immediate learning goals and which directly assist the writing process.

Acknowledgments

I am grateful for the support of the following in the collection and annotation of text:

The Hong Kong Examinations Authority for supplying scripts from the 1992 and 1994 'Use of English' A-level examinations;
The University of Cambridge Local Examinations Syndicate for supplying scripts from the 1994 'General Studies' A-level examination;
The staff and Director of UCREL at Lancaster University for part-of-speech tagging the corpora; and
The University Grants Committee of Hong Kong for their generous funding of research grants DAG92/93.LC01; HKUST 514/94H and DAG94/95.LC01.

Notes

1 Although English is universally held to be important in Hong Kong, even active learners of English complain of inadequate instruction and exposure to the language. In a recent survey of 1,400 EFL learners in Hong Kong (each with about 12 years of conventional classroom instruction in English), 97 per cent indicated strong dissatisfaction with their English skills (Milton forthcoming).
2 Some of the components of this system have been implemented and their effectiveness is being tested; some are still prototypes.
3 Johnson (1994) discusses the need for the teaching of declarative and procedural knowledge of grammar.
4 The two corpora consist of:
   1 about 70,000 words sampled and transcribed from each of seven grade levels of the A-level territory-wide Hong Kong 'Use of English' Examination (a total of about 500,000 words); and
   2 about the same number of words (500,000) from scripts receiving the highest grades (A–B) transcribed from the Cambridge Examinations Syndicate 'General Studies' Examination held in the UK. The topics of each examination were different, but all related to current affairs and students were expected to use an expository style.
5 The POS tagging was done at Lancaster University, using the *CLAWS4* tagger and the expanded tagset *C7*.
6 By 'correctness' I mean what is acceptable to NS intuitions.
7 Such word sequences are sometimes referred to as 'n-grams' by computational linguists, e.g. Church and Gale (1991).
8 These are private institutions at which high school students spend several hours a week cramming vocabulary and 'model answers' before the territory-wide examinations.
9 See Milton and Freeman (1996) for a more detailed analysis of this phenomenon.
10 One of my students recently confided that a teacher had told her that students are told to use these types of expressions because it

makes marking easier: i.e. the marker uses logical connectors as signposts to the students' main content points.

11 This concordancer is 'OLE' enabled ('Object Linking and Embedding' allows programs to 'communicate' with each other so that, for example, the concordancer can be enabled from any program by the user selecting the word or expression to be looked up).

12 Gardner (forthcoming) reports an experiment that confirms the effectiveness of computer-based editing exercises over other types of CALL, although it remains to be established whether they improve learners' abilities to proofread in situ.

13 Of course the text suggested by the concordancer will only be appropriate to the degree that the corpora which it searches are relevant to the writer's textual purposes. Appropriate corpora (e.g. of academic texts) will have to be collected.

CHAPTER FIFTEEN

Learner corpus data in the foreign language classroom: form-focused instruction and data-driven learning

Sylviane Granger and Chris Tribble

1 The relevance of learner corpus data to the language classroom

A discussion of the use of corpus data in the foreign language classroom can imply a shift in the focus of teaching towards form, and the introduction of a more inductive approach to the project of learning and teaching languages than has been common in recent years. We shall begin by reviewing some of the issues that are raised by such a change of focus – and some of the reasons for proposing a move in this direction. We shall then give examples of ways in which corpus-informed learning materials can usefully be included in an EFL programme.

2 Focus on form and corrective feedback

While the communicative approach adopted in current foreign language teaching has undeniably helped improve learners' fluency, in the opinion of some it has been accompanied by a loss of accuracy, especially grammatical accuracy: 'in focusing exclusively on meaning and overall success of communication, we have overlooked the issue of accuracy' (Williams 1995: 13). To remedy this, a number of EFL specialists have advocated integrating form-based activities into the communicative teaching framework.

Recent research into the role played by formal instruction in second language acquisition (SLA) provides growing support for form-focused instruction. In his critical survey of research on consciousness raising in second language learning, Schmidt (1990: 145) stresses the importance of this type of instruction, especially for adults. He states that we can 'predict incomplete acquisition of form by adults to the extent that they do not deliberately attend to form, especially for redundant and communicatively less important grammatical features' and concludes that incidental learning 'appears unlikely for adults.' Likewise Hayashi (1995: 112) finds that 'comprehensible input alone is not enough to ensure grammatical accuracy in L2' and advocates 'form-focused instruction within a communicative context with a combination of lexical and semantic assistance, and the bringing to prominence of the linguistic properties.' Yan-Ping's (1991: 263) findings show that 'form-based classroom instruction is conducive to the success of SLA, be it implicit or explicit'.

Another factor that is clearly brought out by recent SLA studies is the importance of corrective feedback. Rutherford (1987) postulates that one of the instruments to raise learners' consciousness of aspects of the grammatical system could be error identification and correction. Several recent studies support this claim. White (1991) and Trahey and White (1993)'s investigation of adverb placement (*John often kisses Mary* vs. **John kisses often Mary*) shows that learners who received explicit instruction on adverb placement and corrective feedback made progress in eradicating incorrect structures, while learners who received increased input containing correctly placed adverbs but no explicit instruction or feedback showed no improvement. Likewise, Carroll and Swain (1993) find that learners who received negative feedback (either explicit or implicit) performed better on a dative alternation test than learners who received no feedback. Although there is this growing support for form-focused instruction and corrective feedback, a question remains: how should they be implemented in the classroom? Larsen-Freeman and Long (1991: 322) rightly point out that recognising the importance of attention to form in second language acquisition does not justify 'resuscitating some of the teaching practices which SLA research first helped to discredit.'

3 Data-driven learning

A particularly attractive way of providing form-focused instruction is through classroom concordancing or data-driven learning (DDL), which is defined by Johns and King (1991: iii) as 'the use in the classroom of computer-generated concordances to get students to explore regularities of patterning in the target language, and the development of activities and exercises based on concordance output'. Grounded in the wider methodological approaches of 'language awareness' (Hawkins 1984; Van Lier 1995) and 'consciousness raising' (Rutherford 1987; Ellis 1991; James 1992), DDL calls for learners' inductive skills. As Tribble and Jones (1990: 12) say, concordance-based exercises 'favour learning by discovery. The study of grammar (or vocabulary, or discourse, or style) takes on the character of research, rather than spoonfeeding or rote learning'.

So far DDL has almost exclusively made use of native English data. The authenticity of the data ensures that learners are presented with samples of language which reflect the way people actually speak or write. However, native data fails to provide the kind of corrective feedback that has proved to have a positive effect on SLA. While James's (1992: 190) claim that 'the really authentic texts for FL learning are not those produced by native speakers for native speakers, but those produced by learners themselves' may be considered extreme, it is undeniable that in the context of e.g. essay writing, it is learner data and learner data only which will tell us what is difficult for learners in general or a particular group of learners (sharing the same mother tongue, level of proficiency, etc.). It would, therefore, seem fruitful to apply the DDL approach to learner data. Until recently it was difficult to store and process learner data electronically. However, advances in computer technology – both hardware and software – have put corpus compilation within the reach of any motivated EFL specialist. It is now possible to store vast quantities of learner data on computer and make concordances of error-prone items. These concordances can then be presented to learners in parallel with native concordances to make learners aware of grammatical, lexical or discourse features which distinguish their interlanguage from the target norm. This methodology was first described by Tribble (1988) and further illustrated in Tribble and Jones (1990) and Tribble (1991). However, it has not, so far, been applied on a large scale. The use of non-native speaker (NNS) data in the classroom raises two main questions: (1) Which forms should be focused on? (2) Which native speaker (NS) model should be adopted?

4 Which forms?

Until recently the selection of words, phrases and structures for form-focused instruction was largely based on teachers' intuitions. While this approach has its merits, it suffers from one major weakness: teachers' intuitions fail to provide a complete picture of learners' problems. So, for instance, while the confusion between *as* and *like* is invariably present in ELT tools, another corpus-attested error, namely the use of *as* instead of *such as*, is invariably absent. The computerisation of learner data allows for a more systematic account of learner difficulties. By inserting error tags in the learner corpus, it is possible to retrieve comprehensive lists of errors typical of a given learner population (see Milton, Chapter 14, this volume and Dagneaux et al. forthcoming). Parallel NS/NNS concordances of error-prone items can be drawn up and exercises designed on this basis. For instance, in the following exercise the learners are asked to compare the complementation of the words *accept* and *possibility* in NS and NNS data.

Example task

Consider the two examples from native and non-native speaker writing given below.

1. *What grammatical structures appear to follow 'accept'?*
2. *Do any grammatical forms only appear in the non native-speaker examples? If this is the case, check if the students are using an acceptable form.*
3. *Carry out the same investigation of 'possibility' – again, do the non-native speaking writers use a form which is not found in the native speaker data set? If yes, is it an appropriate use of the word?*

(The Longman Language Activator *provides useful advice on the appropriate use of 'accept' and 'possibility')*

Native speaker writing

not being able to accept	>that fulfilment of life is possible
be overcome? Why not accept	>the differences as an intentional
the act. Hugo cannot accept	>that the party line has changed
mothers and learn to accept	>their traditions.
with their emotions and try to accept	>that diversity.
If the peer group doesn't accept	>what the friend is wearing
of a woman, why not accept	>it and consider ways to use

Non-native speaker writing

families, the parents accept	>that new visions of things
think that women must accept	>that some differences exist
nor the children accept	>to recognize that
the parents accept	>that new visions of things may
don't always accept	>that their children also
women have to accept	>the other side of the coin
young. He could never accept	>to be inferior
guinea-pig and accept	>to receive some viruses, some
Feminists have to accept	>to be treated as men
Johnny will not accept	>the Company's decision

Native speaker writing

from the two-fold possibility	>for joining the party: was
earth. There is no possibility	>of his dominant position in
and sensible possibility	>for solving international
There seems every possibility	>that the present Queen will
you die, there is no possibility	>of benefiting from that
deduces the possibility	>of a relatively increasing
mention the possibility	>that one of the motives for
47 that, there is no possibility	>of conversion from one
but there is a possibility	>of entry for those
popular because of the possibility	>for abuse. The second

Non-native speaker writing

January 1993 on, the possibility	>for workers of all kind to
is, however, a strong possibility	>that our society is still
European level, the possibility	>for students to move from
students have the possibility	>to leave for another
of employees, the possibility	>for professional people to
self-confidence and possibility	>of identification. To follow
culture and have the possibility	>to practise their
to young people the possibility	>to enrich their
already explored the possibility	>of forming other such
argument against the possibility	>of an identity
there may be a possibility	>of reducing the
because we have the possibility	>to travel more freely all
of life, i.e. the possibility	>to be in harmony with

This kind of exercise can help students become aware of a fossilised error in their interlanguage, namely the erroneous use of the infinitive after these two words. Exercises of this type should be particularly motivating for learners as they have to do not just with any old grammatical or lexical problem but with their own attested difficulties. Moreover, they constitute a positive way of giving corrective feedback since they do not only display erroneous use but also the structures that the learners have already mastered (such as the *that*-clause after *accept* or the *of*-phrase after *possibility*).

5 Which model?

Studying learner output provides teachers and researchers with significant insights into areas where EFL students face difficulties in matching the performance of their NS peers, but at the same time it is important to have the right control corpus with which to effect a useful NNS/NS comparison. However, opinions as to what constitutes an authoritative corpus differ.

One school of thought holds that an *authoritative* corpus is one which contains expert production relevant to the needs of apprentice writers. Flowerdew (1993) is a proponent of this view and gives a practical example of learners with an interest in business communication studying the use of imperative verbs in a corpus of 'sales letters' (ibid.: 312) to demonstrate his belief that the apprentice writer needs to draw on the writing of accomplished practitioners in a relevant specialised field.

Two different views of corpus authority (particularly for the study of vocabulary) have developed in lexicographically driven studies. One treats authority as analogous to *representativeness*. Early corpora of English such as Brown (US) and LOB (British), and, currently, the British National Corpus (Burnard 1995) have attempted to be as representative as possible of the possible genres of written (and latterly, spoken) language use. This approach has been criticised by Sinclair, for example, who regards *size* as the essential criterion for evaluating the authority of a corpus: '. . . a study of the patterning of infrequent words is doomed [in a sample corpus], and indeed the only words for which it is reliable are those which occur in a good range of genres' (Sinclair, 1991: 24). For Sinclair, the study of *vocabulary* requires a large, even unlimited quantity of texts: the Bank of English has no fixed limit (Sinclair 1991, Chapter 1) and he considers such 'monitor' corpora to be theoretically sounder than any attempt at pre-selection. To some extent, the usefulness of a particular corpus will depend on the type of investigation the student wishes to undertake. If the problem is one of *low-frequency words* – e.g. 'Here the harmony praised by Mrs Ramsay is completely abolished.' (ICLE) – they could either look at a very large corpus which has been designed to let users view the data from a number of perspectives (e.g. genre, thematic area, mode), or study a highly specialised corpus of texts which exemplify genres and contents that are directly relevant to their needs. If, on the other hand, the problem is connected mainly with *high-frequency words*, – e.g. the MAKE/DO contrast – or *grammar*, learners will find most of what they need in a smaller, representative corpus of general English such as LOB.

When, by contrast, the learner's problem relates specifically to genre – a student may for example have difficulty in using argument organising vocabulary in an *essay* – then a small, highly specialised corpus of NS student essays such as the LOCNESS corpus may be a very useful option, and will certainly be the nearest analogue to the texts the learners themselves wish to write. Alternatively, they could turn to a collection of texts which are similar to essays – e.g. newspaper editorials, encyclopaedia entries – but which are written by authoritative, expert writers. Ultimately, it comes down to the question of how specifically genre- or topic-related the feature for investigation is. It is natural for learners to want to base themselves on what Bazerman (1994: 131) calls *expert performance*, but if truly comparable *expert performance* does not exist, then the EFL writer can learn much about a variety of language features from the work of educated non-expert writers.

In summary, there are three broad categories of text collection that learners may wish to investigate as they move towards increased effectiveness in their target language: large general corpora, or highly selective subsets tightly matched to their needs and interests; smaller representative corpora; and collections of comparable NS and NNS learner writing. Given that it is now relatively easy to have access to such text collections (BNC, The Bank of English and many specialised journalistic and academic text sources are now available on the Internet) how can teachers begin to use this sort of information in the language learning classroom?

6 NNS learner data in the language learning classroom

As an example of a working methodology for using NNS learner data in the language classroom we shall focus on problems of under- and overuse. In our opinion, this is one of the main areas where NNS learner data can assist language teachers as it allows teachers to confirm or disconfirm their intuitions about the way in which their students use the target language in comparison with other groups. Indeed, perhaps the greatest gain comes from the way in which the NNS corpus shows what is absent in learner writing. Ham and Rundell (1994: 178) have already clearly demonstrated the relative lexical poverty of most learner output in their discussion of what they call the *default terms* (such as *interesting, important*) which predominate in learner text. We shall consider a practical classroom solution to this sort of problem.

As we saw above, teachers and dictionary makers are aware of the tendency of learners to be too dependent on superordinates in their writing – using words such as *important* to the exclusion of words with a higher degree of specificity such as *critical/crucial/major/serious/significant/vital*, and so on. A comparison of high-frequency vocabulary in the Louvain corpus of advanced French students writing in English (see Table 15.1) revealed the following adjectives as being used markedly more frequently by the NNS group when compared with the wordlist of a core subset of the BNC – i.e. the learners in this group tended to use these words with a significantly greater frequency than proficient NS writers writing in a broad range of genres and text types. This analysis was carried out using Mike Scott's *WordSmith Tools* program (Scott 1996). The program allows for the meaningful comparison of the relative frequency of words in a small corpus (e.g. Louvain French Learners Corpus – 227,964 words) with frequencies in a larger reference corpus (in this instance, Core BNC – 1,080,072 words).

Table 15.1: Adjective overuse in the learner corpus

Word	Louvain	Core BNC	Log-likelihood
real	244 (0.11%)	193 (0.02%)	326.8
different	305 (0.13%)	441 (0.04%)	225.5
important	260 (0.11%)	343 (0.03%)	215.5
longer	162 (0.07%)	176 (0.02%)	165.5
true	173 (0.08%)	212 (0.02%)	156.0

If a teacher decided to focus on students' overuse of *important* the following activity provides a basis for remedial work. Such an activity can easily be adapted to provide vocabulary enhancement exercises to help learners increase their awareness of other words that they tend to underuse. (In the example below, indefinite articles have been edited to prevent learners using them as disambiguators.)

In much student writing 'important' is a word that is used very frequently. The concordance samples below have been edited to remove all instances of 'important'. The attached concordance information will help you to complete the tasks below – as will an appropriate reference work such as the *Longman Language Activator* or the *COBUILD Collocations* CD ROM.

Task 1 Extend your vocabulary by deciding which of the words in the list below would make the best replacement for 'important' in following contexts given here – in some instances it would be better to continue to use 'important'.

Task 2 Using the corpus data you have been studying and other reference works, make a list of the nouns which collocate strongly with each of the adjectives given in the list.

Alternative word list: critical / crucial / major / serious / significant / vital

1.	nd imagine. This is the first and most	________	advantage of science and tech
2.	nimal and human lives. One of the most	________	consequence of pollution is th
3.	shown that they could work hard, take	________	decisions, and become involved
4.	ties seem to ignore completely another	________	factor people are slaves to:
5.	efficiency seem to be some of the all	________	factors in our hypersophistica
6.	television set. This has of course a(n)	________	impact on our mind: we are, ev
7.	e cause of women." This raises an	________	issue: according to me people
8.	g the environment. Air-pollution is a(n)	________	kind of pollution. Without be
9.	e in a world where television plays a(n)	________	part and it is highly probable
10.	ir reintegration in society. This is a(n)	________	point because in a sane and c
11.	itely answer this question. A third	________	problem is the polution due to
12.	the choice of the programmes, the most	________	question seems to be: Does te
13.	s in so critical a situation. The most	________	reason is pollution. Gas from
14.	concerned, it is the object of a very	________	requirement in the world of ad
15.	he influence of the media also plays a(n)	________	role. According to the announ

Example concordance output (two or three pages of this sort of information can be provided for groups of learners)

11 ungal Diseases Fungi cause many **serious** diseases of animals. Aspergillus fungi may
12 ion in the history of medicine. **Serious** diseases were of primary interest to early
13 leukosis complex, resulting in **serious** economic loss. Influenza viruses cause ser
14 hnical offside. If offences are **serious** enough a referee can caution a player (sho
15 ssfully inoculated against many **serious** feline diseases. Kittens should be inocula
16 ge earners are themselves under **serious** financial pressure. It is no easier politi
17 nt of industrial capitalism had **serious** human costs. The early days of the Industr

18 opped by the referee to prevent **serious** injury to contestants who have not been kn
19 ion. Poisonous plants may cause **serious** losses, usually in particular locations or
20 neffective for treating certain **serious** mental disorders. Two early attempts to tr
21 or dangerous fashion. Two more **serious** offences are kicking or trying to kick ano
22 t free kick is awarded for more **serious** offences such as intentional fouls or misc
23 t free kick is awarded for more **serious** offences and if these occur in the penalty
24 ly that rabbit control became a **serious** problem. In Australia a virus deadly only
25 being unable to find a job is a **serious** problem. Because of its human costs in dep
26 rn factories felt the impact of **serious** problems in manufacturing industries, espe
27 c loss. Influenza viruses cause **serious** problems in pigs, horses, and birds. Some
28 rld to revive table tennis as a **serious** sport. A meeting held in 1926 in Berlin am

ETC. . . . ETC. . . .

Source Microsoft Encarta

The example activity above demonstrates ways in which it is possible to combine insights derived from learner text with data taken from a highly specialised micro-corpus (Tribble 1996b). The following activity looks at a different type of vocabulary – that involved in text organisation.

Clearly, the area of text organisation can be a more difficult one to work in (although see Aston 1996) because a wide context is needed and learner text may display other problems which can distract from the main task. However, pronoun use, choice of passive vs. active, and so forth still offer possibilities and the approach can be particularly useful for connectors, a major problem for learners. One way of using data from a NNS and NS essay corpus as means of helping learners to develop an understanding of how essays qua text are organised is to use whole texts in a cycle of reformulation and discussion. Such an approach was originally proposed as a practice in composition classes where students would consider an example of work produced by a member of their class (Cohen 1983; Allwright et al. 1988). However, it has also been successfully applied to examples drawn from collections of texts *not* originating from the group involved in instruction (Tribble 1990, 1996a). Reformulation is in effect a practical genre analysis activity in which students compare two versions of a text – one written by an apprentice, the other a sympathetic reformulation of that text by an expert writer.

If a teacher does wish to consider problems that learners have with explicit text organising vocabulary, a comparison of NS and NNS data can still be very fruitful. The 'keywords' feature of *WordSmith* (Scott 1996) provides a more lexically oriented means of identifying where there may be problems. Applying this tool to the Louvain corpus can reveal words or phrases specifically implicated in text organisation that are significantly overused, as well as those that are used less frequently in the development of learners' arguments. In cases of apparent overuse,

Table 15.2: Frequency of *moreover*

Louvain Corpus	Core BNC
125 (0.05%)	30 (0.003%)

the same technique as that outlined in the *important* activity above can be used. For example, a keyword analysis of the Louvain corpus revealed that *moreover* is used a great deal more frequently in the French learner text when compared with the Core BNC corpus (see Table 15.2).

A potential explanation for this overuse is that French learners tend to see *moreover* as a slightly more elegant synonym for *also* – or even the simple conjunction *and*. What is happening is that learners are missing the main reason for using *moreover* – (and its close equivalent *furthermore*) – which the *Longman Language Activator* describes as 'formal words used to introduce more information that will help persuade people to agree with what you are saying.' A KWIC (Key Word In Context) concordance for *moreover* is not particularly informative as it does not provide sufficient information to the learner. However, if an extended context is provided (using a wordprocessor rather than a concordance to identify appropriate instances in the corpus), it is possible to give learners sufficient spans of text for a useful discussion of which words might be more appropriately used. A list of alternatives such as that provided by the *Longman Language Activator* can also be useful (*and, also, furthermore/moreover, besides, in addition, likewise*). If learners have access to appropriate corpus material, there is enormous scope for their own investigation of the role that vocabulary plays in discourse organisation and the sorts of problems that learners face in making appropriate lexical choice.

7 A word of caution

None of this is to say that corpus studies and DDL are going to have a magical impact on language learning and teaching. As Hawkins (1984: 3) says: 'Awareness of language in the curriculum is no panacea to cure all ills', and the same applies to DDL – it is a new methodology, and raises as many questions as it might appear to answer. First there is the issue of proficiency level raised by Johns (1994: 311) when he comments: 'many questions remain unanswered – for example, whether the approach can be adapted for use with beginners or near-beginners.' Although DDL might seem especially appropriate for advanced learners, Tribble and Jones (1990: 37) give examples of tasks which start students looking at corpora at an early point in language learning.

Perhaps more important is the question of learning style: 'Given the possibility of measuring parameters such as aptitude, intelligence, motivation and cognitive style, is success with DDL associated with a particular parameter or parameters?'(Johns, 1994: 312). In her evaluation of a concordance-based vocabulary package, Packard (1994: 221–2) found that approximately the same number of students found the package 'not very useful' or 'not at all useful' and 'quite useful' or 'very useful'. She concludes that such a package 'will appeal only to a limited number and type of students' and that concordance-based exercises should be viewed as an addition to vocabulary learning techniques: 'They are by no means a replacement for, but could be viewed as complementary to, the traditional, continuous cloze passages, learning of vocabulary through semantic fields, analysis of common roots etc.'

Other considerations include the choice of concordanced items and choice of output format. For example, some linguistic forms lend themselves better to analysis in KWIC format than others. Others, such as use of tenses require a wider context – either sentence or paragraph. As the same caveat applies to major features such as articles (generic vs. specific) or use of pronouns (e.g. *this* vs. *that*), it is important not to 'force' structures into a single type of exercise or to feel that KWIC output is the only way of handling corpus data. The same caveat applies to the issue of concordance editing: concordances need to be carefully edited to help learners find the relevant features. If vast quantities of information is thrown at learners there is a considerable risk that DDL activities can become time-consuming and frustrating for learners. Ma's (1994) investigation has shown that learners sometimes feel confused by concordances, especially when there are many lines in the output.

As a final comment, we would like to stress the importance of follow-up exercises as a way of avoiding the danger of presenting learners with incorrect input when they are working with learner text. When investigative work into learner *problems* is done it is important to stress correct or appropriate use in consolidating exercises. Teachers and learners need to remember that the main interest of NS/NNS comparison is to make learners 'notice' – especially in the case of fossilised errors. After all, the major advantage of DDL is that it presents language as 'an intriguing mystery to be explored' (Hawkins 1984: 138). In such a paradigm learners can become active participants in this 'voyage of discovery into the patterns of the language' (ibid.: 150), a voyage which may induce increased motivation for foreign language learning, including some of its hitherto least popular components, such as grammar.

List of linguistic software mentioned in this book

Birmingham Tagger (POS tagger)
Contact http://www-clg.bham.ac.uk/tagger.html
Brill Tagger (POS tagger)
By anonymous ftp blaze.cs.jhu.edu/pub/brill/Programs
CLAWS (POS tagger)
Contact A.Wilson@lancaster.ac.uk
Combinator (see **Tuples**)
Correct Grammar (grammar and style checker)
Contact Lifetree Software, 33 New Montgomery Street, Suite 1260, San Francisco, CA 94105, USA
ENGCG (POS tagger and parser)
Send an empty subject message to engcg-info@ling.helsinki.fi
Grammatik (grammar and style checker)
Contact Reference Software International, 330 Townsend Street, Suite 123, San Francisco, CA 94107, USA
TACT (text retrieval program)
Contact cch@epas.utoronto.ca
TOSCA analysis environment (POS tagger and parser)
Contact tosca@let.kun.nl
TOSCA Tree Editor (syntactic annotation software)
Contact tosca@let.kun.nl
Tuples (recurrent word combination extractor)
Contact mcenery@comp.lancs.ac.uk
VocabProfile (lexical frequency software)
Contact Paul.Nation@vuw.ac.nz
WordCruncher (text retrieval program)
Contact Johnston and Company, PO Box 446, American Fork, UT 84003, USA
WORDS (word counting program)
E-mail: langners@columbia.dsu.edu
WordSmith Tools (text retrieval program)

Contact http://wwwl.oup.co.uk/cite/oup/elt/software/wsmith
Xanadu (tool for the annotation of cohesive relationships)
Contact rgg@comp.lancs.ac.uk (Roger Garside)
Xerox Tagger (POS tagger)
Contact http://www.xerox.com/lexdemo/xlt-overview.html

Bibliography

Aarts, J. and **Oostdijk, N.** (in preparation) Handling discourse elements in syntax.

Aijmer, K. (1996) *Conversational Routines in English: Convention and Creativity*. Longman, London and New York.

Aijmer, K., Altenberg, B. and **Johansson, M.** (1996) Text-based contrastive studies in English. Presentation of a project. In Aijmer, K., Altenberg, B. and Johansson, M. (eds) *Languages in Contrast. Papers from a Symposium on Text-based Cross-linguistic Studies Lund 4–5 March 1994*. Lund University Press, Lund, pp. 73–85.

Alexander, L.G. (1965) *Essay and Letter Writing*. Longman, London.

Allwright, R.L., Woodley, M-P. and **Allwright, J.M.** (1988) Investigating reformulation as a practical strategy for the teaching of academic writing, *Applied Linguistics* **9(3)**: 237–58.

Altenberg, B. (1984) Causal linking in spoken and written English, *Studia Linguistica* **38**: 20–69.

Altenberg, B. (1986) Contrastive linking in spoken and written English. In Tottie, G. and Bäcklund, I. (eds) *English in Speech and Writing: A Symposium*. Almqvist and Wiksell, Stockholm, pp. 13–40.

Altenberg, B. (1990) Speech as linear composition. In Caie, G., Haastrup, K. Jakobsen, A.L., Nielsen, J.E., Sevaldse, J., Specht, H. and Zettersten, A. (eds) *Proceedings from the Fourth Nordic Conference for English Studies*, Helsingoz, May 11–13, 1989, Department of English, Copenhagen University, pp. 133–43.

Altenberg, B. (1991) A bibliography of publications relating to English computer corpora. In Johansson, S. and Stenström, A-B. (eds) *English Computer Corpora: Selected Papers and Research Guide*. Mouton de Gruyter, Berlin and New York, pp. 355–96.

Altenberg, B. (1993) Recurrent verb-complement constructions in the London-Lund Corpus. In Aarts, J., de Haan, P. and Oostdijk, N. (eds) *English Language Corpora: Design, Analysis and Exploitation*. Rodopi, Amsterdam, pp. 227–45.

Altenberg, B. (1996) Exploring the Swedish subcorpus of ICLE. Paper presented at the 11th World Congress of Applied Linguistics (AILA), Jyväskylä, Finland, 4–9 August.

Altenberg, B. (forthcoming) On the phraseology of spoken English: the evidence of recurrent word combinations. In Cowie, A. (ed.) *Phraseology: Theory, Analysis and Applications*. Oxford University Press, Oxford.

Altenberg, B. and **Eeg-Olofsson, M.** (1990) Phraseology in spoken English: presentation of a project. In Aarts, J. and Meijs, W. (eds) *Theory and Practice in Corpus Linguistics*. Rodopi, Amsterdam and Atlanta, pp. 1–26.

Arnold, J. and **Harmer, J.** (1978) *Advanced Writing Skills*. Longman, London.

Aston, G. (1996) Corpora in language pedagogy: matching theory and practice. In Cook, G. and Seidlhofer, B. (eds) *Principle and Practice in Applied Linguistics: Studies in Honour of H.G. Widdowson*. Oxford University Press, Oxford, pp. 257–70.

Atkins, S. and **Clear, J.** (1992) Corpus design criteria, *Literary and Linguistic Computing* **7(1)**: 1–16.

Atwell, E. and **Elliott, S.** (1987) Dealing with ill-formed English text. In Garside, R., Leech, G. and Sampson, G. (eds) *The Computational Analysis of English*. Longman, London, pp. 120–38.

Baayen, H., Van Halteren, H. and **Tweedie, F.** (1996) Outside the cave of shadows: using syntactic annotation to enhance authorship attribution, *Liter-*

...e pragmatics of formulas in L2

...*of Pragmatics* **10**: 693–723.

...ary tales, *Literary and Linguistic*

...*Discourse*. Macmillan, London.

... Edinburgh University Press,

...*o Better Writing in Course Work*

...thern Illinois University Press,

...tice: an ethnographic appraisal,

...g. Cambridge University Press,

...*: A Cross-linguistic Comparison.*

...ough corpus-based analyses of

...*rpus Linguistics* **1**: 171–97.

...nce types in English, *Discourse*

...pus-based approaches to issues

... 169–89.

...Corpus-based investigations of

...*tics* **16**: 115–36.

...ng) *Corpus-based Perspectives on*

...rsity Press, Cambridge.

Biber, D., Johansson, S., Leech, G., Conrad, S. and **Finegan, E.** (forthcoming) *Longman Grammar of Spoken and Written English*. Longman, London.

Black, E., Garside, R. and **Leech, G.** (1993) *Statistically-driven Computer Grammars of English: The IBM/Lancaster Approach*. Rodspin, Amsterdam.

Bolt, P. (1992) An evaluation of grammar-checking programs as self-helping learning aids for learners of English as a foreign language, *CALL* **5**: 49–91.

Modality in LOCNESS corpus vs Swedish (ICLE) Corpus.

Bradley, J. (1996) TACT and SGML together at last: sgml2tdb. *Conference Abstracts ALLC-ACH '96*. Norwegian Computing Centre for the Humanities, Bergen, pp. 42–3.

Brodda, B. (1991) Doing corpus work with PC Beta; or, how to be your own computational linguist. In Johansson, S. and Stenström, A-B. (eds) *English Computer Corpora: Selected Papers and Research Guide*. Mouton de Gruyter, Berlin and New York, pp. 259–82.

Burnard, L. (1995) *The British National Corpus Users Reference Guide*. SGML Version. Oxford University Computing Services, Oxford.

Carroll, S. and **Swain, M.** (1993) Explicit and negative feedback. An empirical study of the learning of linguistic generalizations, *Studies in Second Language Acquisition* **15**: 357–86.

Carter, R.A. (1987) Is there a core vocabulary? Some implications for language teaching, *Applied Linguistics* **8(2)**: 178–92.

Chafe, W.L. (1982) Integration and involvement in speaking, writing and oral literature. In Tannen, D. (ed.) *Spoken and Written Language: Exploring Orality and Literacy*. Ablex, Norwood, pp. 35–53.

Chafe, W.L. and **Danielewicz, J.** (1987) Properties of spoken and written language. In Horowitz, R. and Samuels, S.J. (eds) *Comprehending Oral and Written Language*. Academic Press, San Diego, pp. 83–113.

Channell, J. (1994) *Vague Language*. Oxford University Press, Oxford.

Church, K. and **Gale, W.** (1991) A comparison of the enhanced good-turing and deleted estimation methods for estimating probabilities of English bigrams, *Computer Speech and Language*, **5(1)**: 19–54.

Cohen, A.D. (1983) Reformulating compositions, *TESOL Newsletter*, **XVII(6)**: 1–5.

Collins Cobuild English Collocations on CD Rom (1995) Harper Collins, London.

Collinson, D.J. (1990) *Writing English. A Working Guide to the Skills of Written English*. Wildwood House, Aldershot.

Connor, U. and **Lauer, J.** (1985) Understanding persuasive essay writing: linguistic/rhetorical approach, *Text* **5(4)**: 309–26.

Corder, S.P. (1981) *Error Analysis and Interlanguage*. Oxford University Press, Oxford.

Crewe, W.J. (1990) The illogic of logical connectors, *ELT Journal* **44**: 316–25.

Crismore, A., **Markkanen, R.** and **Steffensen, M.S.** (1993) Metadiscourse in persuasive writing, *Written Communication* **10(1)**: 39–71.

Crowdy, S. (1994) Spoken corpus transcription, *Literary and Linguistic Computing*, **9(1)**: 25–8.

Crystal, D. (1987) *The Cambridge Encyclopedia of Language*. Cambridge University Press, Cambridge.

Crystal, D. (1991) Stylistic profiling. In Aijmer, K. and Altenberg, B. (eds) *English Corpus Linguistics*. Longman, London and New York, pp. 221–38.

Crystal, D. and **Davy, D.** (1975) *Advanced Conversational English*. Longman, London.

Dagneaux, E., **Denness, S.** and **Granger, S.** (forthcoming) *Computer-aided Error Analysis*.

Davis, P. (1989) *English Structure in Focus*. Newbury House, New York.

De Cock, S. (1996) Formulaic expressions in the speech of native and non-native speakers of English. Unpublished MA dissertation, Lancaster University, Lancaster.

de Haan, P. (1992) The optimum corpus sample size? In Leitner, G. (ed.) *New Directions in English Language Corpora*. Mouton de Gruyter, Berlin and New York, pp. 3–19.

Devito, J. (1966) Psychogrammatical factors in oral and written discourse by skilled communicators, *Speech Monographs* **33**: 73–6.

Devito, J. (1967) Levels of abstraction in spoken and written language, *Journal of Communication* **17**: 354–61.

Dines, E.R. (1980) Variation in discourse 'and stuff like that', *Language in Society* **9**: 13–31.

Dirven, R. (ed.) (1989) *A User's Grammar of English: Word, Sentence, Text, Interaction*. Peter Lang, Frankfurt am Main.

Dulay, H., Burt, M. and **Krashen, S.** (1982) *Language Two*. Oxford University Press, New York.

Dunning, T. (1993) Accurate methods for the statistics of surprise and coincidence, *Computational Linguistics* **19(1)**: 61–74.

Dunning, T. (1994) Statistical identification of language. In *CLR Tech Report*. Computing Research Laboratory, New Mexico State University, Las Crices, pp. 94–273.

Edwards, J. (1992) Design principles in the transcription of spoken discourse. In Svartvik, J. (ed.) *Directions in Corpus Linguistics*. Mouton de Gruyter, Berlin and New York, pp. 129–44.

Ellis, R. (1991) Grammar teaching – practice or consciousness-raising. In Ellis, R. *Second Language Acquisition and Second Language Pedagogy*. Multilingual Matters, Clevedon.

Ellis, R. (1994) *The Study of Second Language Acquisition*. Oxford University Press, Oxford.

Engwall, G. (1994) Not chance but choice: criteria in corpus creation. In Atkins, G. and Zampolli, A. (eds) *Computational Approaches to the Lexicon*. Calderon Press, Oxford, pp. 49–82.

Faerch, C., Haastrup, K. and **Phillipson, R.** (1984) *Learner Language and Language Learning*. Multilingual Matters, Clevedon.

Felton, R. (1996) A new procedure for author attribution. In *ALLC-ACH '96. Conference Abstracts*. Norwegian Computing Centre for the Humanities, University of Bergen, 74–5.

Fillmore, C. (1978) On the organization of semantic information in the lexicon. In Farkas, D., Jacobsen, W. and Todrys, K. (eds) *Papers form the Parasession on the Lexicon*. Chicago Linguistic Society, Chicago, pp. 148–73.

Fillmore, C. (1992) 'Corpus linguistics' or 'Computer-aided armchair linguistics'. In Svartvik, J. (ed.) *Directions in Corpus Linguistics*. Mouton de Gruyter, Berlin and New York, pp. 35–60.

Fitikides, T.J. (1936) *Common Mistakes in English*. Longman, London.

Fligelstone, S. (1992) Developing a scheme for annotating text to show anaphoric relations. In Leitner, G. (ed.) *New Directions in English Language Corpora*. Mouton de Gruyter, Berlin, pp. 153–70.

Flower, L. (1981) *Problem-Solving Strategies for Writing*. Harcourt Brace Jovanovich, New York.

Flowerdew, J. (1993) An educational or process approach to the teaching of professional genres, *ELTJ* **47(4)**: 305–16.

Flowerdew, J. and **Tauroza, S.** (1995) The effect of discourse markers on second language lecture comprehension, *Studies in Second Language Acquisition* **17**: 435–58.

Fowler, H.R. (1986) *The Little, Brown Handbook.* Little, Brown, Boston.

Francis, G. (1986) *Anaphoric Nouns.* English Language Research, Birmingham.

Francis, G. (1994) Labelling discourse: an aspect of nominal-group lexical cohesion. In Coulthard, M. (ed.) *Advances in Written Text Analysis.* Routledge, London, pp. 83–101.

Francis, W.N. and **Kučera, H.** (1982) *Frequency Analysis of English Usage: Lexicon and Grammar.* Houghton Mifflin, Boston.

Fries, P.H. (1994) On theme, rheme and discourse goals. In Coulthard, M. (ed.) *Advances in Written Text Analysis.* Routledge, London, pp. 229–49.

Gardner, K. (forthcoming) Computer-assisted grammar proof-reading.

Garside, R. (1993) The marking of cohesive relationships: tools for the construction of a large database of anaphoric data, *ICAME* **17**: 5–27.

Glover, A. and **Hirst, G.** (1996) Detecting Stylistic Inconsistencies in Collaborative Writing. In Sharples, M. and van der Geest, T. (eds) *The New Writing Environment.* Springer-Verlag, London, pp. 147–67.

Granger, S. (1993) The International Corpus of Learner English. In Aarts, J., de Haan, P. and Oostdijk, N. (eds) *English Language Corpora: Design, Analysis and Exploitation.* Rodopi, Amsterdam, pp. 57–69.

Granger, S. (1994) The learner corpus: a revolution in applied linguistics, *English Today* **39(10/3)**: 25–9.

Granger, S. (1996a) From CA to CIA and back: an integrated approach to computerized bilingual and learner corpora. In Aijmer, K., Altenberg, B. and Johansson, M. (eds) *Languages in Contrast: Papers from a Symposium on Text-based Cross-linguistic Studies Lund 4–5 March 1994.* Lund University Press, Lund, pp. 37–51.

Granger, S. (1996b) Romance words in English: from history to pedagogy. In Svartvik, J. (ed.) *Words. Proceedings of an International Symposium.* Almqvist and Wiksell, Stockholm, pp. 105–21.

Granger, S. (forthcoming a) Automated retrieval of passives from native and learner corpora: precision and recall, *Journal of English Linguistics.*

Granger, S. (forthcoming b) On identifying the syntactic and discourse features of participle clauses in academic English: native and non-native writers compared. In Aarts, J. and Wekker, H. (eds) *Studies in English Language Research and Teaching.* Rodopi, Amsterdam and Atlanta.

Granger, S. (forthcoming c) Prefabricated patterns in advanced EFL writing: collocations and formulae. In Cowie, A. (ed.) *Phraseology: Theory, Analysis and Applications.* Oxford University Press, Oxford.

Granger, S. and **Meunier, F.** (1994) Towards a grammar checker for learners of English. In Fries, U. and Tottie, G. (eds) *Creating and Using English Language Corpora.* Rodopi: Amsterdam and Atlanta, pp. 79–89.

Granger, S. and **Tyson, S.** (1996) Connector usage in the English essay writing of native and non-native EFL speakers of English, *World Englishes* **15**: 19–29.

Granger, S., Meunier, F. and **Tyson, S.** (1994) New insights into the learner lexicon: a preliminary report from the International Corpus of Learner English. In Flowerdew, L. and Tong, A.K.K. (eds) *Entering Text.* The Hong Kong University of Science and Technology, Hong Kong, pp. 102–13.

Hakuta, K. (1974) Prefabricated patterns and the emergence of structure in second language acquisition, *Language Learning* **24(2)**: 491–8.

Halliday, M.A.K. (1985) *An Introduction to Functional Grammar*. Arnold, London.

Halliday, M.A.K. and **Hasan, R.** (1976) *Cohesion in English*. Longman, London.

Ham, N. and **Rundell, M.** (1994) A new conceptual map of English. In Martin, W., Meijs, W., Moerland, M., ten Pas, E., van Sterkenburg, P. and P. Vossen (eds) *Euralex '94 Proceedings*. Papers submitted to the 6th Euralex International Congress on Lexicography. Amsterdam, The Netherlands pp. 172–80.

Hammerly, H. (1991) *Fluency and Accuracy. Towards Balance in Language Teaching and Learning*. Multilingual Matters, Clevedon, Philadelphia and Adelaide.

Hamp-Lyons, L. and **Heasley, B.** (1987) *Study Writing*. Cambridge University Press, Cambridge.

Hanania, A. and **Gradman, H.** (1977) Acquisition of English structures: a case study of an adult native speaker of Arabic in an English-speaking environment, *Language Learning* **27**: 75–91.

Harris, J. (1993) *Introducing Writing*. Penguin English, London.

Hasselgren, A. (1994) Lexical teddy bears and advanced learners: a study into the ways Norwegian students cope with English vocabulary, *International Journal of Applied Linguistics* **4**: 237–58.

Hawkins, E. (1984) *Awareness of Language: An Introduction*. Cambridge University Press, Cambridge.

Hayashi, K. (1995) Form-focused instruction and second language proficiency, *RELC Journal* **26(1)**: 95–115.

Hayward, K. and **Wilcoxon, H.C.** (1994) Connectives in context, *English Teaching Forum* **32(3)**: 20–3.

Herdan, G. (1960) *Type-Token Mathematics: A Textbook of Mathematical Linguistics*. Mouton, The Hague.

Hofland, K. and **Johansson, S.** (1982) *Word Frequencies in British and American English*. The Norwegian Computing Centre for the Humanities, Bergen.

Holmes, D. (1994) Authorship attribution, *Computers and the Humanities* **28**: 87–106.

Huang, J. and **Hatch, E.** (1978) A Chinese child's acquisition of English. In Hatch, E. (ed.) *Second Language Acquisition. A Book of Readings*. Newbury House, Rowley, MA, pp. 118–31.

Hulstijn, J. and **Marchena, E.** (1989) Avoidance: grammatical or semantic causes?, *Studies in Second Language Acquisition* **11**: 241–55.

Hunt, K.W. (1970) Do sentences in the second language grow like those in the first?, *TESOL Quarterly* **4(3)**: 195–202.

Hutchinson, J. and **Barnett, R.** (1996) Review of Karlson et al., 1995, *ICAME* **20**: 77–86.

Isaksson-Wikberg, M. (1992) A Cross-cultural Study of American and Finland-Swedish Rhetoric and Argumentative Composition, with Special Reference to EFL Composition Teaching. Unpublished Licentiate thesis, Åbo Akademi University, Åbo.

Isaksson-Wikberg, M. (1996) Contrastive rhetoric: American and Finland-Swedish school-based argument. Paper presented at the 11th World Congress of Applied Linguistics (AILA), Jyväskylä, Finland, 4–9 August.

Ivanič, R. (1991) Nouns in search of a context: a study of nouns with both open- and closed-system characteristics, *International Review of Applied Linguistics* **29(2)**: 93–114.

Jagtman, M. (1994) COMOLA: a computer system for the analysis of interlanguage data, *Second Language Research* **10(1)**: 49–83.

James, C. (1992) Awareness, consciousness and language contrast. In Mair, C. and Markus, M. (eds) *New Departures in Contrastive Linguistics*. Anglistische Reihe Band 5. Innsbrucker Beiträge zur Kulturwissenschaft, pp. 183–97.

James, K. (1994) Don't shoot my dodo: on the resilience of contrastive and error analysis, *IRAL* **32**: 179–200.

Jarvis, S. (forthcoming) The role of L1-based concepts in L2 lexical reference. PhD thesis, Indiana University, Bloomington.

Johansson, S. (1978) *Some Aspects of the Vocabulary of Learned and Scientific English*. Acta Universitatis Gothoburgensis, Göteborg.

Johansson, S. (1985) Word frequency and text type: some observations based on the LOB corpus of British texts, *Computers and the Humanities* **19**: 23–36.

Johansson, S. (1994) Encoding a corpus in machine-readable form: the approach of the text encoding initiative. In Atkins, B. and Zampolli, A. (eds) *Computational Approaches to the Lexicon*. Calderon Press, Oxford, pp. 83–102.

Johns, T. (1991) Should you be persuaded – two examples of data-driven learning materials, *English Language Research Journal* **4**: 1–16.

Johns, T. (1994) From printout to handout: grammar and vocabulary teaching in the context of data-driven learning. In Odlin, T. (ed.) *Perspectives on Pedagogical Grammar*. Cambridge University Press, Cambridge, pp. 293–317.

Johns, T. and **King, P.** (eds) (1991) Classroom Concordancing, *ELR Journal* (New Series) **4**.

Johnson, E. (1995) Counting words and computing word frequency. Project report: WORDS, *Text and Technology* **5(1)**: 8–17.

Johnson, K. (1994) Teaching declarative and procedural knowledge. In Bygate, M., Tonkyn, A. and Williams, E. (eds) *Grammar and the Language Teacher*. Prentice Hall, London, pp. 121–31.

Jordan, R.R. (1990) *Academic Writing Course* (new edition). Collins ELT, London.

Jörgenson, N. and **Svensson, J.** (1986) *Nusvensk grammatik*. Liber, Malmö.

Källkvist, M. (1993) The characteristics and use of English vocabulary by advanced foreign learners. Unpublished M Phil thesis, University of Cambridge.

Kamimoto, T., Shimura, A. and **Kellerman, E.** (1992) A second language classic reconsidered – the case of Schachter's avoidance, *Second Language Research* **8(3)**: 251–77.

Karlsson, A., Voutilainen, A., Heikkilä, J. and **Antilla, A.** (1995) *Constraint Grammar: A Language-independent System for Parsing Unrestricted Texts*. Mouton de Gruyter, Berlin.

Kellerman, E. (1995) Crosslinguistic influence: transfer to nowhere?. *Annual Review of Applied Linguistics* **15**: 125–50.

Kennedy, G. (1996) The corpus as a research domain. In Greenbaum, S. (ed.) *Comparing English Worldwide*. Clarendon Press, Oxford, pp. 217–26.

Kjellmer, G. (1991) A mint of phrases. In Aijmer, K. and Altenberg, B. (eds) *English Corpus Linguistics*. Longman, London and New York, pp. 111–27.

Koessler, M. and **Derocquigny, J.** (1975) *Les Faux Amis des Vocabulaires Anglais et Américain*. Vuibert, Paris.

Korhonen, R. and **Kusch, M.** (1989) The rhetorical function of the first person in philosophical texts – the influence of intellectual style, paradigm and language. In Kusch, M. and Schröder, H. (eds) *Text, Interpretation, Argumentation*. Helmut Buske, Hamburg, pp. 61–77.

Krashen, S. (1981) *Second Language Acquisition and Second Language Learning*. Pergamon, Oxford.

Krzeszowski, T. (1990) *Contrasting Languages. The Scope of Contrastive Linguistics*. Mouton de Gruyter, Berlin and New York.

Lakoff, R.T. (1982) Some of my favorite writers are literate: the mingling of oral and literate strategies in written communication. In Tannen, D. (ed.) *Spoken and Written Language: Exploring Orality and Literacy*. Ablex, Norwood, pp. 239–60.

Larsen-Freeman, D. (Series Director) (1993) *Grammar Dimensions: Form, Meaning, and Use*. (Four-book series) Heinle and Heinle, Boston.

Larsen-Freeman, D. and **Long, M.** (1991) *An Introduction to Second Language Acquisition Research*. Longman, London and New York.

Laufer, B. and **Eliasson, S.** (1993) What causes avoidance in L2 learning: L1–L2-difference, L1–L2 similarity, or L2 complexity?, *Studies in Second Language Acquisition* **15**: 35–48.

Leech, G. (1992) Corpora and theories of linguistic performance. In Svartvik, J. (ed.) *Directions in Corpus Linguistics*. Mouton de Gruyter, Berlin, pp. 105–22.

Leech, G. (1993) Corpus Annotation Schemes, *Literary and Linguistic Computing* **8(4)**: 275–81.

Leech, G. and **Garside, R.** (1991) Running a grammar factory: the production of syntactically analysed corpora or 'Treebanks'. In Johansson, S. and Stenström, A-B. (eds) *English Computer Corpora: Selected Papers and Research Guide*. Mouton de Gruyter, Berlin and New York, pp. 15–32.

Leech, G. and **Svartvik, J.** (1994) A *Communicative Grammar of English*. Second edition. Longman, London.

Leech, G., Garside, R. and **Bryant, M.** (1994) CLAWS4: the tagging of the British National Corpus. In *Proceedings of the 15th International Conference on Computational Linguistics (COLING 94)*. Kyoto University, Japan, pp. 622–8.

Legat, M. (1989) *The Nuts and Bolts of Writing*. Robert Hale, London.

Lewis, R. (1979) *How to Write Essays*. Heinemann, Oxford.

Linnarud, M. (1975) Lexis in free production. In *Swedish-English Contrastive Studies, Report 6*. English Department, Lund University, Lund.

Linnarud, M. (1986) *Lexis in Composition. A Performance Analysis of Swedish Learners' Written English*. Lund Studies in English 74. Liber förlag, Malmö.

Ljung, M. (1991) Swedish TEFL meets reality. In Johansson, S. and Stenström, A-B. (eds) *English Computer Corpora: Selected Papers and Research Guide*. Mouton de Gruyter, Berlin and New York, pp. 245–56.

Longman Dictionary of Contemporary English (1979) Longman, London. Fourth edition.

Longman Essential Activator (1997) Longman, London.

Longman Language Activator (1993) Longman, London.

Lorenz, G. (1996) Hyperbole in advanced learners' writing: inferences from adjective intensification. Paper presented at the 11th World Congress of Applied Linguistics (AILA), Jyväskylä, Finland, 4–9 August.

Lorenz, G. (1997) *Introducing a Learner Corpus of English Writing: The Hidden Potentials of Adjective Intensification*. Rodopi, Amsterdam.

Lyne, A. (1985) *The Vocabulary of French Business Correspondance*. Slatkin-Champion, Geneva.

Ma, B. (1994) Learning strategies in ESP classroom concordancing: an initial investigation into data-driven learning. In Flowerdew, L. and Tong, A. (eds) *Entering Text*. The Hong Kong University of Science and Technology, Hong Kong, pp. 197–214.

Macpherson, R. (1994) *University English*. Wydawnictwa Szkolne i Pedagogiczne, Warszawa.

Maingay, S. and **Rundell, M.** (1987) Anticipating learners' errors – implications for dictionary writers. In Cowie, A. (ed.) *The Dictionary and the Language Learner – Papers from the EURALEX Seminar at the University of Leeds, 1–3 April 1985*. Max Niemeyer Verlag, Tübingen.

Marius, R. and **Wiener, H.S.** (1988) *The McGraw-Hill College Handbook*. Second Edition. McGraw-Hill, New York.

Mark, K. (1996) Curriculum development issues and the need for a learner corpus. Paper presented at the International Language in Education Conference, University of Hong Kong 16–18 December 1996.

Markkanen, R., Steffensen, M. and **Crismore, A.** (1993) Quantitative contrastive study of metadiscourse: problems in design and analysis of data, *Papers and Studies in Contrastive Linguistics* **28**: 137–51.

Mauranen, A. (1993) *Cultural Differences in Academic Rhetoric: A Textlinguistic Study*. Peter Lang, Frankfurt.

Mauranen, A. (1996) Discourse competence – evidence from thematic development in native and non-native texts. In Ventola, E. and Mauranen, A. (eds) *Academic Writing. Intercultural and Textual Issues*. Benjamins, Amsterdam, pp. 195–230.

McCarthy, M. (1990) *Vocabulary*. Oxford University Press, Oxford.

McEnery, T. and **Wilson, A.** (1996) *Corpus Linguistics*. Edinburgh University Press, Edinburgh.

Meunier, F. (1995) Tagging and parsing interlanguage. In Beheydt, L. (ed.) *La Linguistique Appliquée dans les années 90*. ABLA Review 16, pp. 21–9.

Meunier, F. (in preparation) *Computer corpus linguistics and interlanguage research: a longitudinal and cross-sectional study of the noun phrase.*

Milton, J. (1996) Exploiting L1 and L2 corpora for CALL design: the role of a hypertext grammar. In Botley, S.P., Glass, J., McEnery, T. and Wilson, A. (eds) *Proceedings of Teaching and Language Corpora*. UCREL Technical Papers 9 (Special Issue). Lancaster University, Lancaster, pp. 233–43.

Milton, J. (forthcoming) *Motivation and language learning in Hong Kong*.

Milton, J. and **Chowdhury, N.** (1994) Tagging the interlanguage of Chinese learners of English. In Flowerdew, L. and Tong, K.K. (eds) *Entering Text*. The Hong Kong University of Science and Technology, Hong Kong, pp. 127–43.

Milton, J. and **Freeman, R.** (1996) Lexical variation in the writing of Chinese learners of English. In Percy, C.E., Meyer, C.F. and Lancashire, I. (eds) *Synchronic Corpus Linguistics. Papers from the Sixteenth International Conference on English Language Research on Computerized Corpora*. Rodopi, Amsterdam, pp. 121–31.

Milton, J. and **Hyland, K.** (1997) Qualification and Certainty in L1 and L2 Students' Writing. *Journal of Second Language Writing* **6(2)**: 183–205.

Milton, J. and **Tsang, E.** (1993) A corpus-based study of logical connectors in EFL students' writing. In Pemberton, R. and Tsang, E. (eds) *Studies in Lexis*. Hong Kong University of Science and Technology, Hong Kong, pp. 215–46.

Nattinger, J. and **DeCarrico, J.** (1992) *Lexical Phrases and Language Teaching*. Oxford University Press, Oxford.

Nikula, T. (1996) *Pragmatic Force Modifiers: A Study in Interlanguage Pragmatics*. Studia Philologica Jyväskyläensia 39. University of Jyväskylä, Jyväskylä.

Nolasco, R. (1987) *Writing Upper-Intermediate*. Oxford University Press, Oxford.

O'Donnell, R. (1974) Syntactic differences between speech and writing, *American Speech* **49(1, 2)**: 102–10.

Odlin, T. (1989) *Language Transfer*. Cambridge University Press, Cambridge.

Oosdijk, N. and **de Haan, P.** (1994) Clause patterns in modern British English: a corpus-based (quantitative) study, *ICAME* **18**: 41–79.

Packard, V. (1994) Producing a concordance-based self-access vocabulary package: some problems and solutions. In Flowerdew, L. and Tong, A. (eds) *Entering Text*. The Hong Kong University of Science and Technology, Hong Kong, pp. 215–26.

Partington, A. (1993) Corpus evidence of language change: the case of the intensifier. In Baker, M., Francis, G. and Tognini-Bonelli, E. (eds) *Text and Technology. In Honour of John Sinclair*. Benjamins, Amsterdam, pp. 177–92.

Pery-Woodley, M.M. (1990) Contrasting discourses: contrastive analysis and a discourse approach to writing, *Language Teaching* **23**: 143–51.

Petch-Tyson, S. (forthcoming) Demonstrative expressions in argumentative discourse – a computer-based comparison of non-native and native English. In Botley, S. and McEnery, A. (eds) *Corpus-based and Computational Approaches to Discourse Anaphora*. UCL Press, London.

Pieneman, M. (1992) COALA – a computational system for interlanguage analysis, *Second Language Research* **8(1)**: 59–92.

Poole, M. and **Field, T.** (1976) A comparison of oral and written code elaboration, *Language and Speech* **19(4)**: 305–12.

Porter, N. and **Quinn, A.** (1996) Developing the ICE corpus utility program. In Greenbaum, S. (ed.) *Comparing English Worldwide*. Clarendon Press, Oxford, pp. 79–91.

Quirk, R., Greenbaum, S., Leech, G. and **Svartvik, J.** (1985) *A Comprehensive Grammar of the English Language*. Longman, London.

Raimes, A. (1983) *Techniques in Teaching Writing*. Oxford University Press, New York and Oxford.

Rayson, P., Leech, G. and **Hodges, M.** (forthcoming) Social differentiation in the use of English vocabulary: some analyses of the conversational component of the British National Corpus, *International Journal of Corpus Linguistics*.

Rayson, P. and **Wilson, A.** (1996) The ACAMRIT semantic tagging system: progress report. In Evett, L.J. and Rose, T.G. (eds) *Language Engineering for Document Analysis and Recognition, AISB96 Workshop Proceedings*. Faculty of Engineering and Computing Nottingham, England, pp. 13–20.

Renouf, A. (1992) What do you think of this: a pilot study of the phraseology of core words of English. In Leitner, G. (ed.) *New Directions in English Language Corpora*. Mouton de Gruyter, Berlin and New York, pp. 301–17.

Ringbom, H. (1992) On L1 Transfer in L2 Comprehension and L2 Production, *Language Learning* **42**: 85–112.

Ringbom, H. (ed.) (1993) *Near-native Proficiency in English*. English Department Publications, Åbo Akademi University, Åbo.

Roventini, A. (1996) Palomar: a computer-aided analysis of some lexical and stylistic features. In *ALLC-ACH '96. Conference Abstracts*. Norwegian Computing Centre for the Humanities, University of Bergen, pp. 232–7.

Rundell, M. and **Stock, P.** (1992) The corpus revolution, *English Today* **30**: 9–14.

Rutherford, W. (1987) *Second Language Grammar: Learning and Teaching*. Longman, London.

Scarcella, R. (1979) 'Watch up!': a study of verbal routines in adult second language performance, *Working Papers on Bilingualism* **19**: 79–88.

Schills, E. and **de Haan, P.** (1993) Characteristics of sentence length in running text, *Literary and Linguistic Computing* **8(3)**: 20–6.

Schmidt, R. (1990) The role of consciousness in second language learning, *Applied Linguistics* **11(2)**: 129–58.

Scholfield, P. (1995) *Quantifying Language*. Multilingual Matters, Clevedon.

Scott, M.R. (1996) *WordSmith Tools*. Oxford University Press, Oxford.

Selinker, L. (1989) CA/EA/IL: the earliest experimental record, *IRAL* **27**: 267–91.

Shimazumi, M. and **Berber Sardinha, A.P.** (1996) Approaching the assessment of performance unit archive of schoolchildren's writing from the point of view of corpus linguistics. Paper presented at TALC (Teaching and Language Corpora), University of Lancaster 3–12 August 1996.

Silva, T. (1990) Second language composition instruction: developments, issues, and directions in ESL. In Kroll, B. (ed.) *Second Language Writing*. Cambridge University Press, Cambridge, pp. 11–23.

Sinclair, J. (1986) Basic computer processing of long texts. In Leech, G. and Candlin, C. (eds) *Computers in English Language Teaching and Research*. Longman, London and New York, pp. 185–203.

Sinclair, J. (1991) *Corpus, Concordance, Collocation*. Oxford University Press, Oxford.

Sinclair, J. (1995) Corpus typology – a framework for classification. In Melchers, G. and Warren, B. (eds) *Studies in Anglistics*. Almqvist and Wiksell International, Stockholm, pp. 17–33.

Sjöholm, K. (1995) *The Influence of Crosslinguistic, Semantic and Input Factors on the Acquisition of English Phrasal Verbs. A Comparison between Finnish and Swedish Learners at an Intermediate and Advanced Level*. Åbo Akademi University Press, Åbo.

Smalley, R.L. and **Ruetten, M.K.** (1990) *Refining Composition Skills. Rhetoric and Grammar for ESL Students*. Heinle and Heinle, Boston.

Smalzer, W.R. (1996) *Write to be Read: Reading, Reflection, and Writing*. Cambridge University Press, Cambridge.

Smith, E.L. (1986) Achieving impact through the interpersonal component. In Couture, B. (ed.) *Functional Approaches to Writing*. Pinter, London, pp. 108–19.

Spitzbardt, H. (1965) English adverbs of degree and their semantic fields, *Philologia Pragensia* **8**: 349–59.

Stark, H.A. (1988) What do paragraph markings do?, *Discourse Processes* **11**: 275–303.

Stenström, A-B. (1990) Lexical items peculiar to spoken discourse. In Svartvik, J. (ed.) *The London-Lund Corpus of Spoken English. Description and Research*. Lund University Press, Lund, pp. 137–75.

Strunk, W. and **White, E.B.** (1972) *The Elements of Style*. Macmillan Publishing, New York.

Stubbs, M. (1986) Language development, lexical competence and nuclear vocabulary. In Durkin, K. (ed.) *Language Development in the School Years*. Croom Helm, London, pp. 57–76.

Stubbs, M. (1996) *Text and Corpus Analysis*. Blackwell, Oxford.

Svartvik, J. (1993) Lexis in English language corpora, *Zeitschrift für Anglistik und Amerikanistik* **41**: 15–30.

Svartvik, J. and **Ekedahl, O.** (1995) Verbs in public and private speaking. In Aarts, B. and Meyer, C. (eds) *The Verb in Contemporary English*. Cambridge University Press, Cambridge, pp. 273–89.

Swales, J.M. and **Feak, C.B.** (1994) *Academic Writing for Graduate Students: A Course for Non-native Speakers of English*. University of Michigan Press, Ann Arbor.

Tannen, D. (1982) The oral/literate continuum in discourse. In Tannen, D. (ed.) *Spoken and Written Language: Exploring Orality and Literacy*. Ablex, Norwood, pp. 1–17.

Tannen, D. (1989) *Talking Voices: Repetition, Dialogue and Imagery in Conversational Discourse*. Cambridge University Press, Cambridge.

Thomas, J. and **Wilson, A.** (1996) Methodologies for studying a corpus of doctor–patient interaction. In Thomas, J. and Short, M. (eds) *Using Corpora for Language Research*. Longman, London and New York, pp. 92–109.

Trahey, M. and **White, L.** (1993) Positive evidence and preemption in the second language classroom, *Studies in Second Language Acquisition* **15**: 181–204.

Tribble, C. (1988) The use of text structuring vocabulary in native and non-native speaker writing, *MUESLI News*, June 1989.

Tribble, C. (1990) *Reformulation in a General English Setting*. Bell Educational Trust, Occasional Papers, Cambridge.

Tribble, C. (1991) Some uses of electronic text in English for academic purposes. In Milton, J. and Tong, K. (eds) *Text Analysis in Computer Assisted Language Learning*. The Hong Kong University of Science and Technology, Hong Kong, pp. 4–14.

Tribble, C. (1996a) *Writing*. Oxford University Press, Oxford.

Tribble, C. (1996b) Corpora for language teaching: building and using small corpora for general and specific language teaching purposes. Paper presented at the TALC Conference Workshop, Lancaster University 9–12 August 1996.

Tribble, C. and **Jones, G.** (1990) *Concordances in the Classroom*. Longman, London.

Tyler, A. (1994) The role of syntactic structure in discourse structure: signalling logical and prominence relations, *Applied Linguistics* **15**: 243–62.

Ur, P. (1996) *A Course in Language Teaching*. Cambridge University Press, Cambridge.

Ure, J. (1971) Lexical density and register differentiation. In Perren, G.E. and Trim, J.L.M. (eds) *Applications of Linguistics*. Cambridge University Press, Cambridge, pp. 443–52.

Van Els, T., Bongaerts, T., Extra, G., van Os, C. and **Janssen-van Dieten, A.M.** (1984) *Applied Linguistics and the Learning and Teaching of Foreign Languages*. Edward Arnold, London.

Van Halteren, H. (1996) Review of Karlsson et al. 1995, *International Journal of Corpus Linguistics* **1(1)**: 148–54.

Van Lier, L. (1995) *Introducing Language Awareness*. Penguin English, London.

Vande Kopple, W.J. (1985) Some exploratory discourse on metadiscourse, *College Composition and Communication* **36**: 82–93.

Vihman, M. (1982) Formulas in first and second language acquisition. In Menn, L. and Obler, L. (eds) *Exceptional Language and Linguistics*. New York Academic Press, New York.

Virtanen, T. (1996) Exploiting the International Corpus of Learner English (ICLE). In Harakka, T. and Koskela, M. (eds) *Kieli ja tietokone: AFinLAn vuosikirja 1996* [Language and the Computer: AFinLA Yearbook 1996]. Yliopistopaino, Jyväskylä, [Jyväskylä University Press] pp. 157–66.

Warner, A. (1961) *A Short Guide to English Style*. Oxford University Press, London.

Weinert, R. (1995) The role of formulaic language in second language acquisition: a review, *Applied Linguistics* **16(2)**: 180–205.

West, M. (1935) *The New Method English Dictionary*. Longman, London.

West, M. (1936) *A General Service List of English Words*. Longman, London.

White, L. (1991) Adverb placement in second language acquisition: some effects of positive and negative evidence in the classroom, *Second Language Research* **7**: 133–61.

White, R. (1987) *Writing Advanced*. Oxford University Press, Oxford.

White, R. and **Arndt, V.** (1991) *Process Writing*. Longman, London and New York.

Wikborg, E. (1985) Types of coherence breaks in university student writing. In Enkvist, N.E. (ed.) *Coherence and Composition: A Symposium*. Publications of the Research Institute of the Åbo Akademi Foundation. Åbo Akademi, Åbo, pp. 93–133.

Wikborg, E. and **Björk, L.** (1989) *Sammanhang i text. En empirisk undersökning och skrivpedagogiska konsekvenser*. [Coherence in text. An empirical study with pedagogical consequences for composition teaching.] Hallgren and Fallgren, Uppsala.

Wilkins, D.H. (1974) *Notional Syllabuses*. Oxford University Press, London.

Williams, J. (1995) Focus on form in communicative language teaching: research findings and the classroom teacher, *TESOL Journal* **4(4)**: 12–16.

Wilson, A. and **Rayson, P.** (1993) The automatic content analysis of spoken discourse. In Souter, C. and Atwell, E. (eds) *Corpus-based Computational Linguistics*. Rodopi, Amsterdam, pp. 215–26.

Wong-Fillmore, L. (1979) Individual differences in second language acquisition. In Fillmore, C., Kempler, D. and Wang, W. (ed.) *Individual Differences in Language Ability and Language Behavior*. Academic Press, New York, pp. 203–28.

Wu, S. (1995) *Transfer in Chinese students' academic English writing*. Unpublished PhD dissertation, Northern Arizona University.

Yan-Ping, Z. (1991) The effect of explicit instruction on the acquisition of English grammatical structures by Chinese learners. In James, C. and Garrett, P. (eds) *Language Awareness in the Classroom*. Longman, London and New York, pp. 254–77.

Yip, V. (1995) *Interlanguage and Learnability. From Chinese to English*. John Benjamins, Amsterdam and Philadelphia.

Yorio, C. (1989) Idiomaticity as indicator of second language proficiency. In Hyltenstam, K. and Obler, L. (eds) *Bilingualism Across the Lifespan: Aspects of Acquisition, Maturity and Loss*. Cambridge University Press, Cambridge, pp. 55–72.

Index